AF863275

The Urban Book Series

Editorial Board

Margarita Angelidou, Aristotle University of Thessaloniki, Thessaloniki, Greece

Fatemeh Farnaz Arefian, The Bartlett Development Planning Unit, UCL, Silk Cities, London, UK

Michael Batty, Centre for Advanced Spatial Analysis, UCL, London, UK

Simin Davoudi, Planning & Landscape Department GURU, Newcastle University, Newcastle, UK

Geoffrey DeVerteuil, School of Planning and Geography, Cardiff University, Cardiff, UK

Jesús M. González Pérez, Department of Geography, University of the Balearic Islands, Palma (Mallorca), Spain

Daniel B. Hess, Department of Urban and Regional Planning, University at Buffalo, State University, Buffalo, NY, USA

Paul Jones, School of Architecture, Design and Planning, University of Sydney, Sydney, NSW, Australia

Andrew Karvonen, Division of Urban and Regional Studies, KTH Royal Institute of Technology, Stockholm, Stockholms Län, Sweden

Andrew Kirby, New College, Arizona State University, Phoenix, AZ, USA

Karl Kropf, Department of Planning, Headington Campus, Oxford Brookes University, Oxford, UK

Karen Lucas, Institute for Transport Studies, University of Leeds, Leeds, UK

Marco Maretto, DICATeA, Department of Civil and Environmental Engineering, University of Parma, Parma, Italy

Ali Modarres, Tacoma Urban Studies, University of Washington Tacoma, Tacoma, WA, USA

Fabian Neuhaus, Faculty of Environmental Design, University of Calgary, Calgary, AB, Canada

Steffen Nijhuis, Architecture and the Built Environment, Delft University of Technology, Delft, The Netherlands

Vitor Manuel Aráujo de Oliveira, Porto University, Porto, Portugal

Christopher Silver, College of Design, University of Florida, Gainesville, FL, USA

Giuseppe Strappa, Facoltà di Architettura, Sapienza University of Rome, Rome, Roma, Italy

Igor Vojnovic, Department of Geography, Michigan State University, East Lansing, MI, USA

Claudia van der Laag, Oslo, Norway

Qunshan Zhao, School of Social and Political Sciences, University of Glasgow, Glasgow, UK

The Urban Book Series is a resource for urban studies and geography research worldwide. It provides a unique and innovative resource for the latest developments in the field, nurturing a comprehensive and encompassing publication venue for urban studies, urban geography, planning and regional development.

The series publishes peer-reviewed volumes related to urbanization, sustainability, urban environments, sustainable urbanism, governance, globalization, urban and sustainable development, spatial and area studies, urban management, transport systems, urban infrastructure, urban dynamics, green cities and urban landscapes. It also invites research which documents urbanization processes and urban dynamics on a national, regional and local level, welcoming case studies, as well as comparative and applied research.

The series will appeal to urbanists, geographers, planners, engineers, architects, policy makers, and to all of those interested in a wide-ranging overview of contemporary urban studies and innovations in the field. It accepts monographs, edited volumes and textbooks.

Indexed by Scopus.

Ibrahim Rotimi Aliu

Urban Private Housing in Nigeria

Understanding Residential Quality and Housing Preference Dynamics in Metropolitan Lagos

Springer

Ibrahim Rotimi Aliu
Department of Geography and Planning
Lagos State University Ojo Lagos
Ojo Lagos, Nigeria

ISSN 2365-757X ISSN 2365-7588 (electronic)
The Urban Book Series
ISBN 978-3-031-47431-6 ISBN 978-3-031-47432-3 (eBook)
https://doi.org/10.1007/978-3-031-47432-3

© The Editor(s) (if applicable) and The Author(s), under exclusive license to Springer Nature Switzerland AG 2024

This work is subject to copyright. All rights are solely and exclusively licensed by the Publisher, whether the whole or part of the material is concerned, specifically the rights of translation, reprinting, reuse of illustrations, recitation, broadcasting, reproduction on microfilms or in any other physical way, and transmission or information storage and retrieval, electronic adaptation, computer software, or by similar or dissimilar methodology now known or hereafter developed.
The use of general descriptive names, registered names, trademarks, service marks, etc. in this publication does not imply, even in the absence of a specific statement, that such names are exempt from the relevant protective laws and regulations and therefore free for general use.
The publisher, the authors, and the editors are safe to assume that the advice and information in this book are believed to be true and accurate at the date of publication. Neither the publisher nor the authors or the editors give a warranty, expressed or implied, with respect to the material contained herein or for any errors or omissions that may have been made. The publisher remains neutral with regard to jurisdictional claims in published maps and institutional affiliations.

This Springer imprint is published by the registered company Springer Nature Switzerland AG
The registered company address is: Gewerbestrasse 11, 6330 Cham, Switzerland

Paper in this product is recyclable.

Dedication

I dedicate this treatise to the lovely memories of my biological parents, Lawal Abe Aliu and Madam Seliat Oguntunke Aliu (nee Jegede) who died in 2015 and 2022 respectively. They both laid the foundation for my endearing traits of curiosity, persistence, candor, tenacity, endurance, honesty and industriousness. I wish that their lovely souls rest in peace.

Preface

Urban housing markets typically comprise both public and private housing with majority of urban residents being sheltered in private housing apartments. The public housing market consists of residential property produced, sold and leased by the government, while the private housing market comprises residential property produced, sold and rented by the individuals and the organized property developers. Urban housing markets vary in terms of quality, quantity and prices which affect urban residents' preferences and choices. At research level, scholars have focused majorly on explaining urban public housing problems but ignoring inherent issues in urban private housing markets. In Nigeria particularly, residential quality and housing preferences of urban residents within the private housing markets have been largely ignored. Of course, urban residents' housing quality and preferences in the private housing markets should be of concerns to urban stakeholders and scholars as they are indicators of urban quality of life and sustainability. This book uses multiattribute and neo-classical choice decision theories to examine residential quality indicators and housing preferences in Metropolitan Lagos private housing markets.

The fundamental questions addressed in this book are: what are the sociodemographic characteristics of urban Lagos households that operate within the private housing market? What are the patterns of their residential quality and home choices? What are the dominant residential factors that shape urban residents' home choices? In this book it is argued that though sociodemographic attributes of residents do influence home choices but residential type, neighborhood conditions and dwelling structural features also influence residential preferences. Incidentally, books on dynamics of urban housing quality and preferences of urban residents in polarized societies of the developing world are quite insufficient both in scope and subject matter. Housing quality is an essential measure of human quality of life and the ability or otherwise of urban residents to make choices given available housing conditions goes a long way to redefine the quality of lives in the city. This book therefore provokes critical discourse on the nature of urban private housing markets in the contexts of residential quality and preferences as underlined by household socioeconomic and demographic characteristics. This book is of immense importance to all students and researchers as well as professionals in the built environment who are curiously seeking to understand the private housing market dynamics and housing conditions of urban dwellers especially in Nigeria and other developing economies.

This book is organized in ten chapters. Chapter 1 introduces the background issues in housing, residential quality and housing preferences. This section also highlights the focus and the scope of the book. Chapter 2 deals with the physical, human and housing development in Lagos Nigeria. Chapter 3 deals with theoretical foundations of residential quality and housing preferences. Several concepts such as meaning of housing, residential quality, housing need, housing preference, models of the spatial pattern of urban residential quality, residential choice decision theory and hypotheses are discussed in the study. Chapter 4 dwells on the empirical studies on housing polarization and housing preferences, residential quality and modeling of housing preference. Chapter 5 deals with the research methods used for assessing housing quality and residential preferences in Lagos. It addresses types, sources, strategies and analysis of housing quality and preference data. Chapter 6 describes the Lagos households' sociodemographic and residential characteristics. Results from the analysis of residential quality and housing preference data in Lagos are contained in Chapters 7, 8 and 9 of the book. Chapter 10 consists of discussion of research findings, implications of findings, recommendations and conclusions. This book was written with three missions namely to provide a reading book on the nature of urban private housing in Nigeria; produce a treatise that profiles the sociodemographic peculiarities, residential quality and preference making decisions of urban residents in Lagos megacity; and to foster an empirically based housing study that engages in the analysis of housing quality and residential preferences from different quantitative perspectives.

Ojo Lagos, Nigeria Dr. Ibrahim Rotimi Aliu

Acknowledgements

This book "Urban Private Housing in Nigeria" is an outcome of a five-year intensive re-organization, moderation and reconstruction of my PhD thesis. I therefore wish to acknowledge the supports received from my undergraduate students during primary data collection, Professor Olayinka Ajala my PhD supervisor and Professor Remi Adediji both of the Obafemi Awolowo University Ile Ife Nigeria for their academic advice and Lagos State University Management for giving me academic tenure.

I also thank my wife and my little three children for their understanding and moral support during the research and writing stages of this book. I equally thank the Springer's Urban Book Series Editorial Board, the Collection Editor and two anonymous Springer Urban Book Series reviewers who meticulously read through and provided useful comments on the first draft of the book.

Lastly, I acknowledge that the maps in this book were created using ArcGIS® software by Esri. ArcGIS® and ArcMap™ are the intellectual property of Esri and are used here under license. Copyright© Esri All rights reserved. For more information about Esri software please visit, https://www.esri.com.

Contents

About the Author

Ibrahim Rotimi Aliu is Associate Professor of Housing and Urban Studies at the Department of Geography and Planning, Lagos State University, Ojo, Lagos, Nigeria. He obtained his Ph.D. Degree in Geography from Obafemi Awolowo University (OAU), Ile-Ife, Nigeria, specializing in housing and urban studies. His research interests cover urban analysis, housing studies, urban design, the built environment, urban management and sustainability. A proponent of high-quality research, Dr. Aliu has to his credit about 50 exceptional publications in reputable international and local journals including *Journal of Housing and the Built Environment, Property Management, Habitat International, Cities, Waste Management and Research, Environment Development and Sustainability, Sage Open, Indoor and Built Environment, African Geographical Review, South African Geographical Journal, Bulletin of Geography, Energy Efficiency, Journal of Poverty* and so on. Some of his recent publications include *Gender, Ethnicity and Residential Discrimination: Interpreting Implicit Discriminations in the Lagos Housing Market (Journal of Housing and the Built Environment, Vol. 39), Living on the Margins: Socio-environmental Characterization of Residential and Water Deprivations in Lagos Informal Settlements, Nigeria (Habitat International, Vol. 107), Unpacking the Dynamics of Intra-urban Residential Mobility in Nigeria: Analysis of Low Income Families in Ojo Lagos (Cities, Vol. 85), Municipal Household Solid Waste Management Strategies in an African Megacity: An Analysis of Public Private Partnership Performance in Lagos (Waste Mgt and Research, Vol. 32), Energy Efficiency in Prepaid-Postpaid Metered Homes: Analyzing Effects of Socioeconomic, Housing and Metering Factors in Lagos Nigeria (Energy Efficiency, Vol. 11), Sustaining Urbanization While Undermining Sustainability: A Socio-environmental Characterization of Sand Mining in Lagos (Geo Journal, Vol. 86), Intra-city Polarization, Residential Type and Attribute Importance: A Discrete Choice Study of Lagos (Habitat International, Vol. 42), Residential Polarization in an African megacity: An Exploratory Study of Lagos (South African Geographical Journal, Vol. 97), Housing Policy Debacle in Sub-Saharan Africa: An Appraisal of Three Housing Programmes in Lagos Nigeria (African Geographical Review, Vol. 37), Establishing the Nexus Between Residential Quality and Health*

Risk in Lagos Nigeria: An Exploratory Analytical Approach (Indoor and Built Environment Vol. 22), Sustainable Housing Development Dynamics in the Global South (Bulletin of Geography, Vol. 56), Beach Recreation Among Lagos Urban Residents: A Multivariate Analysis of Preferences and Decision Making Process (Tourism Analysis, Vol. 20), Marginal Land Use and Value Characterizations in Lagos: Untangling the Drivers and Implications for Sustainability (Environment Development and Sustainability, Vol. 18), Understanding Residential Polarization in a Globalizing City: A Study of Lagos (SAGE Open, Vol. 3), Nutritional Insecurity in Ojo Lagos: Redefining Food Security in the Context of Social Deprivation (Journal of Poverty, Vol. 20), all published with Web of Science Impact Factors. Dr. Aliu reviews for a number of outstanding international journals worldwide. Many of his works are found on researchers' platforms such as ResearchGate, Web of Science Publons, Scopus, Google Scholar, ORCID and Kudos. He has attended and presented papers at several international and local conferences. He won two research grants from TETFund Institutional Based Research (IBR) in 2016 and 2019 and a grant from TETFund National Research Fund (NRF) in 2021. Dr. Aliu belongs to a number of academic associations including the African Urban Planning Research Network (AUPRN), Association of Nigerian Geographers (ANG), Association of American Geographers (AAG) and Nigerian Institute of Town Planners (NITP). His recent research focuses on sustainable housing and urban sustainable development in the Global South. He is the lead author of the book *Sand Mining in African Coastal Regions* published by Springer in 2022.

List of Figures

List of Tables

Chapter 1
Introduction to Housing

Abstract At ontological realm, housing has two notional connotations: housing as a physical structure and housing as a social process of providing shelter. In both senses, housing is a distinctively complex phenomenon whose utility is often taken for granted perhaps because of the narrow idea that it represents shelter or mere physical structure against the natural elements of weather including torrential rain, scorching sun, buffeting wind and trebling gale. As a physical structure, housing represents homes and dwellings for a varied category of human beings. In a deeper sense, housing is more than mere shelter but a socially produced and physically constructed space/armature that guarantees safety, security, health, social privacy and economic well-being for inhabitants. In the urban area, housing plays huge role in boosting nation's economy and sustainable urbanization. However, due to high population density, imbalances between housing supply and demand, urban housing usually displays variations in quality, quantity, prices and preferences. In all jurisdictions, housing is produced by the government (public housing), individuals and property developers (private housing). Housing quality and preferences in both public and private housing markets are underlined by sociodemographic and economic status of the people. The choices that residents make are limited by their sociodemographic and economic background, quality of houses, available dwelling units, enlightenment, lifestyles and taste. In the Global South cities, public housing markets only cater for the few privileged urban residents while the majority of urban residents are accommodated in private housing markets.

Keywords Urban housing market · Private housing market · Public housing market · Urban residential quality · Housing preference

© The Author(s), under exclusive license to Springer Nature Switzerland AG 2024

I. R. Aliu, *Urban Private Housing in Nigeria*, The Urban Book Series,
https://doi.org/10.1007/978-3-031-47432-3_1

1.1 Background to Residential Quality and Housing Preference

Housing as a form of shelter is an indispensable man's basic need and central to his economic, social and physiological well-being (Aliu 2022; Aliu and Ajala 2014; Mabogunje et al. 1978). Incidentally, housing is traditionally provided by government, individuals and private organized sector. While housing from the first provider is also known as public housing, housing from the second and the third providers are collectively known as private housing (Aliu et al. 2018; Aliu 2022). In all jurisdictions, the private housing market predominates and provides shelter for the greater number of urban residents. However, for the complexity of its provision process, housing is characterized by constant scarcity and sometimes quality variation (Ndulo 1985; Aluko 2000; Agbola 2005; Ajala and Adelodun 2007). The variation in residential quality has created diversity of preferences and choices, which though is dictated by the heterogeneity of housing but perhaps is determined by the individual socioeconomic status. Studies on housing preferences have proliferated more in the last few decades in the advanced and some rapidly growing economies, due perhaps to their implications for urban planning, quality of life and sustainable development (Galster 1979; Clark 1992; Serim and Seung 1997; Cho 1997; Wang and Li 2004; Leishman et al. 2004; Cirman 2004, 2006; O Connel 2006; Kauko 2006; Garcia and Hernandez 2007; Sue 2008; Gibler et al. 2009; Opoku and Abdul-Muhmin 2010; Fong and Chan 2011). In all contemporary societies of today, housing preferences are hinged on consumers' socioeconomic status, neighborhood conditions and residential quality.

Generally, in terms of quantity, price and quality, the urban housing market is never a monolithic structure, but a set of submarkets that display complex spatial variation (World Bank 1993; Abumere 1994; Clark and Dieleman 1996; Aluko 2000; Wang and Li 2004). Residential quality evinces three quality components of a dwelling, namely neighborhood, location and structural quality (Kain and Quigley 1970; Goodwin 1977; Sumka 1979; Quigley 1976, 1985; Can 1991; Aluko 2000; Kearns and Parkinson 2001; Rapoport 2001; Hwang and Quigley 2004; Aliu and Adebayo 2010). Neighborhood quality refers to the quality conferred on a dwelling by virtue of the surrounding environment in which it is built. The nature of the surrounding in terms of sanitation, parking space, accessibility, light, drainage and security determines the neighborhood or environmental quality of a dwelling (Ndulo 1985; Can 1991; Aluko 2000; Rapoport 2001). Location quality describes the value attached to a dwelling by its position relative to other activity places such as workplaces, markets, friends and relations. Structural quality refers to the attributes of dwellings through their external and internal designs. Some of the structural components include type of house, number of rooms, room space, toilets, baths, water sources, doors, windows, electricity, patio, kitchen and aesthetics (Goodwin 1977). Residential quality therefore is the collective description of the location, neighborhood, and structural quality components of a dwelling unit. The residential quality components form the basis upon which individuals predicate their choices and preferences.

Housing preferences are predilections expressed by consumers for a particular set of attributes of housing products within the context of underlying tastes which exist independently of constraints (Maclennan 1977). According to Kardes (1999), preferences are evaluative judgements concerning two or more objects and are measured based on comparison of attributes or features of the objects. Two theoretical approaches have dominated contemporary studies on housing preference measurement: attitudinal-behavioral models which estimate preferences by stated part-worth analysis and rational-economic choice models which estimate preferences by revealed-hedonic utility maximization. Most of the studies in housing preferences have been situated in at least one of these theoretical frameworks (see Maclennan 1977; Megbolugbe 1989; Arimah 1997; Wang and Li 2004). The orientation of housing studies in the contemporary time borders on the measurement of the consumers' expanding preference and choice profiles. The issue therefore is how to explain the differences between "what ought to be" and "what it is" with regard to housing characteristics of different groups within the housing market. Even when previous studies have provided useful insights into the factors that determine housing choices, they however reflect several limitations.

Existing studies have largely focused upon housing purchase preferences in relation to household characteristics, with little consideration for how the quality variation in submarkets influences tenure, location and residential type preferences in rental housing markets. Most previous studies have also concentrated on public housing markets with little consideration for the dynamics in private housing markets. Again, there are problems with methodologies that clearly explain housing preference behavior of households. Even though few studies have made use of revealed and stated preference methodologies at the same time, there are no known studies that have employed the combined methods for housing preferences using residential quality variables within private housing submarkets in Nigeria. Given the perceived inadequacies in previous studies, this book therefore examines the pattern of residential quality and preferences in Lagos private housing markets. It seeks to achieve this goal by providing information on housing preferences in different residential density areas of the megacity namely high, medium and low residential density districts using Multi-Attribute Residential Preference Model (MARP) framework.

1.2 The Housing Research Problem

Despite the fact that private housing dominates the urban setting, ironically the dynamics of residential quality and housing preferences of urban residents operating within the urban private housing market have shown to be grossly underexplored in the developing world. Majority of the studies on housing has been focused on the analysis of public housing which accounts for less than 10% of the urban housing demand. Even housing policy in the Global South rarely incorporates the significant aspect of the private housing markets. Nonetheless, some existing works on housing have focused on the analysis of housing demand and choice from residential tenure, type and locational perspectives in relation to household characteristics in poorly organized housing markets of the developing economies. For instance, some empirical studies have found out that there is a connection between housing tenure and neighborhood attributes (Henderson and Ioannides 1983; Huff 1996; Wang and Li 2004; Gbakeji and Ojeifo 2009). According to these studies, neighborhood variables such as distance, closeness to CBD, environmental sanitation, security, accessibility, recreational facilities and so on bear significant correlation with housing tenure choice. The role played by dwelling characteristics such as house type, number of rooms, room space, toilet and bath, kitchen and presence of water in determining housing preferences has also been identified by previous studies (Borukhov et al. 1978; Megbolugbe 1989).

Other studies have established socioeconomic status of home buyers such as race, age, income, household size, stage in lifecycle, educational level and occupation of household head, school-age children, and the ratio of housing price to household income as important determinants of housing preferences (see Timmermans et al. 1996; Andrejs 1996; Clark et al. 1997; Arimah 1997; Cho 1997; Tita et al. 2006; Rhodes 2007; Tayyaran and Khan 2007; Sue 2008; Opoku and Abdul-Muhmin 2010). Observation from previous studies points to the fact that scholars have concentrated on the analysis of the criteria for and determinants of either housing type or tenure choice. Most of these studies are predicated on situations in the developed Western and rapidly growing Asian economies. There is every reason to follow with utmost caution in developing countries like Nigeria the orientation of these studies in explaining residential quality and housing preferences. Both from the cultural and policy perspectives, the situations in the African countries are different from that of the developed countries. Therefore, there is only little to gain by relying totally on the studies that are well entrenched in Western culture and economies to relate to the African condition.

In Nigeria, housing as a complex, multidimensional product has been extensively investigated. Some of the past studies consider various issues such as housing and spatial pattern of modernization (Sada 1975; Abumere 1994), conditions of residential houses in Nigerian cities (Abiodun 1976; Onibokun 1985), the impact of subsidies on low-income public housing (Sule 1981; Anusionwu 1982), determinants of housing values (Arimah 1992; Ekanem 1995; Aluko 2000; Ajala and Adelodun 2007), housing affordability and urban development (Ajala et al. 2010), housing policy and housing delivery (Aribigbola 2008; Towry-Coker 2012), yet few actually deal with housing preferences and their determinants in Nigerian cities' private housing markets (Aminu 1977; Megbolugbe 1989; Arimah 1997; Aribigbola 2005; Sanni and Akinyemi 2009; Ajala and Olayiwola 2011). Majority of these existing literatures have focused more on the public housing markets than on the private housing markets. In spite of what has been done on housing in Nigeria, certain aspects of housing preference analysis are still insufficiently studied. Two significant areas have been largely ignored in recent housing studies in Nigeria: the nexus between residential quality and rental choices, and the extension of eclectic methodological frameworks that could facilitate the prediction of preference behavioral patterns of consumers in the private housing market.

Firstly, adequate attention has not been given to the influence of residential quality on housing choice formation in Nigeria in recent times. While old housing studies in Nigerian cities have alluded to the urban residents' predisposition to multiple dwelling units, high room density and dwellings with low facility quality (Adeniyi 1972; Abiodun 1976), the idea that this condition still persists in Lagos is too tenuous to hold on to. Recent trends in housing consumption in Lagos have indicated a shift from preferences for just any house, to a home that can provide suitable structural quality, convivial environmental values and reasonable affordability (Jiboye 2009). Secondly, existing studies on housing preferences in Nigeria have majorly employed revealed-hedonic framework using ordinary least square (OLS) statistical techniques (see Megbolugbe 1989; Arimah 1992; Ekanem 1995; Aluko 2000) and only a paltry number of studies have employed stated-utility model using logit techniques (Arimah 1997). The limitations of both of these methodologies have been long revealed (see Mason and Quigley 1990; Timmermans et al. 1994; Cho 1997; Earnhart 2002; Wang and Li 2004). According to Wang and Li (2004), perhaps the hedonic ordinary least square regression OLS methodology does not estimate choices but rather the implicit price implications of housing characteristics, and studies based on this technique can therefore be hardly taken as housing preference studies. Recent studies have shown that the beta coefficients yielded by the OLS regression model with multiple variables are often incorrect, suffer from multicolinearity and could be misleading in explaining categorical dependent variables (Earnhart 2002; Walker et al. 2002). Of course, the stated approach has been criticized for being experimentally dependent, employing too few variables, considering hypothetical choice alternatives and may not capture real choices of consumers due to information loss (Timmermans et al. 1994; Earnhart 2002). However, for these inherent drawbacks, a group of scholars have seen the need for the combination of the two methodologies (Earnhart 2002; Tayyaran and Khan 2007). Incidentally, very few housing preference studies have been based on the combined method in Lagos Nigeria.

In advanced economies, few scholars have used the combined method but with some obvious limitations. For instance, a study by Earnhart (2002) focused only on a small single-family dwelling market in the USA using environmental amenity variables that drive housing purchases while Tayyaran and Khan (2007) only considered telecommuting and residential location decisions in Canada. Both of these foreign studies have spatial limitations as they are restricted to too small locations thereby lacking discernible differentiation. Some other researchers, including those in Nigeria, have used exclusively either revealed or stated model in their studies and arrived at different results. It is believed that a combination of the two techniques in a single book like this will give a better idea about the underlying factors influencing housing preferences in different residential density districts in Lagos. Since housing preferences are made with due recourse to a combination of dwelling and neighborhood attributes, it is perhaps important that they are essentially considered as complex decision-making processes and this calls for an understanding of how multicriteria decisions are made. Hence, this book also employed multicriteria decision-making models such as Multi-Attribute Utility Theory MAUT (see Edwards and Barron 1994; Barron and Barrett 1996; Figueira et al. 2004; Linkov et al. 2004; Sylvia et al. 2010).

Geographical and social studies on residential pattern have generally taken two orientations: those that focus on revealing the residential pattern based on dwelling and neighborhood quality and those that strive to provide explanations for such pattern (Abumere 1994). While the sociologists attempt to view residential differentiation as resulting from the tendency for racial segregation (Krivo 1986; Rosenbaum 1995, 1996), the economists tend to look at residential differentiation as an outcome of choice behaviors resulting from the tendency to maximize utility (Quigley 1976, 1985; Cirman 2006). Both sociological and economic explanations of residential differentiation are fraught with serious inadequacies (Harvey 1975). First, sociological explanation does not provide insight beyond emphasizing the rather simplistic notion that people of the same racial provenance live closely together, and second, the neo-classical economic theory of utility maximization behavior on the part of individual consumers does not explain the spatial pattern of human activities sufficiently. However, the geographic view of residential differentiation assumes that the spatial aspect of housing quality is often masked by the socioeconomic peculiarities and idiosyncrasies of the city dwellers and this influences choices (Briggs 2005; Jerry 2007). There are three discernible spatial patterns of private housing structures in Lagos: the high-density-low-quality residential area, the medium-density-medium-quality residential area and the low-density-high-quality residential area (Aluko 2000; Oduwaye 2005). These are also differentiated submarkets with peculiar quality, housing price and socioeconomic characteristics. Preferences for housing within these residential areas are dictated by many factors such as the location, accessibility, affordability and social status. The way urban residents perceive different housing opportunities (personal, private or public) is related to the quality of available dwelling units within the housing submarkets. There is need therefore to examine the preferences for housing quality within these residential submarkets.

The research questions arising from the above raised problems therefore are multifarious: What are the influential residential attributes that shape housing preference formations within different residential density areas in Lagos? What is the nature of interrelationship among household characteristics and residential variables that influence housing preferences? What are the spatial patterns of residential quality and housing preferences in Lagos? In what ways, do home seekers combine the multiple variables in their decisions to choose desired dwellings?

1.3 The Focus and Scope of the Book

The focus of this book is to profoundly examine the pattern of residential quality and housing preference exhibited in Lagos private housing markets, Nigeria, with a view to understanding the underlying factors that shape choice behaviors among urban residents. The specific objectives are to:

- Describe the demographic and the socioeconomic attributes of urban residents in Lagos private housing market
- Analyze the structural and the neighborhood quality of urban residents' housing units
- Analyze the housing preferences of urban residents in Lagos private housing market
- Analyze the association between the preferred residential quality variables and socioeconomic attributes
- Ascertain the spatial pattern of residential quality and preferences using key variables
- Determine the factors responsible for the housing preference behaviors exhibited by the urban residents.

This book covers private housing market comprising both formal and informal properties provided and occupied by individuals in Metropolitan Lagos, Nigeria. It is instructive to note that the private housing market in Nigeria is populated by varying types of housing with formal and informal status and housing provision players who are from different strata of the society. These mixed sets of housing stakeholders create a private property market that is characterized by multiple housing types, distinct quality levels and varying prices. While many of the properties are from formal sources, a huge proportion is from informal sources. However, in Nigeria and indeed in all African countries, speaking about housing informality requires some level of caution as a lot of controversies have surrounded the use of the term informal housing.[1] Housing is an expansive field of study that has accommodated a variety of scientific inquiries and multiplicity of methodologies. This book employed varied methods ranging from revealed to stated preference methodologies using

[1] Informal housing theoretically connotes sets of homes built on unauthorized public or private land. Housing informality therefore refers to illegal or lack of proper tenure rights, unofficial appropriation and occupation of land or lack of formal documentation of land upon which a piece of housing property is built. The causes of housing informality within the urban property space are numerous. Sometimes, informal housing may arise as a result of the inability of the city housing market to meet the housing demand of urban residents thereby creating an inescapable option for the underserved residents to get accommodated in substandard but cheaper houses. In this way, informal housing is seen as a strategy employed by the urban land speculators to provide affordable housing to the low-income workers of the city. Added to this is the complexity of the process and cost of land acquisition and regularization in urban areas of the developing world. The monetary cost of acquisition and the bureaucracies involved in the regularization of land in the city are just too much to discourage the poor from having access to decent housing especially as property owners. Again informality may be an outcome of poor urban planning and land use policy. Hence, informal housing is a distinctive urban housing market where affordability accrues through constraints or absence of formal planning and regulation. More so, urban land markets are typically in crisis in most parts of the developing economies. In this region, informal housing is a means for both elite and subaltern groups to make profit out of unorganized urban housing and land markets. In virtually all urban communities in Nigeria including Lagos, informal housing constitutes the largest proportion of the private housing market, and government has cautiously refrained from enforcing rules and regulations to dispossess the homeowners of their properties.

conjoint analysis. The variables used in the book ranged from residential structural, neighborhood, location quality factors to socioeconomic indicators. These variables are very crucial to the understanding of the challenges which urban dwellers are facing concerning ideal housing that meets their aspirations and expectations. The relevance of housing preference and residential quality dynamics to urban housing analysis makes this book an important contribution to housing research. The book deals with the influence of the quality of houses being provided by all the private stakeholders in the state on residents' housing rental preferences. The geographic area covered in this book is the Metropolitan Area of Lagos in Nigeria. The spatial dimension of residential quality and housing preferences in this region has not been well explored in housing studies.

Few years to the end of the last millennium, the Nigerian physical and fiscal environment witnessed rapid changes, some of which altered the socioeconomic opportunities and residential conditions of urban dwellers. These changes have also affected the perceptive dynamics of the individual in the city. The conditions of the city are in a state of flux, and it is not clear how these have affected the orientation of Lagos residents. Hence, there is a need for a new inquiry into how housing decisions in Lagos are made, what the people's preferences are and what factors influence their housing rental choices in contemporary time. Because of the complexity of the relationships that exist between residential quality and housing preferences, it is pertinent to examine housing preferences in different residential density areas of Lagos. A new book of this nature is quite important for three reasons namely: It gives critical insights into the ways urban residents' housing preferences are formed in the contemporary period, it identifies the residential quality attributes that are essential in explaining preferences, and it describes the spatial variations in preferences among varying groups in the city.

This book differs from other previous efforts by focusing on housing preferences within differentiated density areas in which residential quality is recognized as important in the competition for residential choices. The findings from the study reported in this book have policy, practical and theoretical implications for housing in Lagos and other cities in the Global South region. In terms of policy development, governments have to understand the existing pattern of housing quality in Lagos as well as the preferences of residents in order to plan for housing that would meet their aspirations and needs. To the builders, the results provide the factual foundation to base their home construction efforts for the Lagos urban residents. This book also increases the horizon of housing research frontier as it emphasizes the place of spatial differentiation in housing preference behavior.

1.4 Summary

Housing quality and residential preferences are two terms that have received tremendous inquiries for long time. Although they are not essentially the same conceptually, they are very interlinked especially when residents make decisions on home choices.

This book intends to make additional contributions to housing research by linking the personal and housing contextual quality factors that facilitate housing preference decision-making process.

References

Abiodun OJ (1976) Housing problems in Nigerian Cities. Town Plann Rev 47(4):330–348

Abumere IS (1994) Residential differentiation in Ibadan: some sketches of an explanation. In: Filani MO, Akintola FO, Ikporukpo CO (eds) Ibadan region. Rex Charles, Ibadan (85–97)

Adeniyi EO (1972) Housing in Nigerian development. Niger J Econ Soc Stud 14(3):239–250

Agbola T (2005) Nigerian housing debacle, an inaugural lecture Department of Urban and Regional planning University of Ibadan, Nigeria

Ajala OA, Adelodun OA (2007) Determinants of housing quality in Ibadan North Local Government Area of North Western Nigeria. Baselius Res 8(2):72–84

Ajala OA, Olayiwola MA (2011) Choice of residential locations in selected urban centres in South Western Nigeria. Ile-Ife Plann J 4(1):1–14

Ajala OA, Aigbe GO, Aliu IR (2010) Affordable housing and urban development in Nigeria: contemporary issues, challenges and opportunities. Ilorin J Bus Soc Sci 14(1):1–13

Aliu IR, Adebayo A (2010) Evaluating the influence of residential quality on urban residents' wellbeing: the case of Lagos Nigeria. Int J Acad Res 2(6):400–410

Aliu IR, Ajala OA (2014) Intra-city polarization, residential type and attribute importance: a discrete choice study of Lagos. Habitat Int 42(2):11–20. https://doi.org/10.1016/j.habitatint.2013.10.002

Aliu IR, Towry-Coker L, Odumosu T (2018) Housing policy debacle in Sub-Saharan Africa: an appraisal of three housing programmes in Lagos Nigeria. Afr Geogr Rev 37(3), 241–256. https://doi.org/10.1080/19376812.2017.1284005

Aliu IR (2022) Sustainable housing development dynamics in the Global South: reflections on theories, strategies and constraints. Bulleting Geogr Socioeconomic Ser 56:83–100. https://doi.org/10.12775/bggs-2022-0014

Aluko EO (2000) Urban market segmentation and house values in metropolitan Lagos. Niger Geogr J 3&4:148–157

Aminu FA (1977) The social and cultural bases for housing preferences in Ibadan Nigeria. PhD thesis, University of Michigan USA Microfilms International 30(3):1701

Andrejs S (1996) Race and tenure in Toronto. Urban Stud 33(2):223–252

Anusionwu EC (1982) Low cost housing in Nigeria: problems and new perspectives. Niger J Econ Soc Stud 24(3):299–316

Aribigbola A (2008) Housing policy formulation in developing countries: evidence of program implementation from Akure Ondo State, Nigeria. J Hum Ecol 23(2):125–134

Aribigbola A (2005) Housing choices in Akure Ondo State, Nigeria. A PhD thesis Obafemi Awolowo University, Ile-Ife

Arimah B (1992) Variations in housing values in a Nigerian City: the case of Ibadan. Malays J Trop Geogr 23(1):1–12

Arimah BC (1997) The determinants of housing tenure choice in Ibadan Nigeria. Urban Stud 31(4):105–124

Barron FH, Barrett BE (1996) The efficacy of SMARTER. Simple multi-attribute rating technique extended to ranking. Acta Psychol 93:23–36

Borukhov E, Ginsberg Y, Werczberger E (1978) Housing prices and housing preferences in Israel. Urban Stud 15:187–200

Briggs XS (2005) The geography of opportunity: race and housing choice in Metropolitan America reviewed by Reginald Tucker Seeley: Brookings institution press U.S.A.

Can A (1991) The measurement of neighborhood dynamics in urban housing prices. J Urban Econ 1:254–272
Cho C (1997) Joint choice of tenure and dwelling type: a multinomial logit analysis for the city of Chongju. Urban Stud 34(9):1459–1473
Cirman A (2006) Housing tenure preferences in the post-privatization period: the case of Slovenia. Hous Stud 21(1):113–134
Cirman A (2004) Housing tenure preferences in society with marginal rental sectors: the case of Slovenia, A paper delivered at the conference on adequate and affordable housing for all, 24–26 June, Toronto, Canada
Clark WAV, Dielemann FM (1996) Households and housing: choices and outcomes in the housing market. New Jersey: Centre for Urban Policy Research Rutgers University
Clark WAV (1992) Residential preferences and residential choices in a multi-ethnic context. Demography 29(3):451–466
Clark WAC, Derloo MC, Dieleman FM (1997) Entry to home-ownership in Germany: some comparisons with the United States of America. Urban Stud 34(1):7–19
Earnhart D (2002) Combining revealed and stated data to examine housing decisions using discrete choice analysis. Journal of Urban Economics 51:143–169
Edwards W, Barron FH (1994) SMARTS and SMARTER: improved simple methods for multi-attribute utility measurements. Organ Behav Hum Decis Process 60:306–325
Ekanem FN (1995) Determinants of the price of homes in a suburban area of Washington D.C Compared with Those in a Suburban Area of Lagos, Nigeria. Niger J Econ Soc Stud 37(1):1–11
Figueira J, Greco S, Ehrgott M (eds) (2004) Multiple criteria decision analysis: state of the art surveys. Springer, New York
Fong E, Chan E (2011) Residential patterns among religious groups in Canadian Cities. City Community 10(4):393–412
Galster G (1979) Interracial variations in housing preferences. Reg Sci Perspect 9:1–17
Garcia JAB, Hernandez RJE (2007) Housing and urban location decisions in Spain: an econometric analysis with unobserved heterogeneity. Urban Stud 44(9):1657–1676
Gbakeji OJ, Ojeifo OM (2009) Aspects of residential and neighborhood preferences in the Warri metropolis Delta State Nigeria. Stud Home Community Sci 1(2):121–126
Gibler KM, Taltavul P, Casado-Diaz JM, Casado-Diaz AM, Rodriguez V (2009) Examining retirement housing preferences among international retirees' migrants. Int Real Estate Rev 12(1):1–22
Goodwin AS (1977) Measuring the values of housing quality—a note. J Reg Sci 17(1):107–115
Harvey D (1975) Class structure in a capitalist society and the theory of residential differentiation. In: Peel R et al (eds) Processes in physical and human geography: Bristol Essays. Heinemann, London
Henderson VJ, Ioannides YM (1983) A model of housing tenure choice. Am Econ Rev 73(1):98–113
Huff JO (1996) Geographic regularities in residential search behavior. Ann Assoc Am Geogr 76(2):208–227
Hwang M, Quigley JM (2004) Selectivity, quality adjustment and mean reversion in the measurement of house values. J Real Estate Financ Econ 28(2/3):161–178
Jerry A (2007) The geography of opportunity: race and housing choice in Metropolitan America, edited by Xavier de Souza Briggs. 2005. Series: James A. Joaszhnson Metro Series. Brookings Institution Press, Washington, p 353 (reviewed) J Reg Sci 47(2):405–407
Jiboye AD (2009) Evaluating tenants' satisfaction within public housing in Lagos, Nigeria. Town Plann Archit 33(4):239–247
Kain JF, Quigley JM (1970) Measuring the value of house quality. J Am Stat Assoc 65(330):532–548
Kardes FR (1999) Consumer behavior and management decision making. Addison Willey, London
Kauko T (2006) Expression of housing consumer preferences: proposition for a research agenda. Hous Theory Soc 23(2):92–108

Kearns A, Parkinson M (2001) The significance of neighborhood. Urban Stud 38(12):2103–2110
Krivo JL (1986) Home ownership differences between Hispanics and Anglos in the United States. J Soc Soc Probl 33(4):319–333
Leishman C, Aspinall P, Munoro M, Warren FJ (2004) Preferences, quality and choice in new-build housing. Joseph Rowntree Foundation, London. www.jrt.org.uk. Accessed 23 March 2010
Linkov I, Varghese A, Jamil S, Seager TP, Kiker G, Bridges T (2004) Multi-criteria decision analysis: a framework for structuring remedial decisions at the contaminated sites. In: Linkov I, Ramadan AB (eds) Comparative risk assessment and environmental decision making. Springer, New York, pp 15–54
Mabogunje AL, Hardoy JE, Misra RP (1978) Shelter provision in developing countries. Scientific committee on problems of the environment SCOPE. Wiley, New York
Maclennan D (1977) Information, space and the measurement of housing preferences and demand. Scott J Polit Econ 24(2):97–115
Mason C, Quigley JM (1990) Comparing the performance of discrete choice and hedonic models. In: Fischer MM, Njikamp P, Papageorglou (eds) Spatial choices and processes. Holland, Elsevier, pp 219–246
Megbolugbe IF (1989) A hedonic index model: the housing market of Jos. Urban Stud 26:486–494
Ndulo M (1985) The determinants of urban housing value: the evidence from Zambia. Malays J Trop Geogr 12:31–36
Oduwaye L (2005) Residential land values and their determinants in high density residential neighbourhoods of the Lagos Metropolis. Res Rev 21(2):37–53
Onibokun A (ed) (1985) Housing in Nigeria. Nigerian Institute of Social and Economic Research NISER, Ibadan
Opoku RA, Abdul-Muhmin AG (2010) Housing preferences and attribute importance among low-income consumers in Saudi Arabia. Habitat Int 34:219–227
Quigley J (1976) Housing demand in the short run: an analysis of polytomous choice. In: Winter S (ed) Explor Econ Res 3(1):76–102
Quigley J (1985) Consumer choice of dwelling, neighborhood and public services. Reg Sci Urban Econ 15:41–63
Rapoport A (2001) Theory, culture and housing. Hous Theory Soc 17:145–165
Rhodes LM (2007) Strategic choice in Irish housing system: taming the complexity. Hous Theory Soc 24(1):14–31
Rosenbaum J (1995) Changing the geography of opportunity by expanding residential choice: lessons from the Gatreaux Program. Hous Policy Debate 6(1):231–269
Rosenbaum J (1996) The influence of race on Hispanic housing choices in New York City 1978–1987. Urban Aff Rev 32(2):217–243
Sada PO (1975) Urban housing and spatial pattern of modernization in Benin City. Niger Geogr J 18(1):39–55
Sanni L, Felicia A (2009) Determinants of household residential districts preferences within metropolitan city of Ibadan, Nigeria. J Human Ecol 25(2):137–141
Serim H, Seung JK (1997) The choice of functional form and variables in the hedonic price model in Seoul. Urban Stud 34(7):989–998
Sue H (2008) Housing choices and issues for young people in the UK. Joseph Rowntree Foundation, London. www.jrt.org.uk. Accessed 23 March 2010
Sule RA (1981) The future of the Nigerian housing subsidy: the unanswered questions. Niger J Econ Soc Stud 23(1):109–128
Sumka HJ (1979) Measuring the quality of housing: an econometric analysis of tax appraisal records. Land Econ 53:293–309
Sylvia J, Henny C, Roland G (eds) (2010) Methodology for research into housing preferences and choices. Springer, New York
Tayyaran MR, Khan MA (2007) Telecommuting and residential location decisions: combined stated and revealed preferences model. Can J Civil Eng 34:1324–1333

Timmermans H, Molin E, van Nootwijk L (1994) Housing choice processes: stated versus revealed modeling approaches. Neth J Hous Built Environ 9(3):215–227
Timmermans H, van Nootwijk L, Oppewal L, van der Waerden P (1996) Modeling constrained choice behavior in regulated housing markets by means of discrete choice experiments and universal logit models: an application to the residential choice behavior of divorcees. Environ Plann A 28:1095–1112
Tita EG, Petras TL, Greenbaum RT (2006) Crime and residential choice: a neighborhood level analysis of the impact of crime on housing prices. J Quant Criminol 22:299–317
Towry-Coker L (2012) Housing policy and the dynamics of housing delivery in Nigeria: a case study of Lagos State. Makeway publishing, Ibadan
Walker B, Marsh A, Wardman M, Niner P (2002) Modelling tenant choices in the public rented sector: a stated preference approach. Urban Stud 39(4):665–688
Wang D, Li S-M (2004) Housing preferences in a transitional housing system: the case of Beijing, China. Environ Plann A 36:69–87
World Bank (1993) Housing: enabling markets to work a policy paper. International Bank for Reconstruction and Development IBRD, New York

Chapter 2
Lagos Metropolitan Area: Physical, Historical and Housing Development

Abstract Lagos Metropolitan Area (LMA) is the greater Lagos Megacity Region. This city has been playing a vital role in the economic and political lives of Nigerian. Although located in the South Western Nigeria, Lagos metropolis is a melting pot of all ethnic groups in Nigeria. It is a slave trade port that grew in the fifteenth century into a strong virile super economic power in the African sub-Saharan region. Probably, it is the most industrialized city in Africa and certainly the most populous in Nigeria. Lagos megacity remains as the main economic nerve of the nation and also a relatively stable city over time. Historically, Lagos grew as a slave trade port in the fifteenth century, and at the point of colonial administration in 1914, it assumed the capital city of Nigeria, and after in independence 1960, Lagos naturally retained the capital city until 1991 when Abuja took over as the seat of power in Nigeria. Located in the tropics, Lagos enjoys wonderful climatic and geological stability. Its proximity to the Atlantic Ocean confines its opportunities in maritime and banking activities. The housing condition of Lagos has its root in the colonial Government Reserve Areas (GRAs) which created more exclusive regions of special housing for the more privileged rich Nigerians. However, the exponential growth of Lagos has created some residential polarization leading to segmented housing markets. While Lagos enjoys some exquisite residential neighborhoods, a greater part of the city lies on the downtown where there are low-priced homes and poor-quality private housing.

Keywords Lagos metropolitan area · Lagos crown colony · Housing development · Lagos megacity · Lagos residential density areas (LRDA)

2.1 Lagos Metropolitan Area Location and Physical Attributes

This book is predicated upon and written in the context of urban housing in Lagos the most urbanized and economically advanced city in Nigeria and perhaps in the whole West African subregion. Lagos is the face of all urban communities in Nigeria. As

© The Author(s), under exclusive license to Springer Nature Switzerland AG 2024

I. R. Aliu, *Urban Private Housing in Nigeria*, The Urban Book Series,
https://doi.org/10.1007/978-3-031-47432-3_2

depicted in Figs. 2.1 and 2.2, geographically, Lagos in Nigeria is located between longitudes 2°42′–4°20′ East and latitudes 6°22′–6°42′ North. Located in the South Western region of Nigeria, Lagos is bounded in the East and in the North by Ogun State, in the South by the Atlantic Ocean and on the Western flank by the Republic of Benin. It occupies a total land area of 3577 km^2 representing 0.4% of Nigeria. Given the small land area of Lagos, it invariably remains the smallest state in Nigeria. The soil that characterizes the region is sandy along the coastal low plains extending from Badagry in the West to Epe in the far Eastern flank and reddish loamy soil along the upland areas of Ikeja, Agege and Ikorodu.

The larger part of Lagos State belongs geologically to the sedimentary rock of the Holocene deposit (Jeje 1978). The sedimentary deposits are made of silt, clay, peat and unconsolidated sand. This geological attribute makes the construction of dwellings more challenging and invariably accounts for perennial residential quality problems as strong materials need to be used in building safe and durable housing for the urban residents. Perhaps, the soil conditions might account for incessant housing collapse in many parts of Lagos metropolis. Because of its proximity to the Atlantic Ocean, the coastal fringe of Lagos State is characterized by creeks and lagoons; features that endow Lagos with natural ports among which Apapa wharf stands as the largest and the busiest in the sub-Saharan West African region. The strategic location of Lagos both as a coastal settlement and an integral part of the South Western region of Nigeria bestows on it a critical place in the socioeconomic and political development of the country. The topography of Lagos is dominated by its system of islands, sandbars and lagoons. The city itself sprawls over what used to be the four main islands: Lagos, Iddo (now attached to the mainland), Ikoyi (now attached to Lagos Island) and Victoria (now the tip of the Lekki Peninsula); because of land reclamation efforts over the years, some of the original main islands are no longer true islands. A system of bridges connects some of Lagos's islands to each other and to the mainland. All the territory is low-lying, the highest point on Lagos

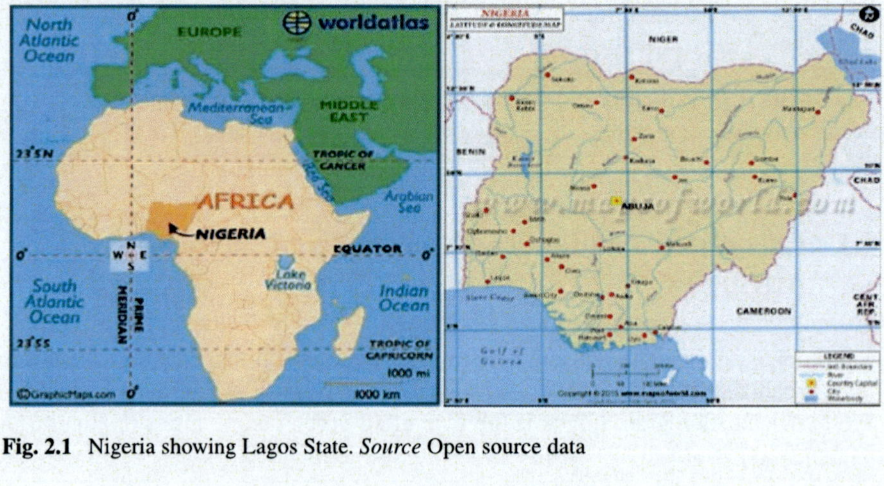

Fig. 2.1 Nigeria showing Lagos State. *Source* Open source data

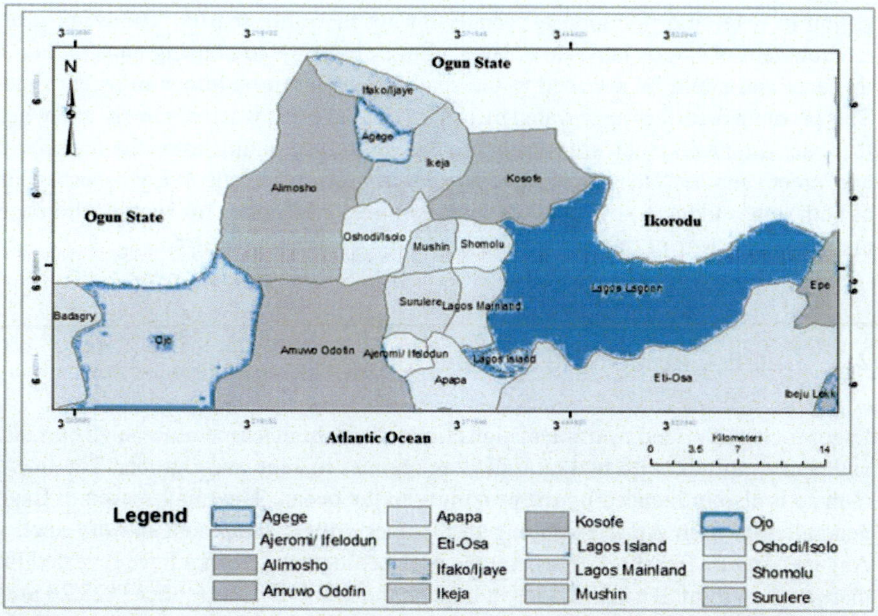

Fig. 2.2 Lagos metropolitan area (LMA). *Source* https://www.the-sixteen-metropolitan-local-government-areas-in-Lagos-state-Source-Lagos-state.png

Island being only 22 ft. above sea level. Lagos coastal regions consist of littoral and lagoon sediments resulting from the weathered coastal belt and the alluvial deposit of the Ogun River flood plain. The coastal plain sand deposit was eroded to a depth far below the present sea level due to the global changes in the ice age. At the beginning of the Holocene era, the sea level rose again to the present level. In this seemingly uniformity of geologic process, there is a wide variation. The variation is in the contrast between certain areas of Ikorodu and Epe in the East compared with the other parts along the Northern region of the state.

According to Abegunde (1987), Lagos State can be categorized based on the geomorphologic characteristics into five zones. The first geomorphologic zone is the Sandy Barrier Beaches that run parallel to the Atlantic Ocean, covering Badagy, Victoria Island and Ikoyi surroundings as well as Lekki-Ajah environments. The second geomorphological zone is the Sandy Barrier Island, found in the lagoon creeks, covering Iddo, Topo, Victoria Island and Lagos Islands. The third zone is the Lowland Sandy Plains prevalent in the mangrove swamps of Badagry, and Ojo. The fourth zone is the Coastal Uplands zone found in the Northern regions of the state such as Ikorodu, Epe settlements and usually about 45 m above sea level. The fifth zone is the Coastal Lowlands, which lies between the sandy plain and Coastal Uplands covering such areas as Isolo, Mushin, Oshodi, Ikeja, Alimoso, Ilupeju, and Ketu with the altitude always below 15 m above sea level. The peculiar soil characteristics of Lagos and its proximity to the ocean which gives a high water table expose the region to perennial flooding, especially during the rainy season. The water-prone environment of Lagos has also created a huge challenge to housing construction in the state and could be ascribed to the spate of collapsed buildings in recent times. This problem is further aggravated by lack of drainage and water channels, and where there are drainages, they are mostly blocked by refuse dumps from the households and street vendors. Therefore, the rainy season is always hectic in Lagos, especially as both state and local governments shirk their responsibilities for keeping drainages and channels clear of refuse.

2.2 Lagos Climate and Microclimate

Lagos is characterized by tropical high climate, with high temperature, high humidity and heavy rainfall, with two rainfall peak regimes in June and October. The microclimate is also influenced by the proximity to the ocean. The rainy season in Lagos generally starts in April extending to October with a short cool but dry spell in August (August Break). Reports by the Meteorological Services have revealed that there are two rainfall peak periods in Lagos. The first is in June (about 1125.28 mm), and the second usually in October (about 409.14 mm). The mean annual rainfall for Lagos State is about 1620.59 mm. According to the Nigerian Meteorological Services (NMS) Oshodi, rainfall in Lagos State experiences a wide spatial variation. Along the coastal settlements, rainfall is pervasively high but generally decreases toward the Northern region of the state. For example at Apapa, the Mean Monthly Rainfall was 1854.4 mm, Lagos Island 1841.7 mm, Ikoyi 1761 mm (all locations very close to the coast) while Agege had 1394.5 mm, Iju 1410.5 mm and Ikorodu 1441.3 mm (all far from the Coast), but for the effect of relief at Epe, which enhanced its Mean Monthly Rainfall of 1671.1 mm, compared with Ikorodu on the same latitude with 1441.3 mm, rainfall should have expectedly reduced northwards (Balogun et al. 1999). The diurnal temperature is constantly high in Lagos. This is in perfect conformity with the tropical climate of the region. The average diurnal temperature is 27.6 °C. The minimum and maximum daily temperatures are 29.6 °C and 24.5 °C, respectively, with the daily range of 5.1 °C. The lowest temperature is recorded in August, and the highest temperature about 34 °C is usually recorded between December and March. The general humidity in Lagos State is very high, although there are variations from place to place and from time to time. The mean humidity in the state ranges between 76 and 80.5%. Usually, the morning humidity is higher than the afternoon humidity.

The main continental winds that affect the climatic and weather conditions of Lagos State are: South West Trade Wind (SWTW) and North East Trade Wind (NETW). The extent of influence of these winds is determined by the Intertropical Converge Zone (ITCZ) or Intertropical Front or Discontinuity (ITF or ITD). The South West Trade Wind sweeps over the ocean and thus carries warm, moisture-laden air to the hinterland. This wind brings rainfall to the Lagos settlement and beyond. The SETW pushes the ITCZ to the North from April to October. But from

October to February, the North East Trade Wind pushes the ITCZ to the South reaching Lagos sparingly in December. The NETW is localized as Harmattan which is a dusty, dry and cold wind. It is not usually accompanied by rain. Due partly to the climate of Lagos and partly to its soil characteristics, the state is characterized by diverse biodiversities. Naturally, Lagos is characterized in the coastal areas by mangrove plants, raffia palms, bamboo and short trees. In the Northern region such as Ikorodu, Epe and Agege, the vegetation is characterized by tall trees, palm trees and fibers. The condition in the Northern region permits the growth of cassava, yams and vegetables. On the coastal area, it is the coconut trees that are more found and interspersed with short-time vegetables and sugarcane. The vegetation is luxuriant both during rainy and dry seasons. However, due to rapid urbanization, the present area regarded as Lagos metropolis has lost a large portion of its vegetative cover to industrial and residential buildings. The natural vegetative characteristics of Lagos only make room for the procurement of soft materials for shelter construction and in the early period of settlement evolution in Lagos, mud houses and leave-thatched structures were common. The recurrent problem of loss of vegetation has created a lack of sufficient trees that could be used for housing construction, especially bamboo and planks. Most of the roofing planks are brought from the neighboring states of Ogun, Oyo and Ondo. The early houses built in Lagos were dictated not by the climate alone, but also by the materials available—sand, mud, from the lagoon, palm leaves, bamboo poles, raffia palm, decayed vegetables and clay—they resembled rectilinear tents interlaced with nets, leaves, bark of trees and bamboo fronds (Adefuye et al. 1987). The traditional built environment that predated the colonial era in Lagos was both in design and standard marked by a process intimately related to the user's needs and very much in the user's control.

2.3 Urbanization in Lagos

Urbanization as a process of population concentration, economic agglomeration and political change is very long and prominent in Lagos. Urban growth in Lagos dates back to the late fifteenth century (1472) when the Portuguese started using the Lagos Port as a slave trade market deport across West African subregion. All slaves gathered in the region were ferried to Europe and America through Lagos Port. This was one major factor that initiated and launched Lagos urbanization (Mabogunje 1968; Peil 1991, 1994; Odumosu, 2004). After the abolition of slavery, Lagos grew as a foremost capital city, industrialized hub and major commercial center that attracted a huge population from other parts of the country and West African subregion. Since the mid-twentieth century, Lagos had witnessed steady and exponential population growth from mere 325,000 in 1950 to about 16 million people in 2022 (see Table 2.1 and Fig. 2.3). Presently, Lagos is the most urbanized and industrialized region in Nigeria and in the entire sub-Saharan Africa. In 2006, it had a population of about 10 million people and in 2022 a population of about 15,726,000 million people out of which 12.8 million (80%) live in the metropolis (NPC 2006; UNHABITAT 2008;

UN World Population Prospects 2022). Lagos entered the new millennium in the year 2000 as a megacity, with about 10 million people (UNHABITAT 2008).

Lagos is a sociodemographically and ethnically varied community. The dominant ethnic group is Yoruba, although, as a cosmopolitan city, many other ethnic groups are found in Lagos. What is known as Lagos today began as a Crown Colony in 1851 when the then Oba of Lagos, Oba Dosumu, ceded the territory to the British colonialists, having banished the erstwhile monarch Oba Kosoko to Epe a closer community in the neighborhood (Adefuye et al. 1987). The year 1950 marked a unique epoch in the development of Lagos. By the ordinance no. 17 of 1950, the Mayoral chair was introduced into Lagos town council. The mayoralty signified the beginning of the independent political demarcation of Lagos for future relevance. Dr. Olorunimbe was the first and the only mayor of Lagos as mayoralty was abolished in 1953 and replaced by a minister for Lagos Affairs as recommended by the 1954

Table 2.1 Lagos state population distribution

LGA	Population 2006	Male (2006)	Female (2006)	Projection 2022
Agege	459,939	242,520	217,419	802,473
Ajeromi-Ifelodun	684,105	352,238	331,867	1,193,585
Alimosho	1,277,714	649,460	628,254	2,229,278
Amuwo-Odofin	318,166	167,856	150,310	555,117
Apapa	217,362	119,556	970,86	379,240
Badagry	241,093	121,232	119,861	420,645
Epe	181,409	91,105	90,304	316,511
Eti-Osa	287,785	160,396	127,389	502,110
Ibeju-Lekki	117,481	59,544	59,737	204,974
Ifako-Ijaye	427,878	218,993	208,885	746,536
Ikeja	313,196	169,233	143,963	546,445
Ikorodu	535,619	272,569	263,050	934,516
Kosofe	665,393	350,120	315,273	1,160,937
Lagos Island	209,437	108,057	101,380	365,413
Lagos Mainland	317,720	166,163	15,557	554,339
Mushin	633,009	328,197	394,812	1,104,436
Ojo	598,071	310,100	287,971	1,043,478
Oshodi-Isolo	621,509	321,767	299,742	1,084,371
Shomolu	402,673	207,649	195,024	702,559
Surulere	503,975	261,265	242,710	879,305
Total	9,013,534	4,678,020	4,335,514	15,726,268

Source National Population Census NPC 2006 as projected for 2022@ 3.54% rate. United Nations World Population Prospects: <https://www.macrotrends.net/cities/22007/lagos/population> Lagos, Nigeria Metro Area Population 1950–2023. www.macrotrends.net. Retrieved 2023-06-29

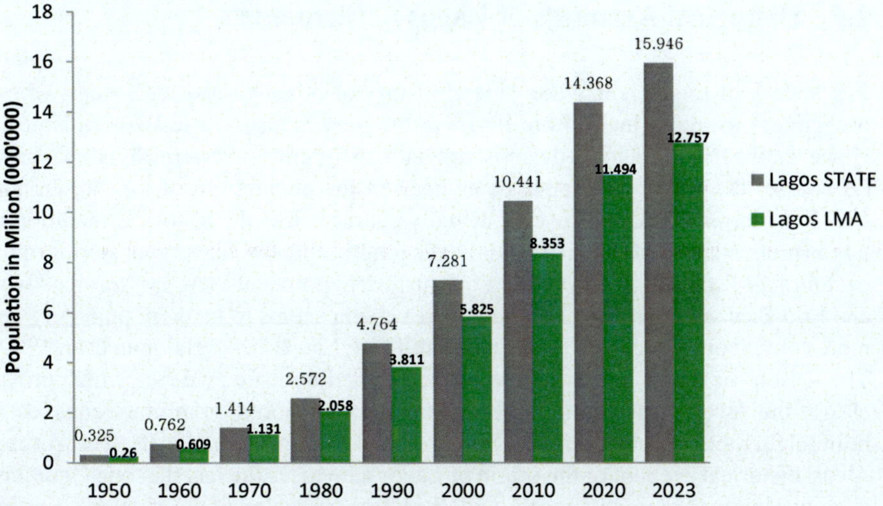

Fig. 2.3 Lagos population growth from 1950 to 2023

Macpherson Constitution. The spatial growth of Lagos has been very rapid. Over time, Lagos grew from Lagos Island to include other areas such as Ikoyi, Obalende and Victoria Island where the British expatriates had their earlier abodes. This trend continued until 1960 when Lagos became the capital city of the emergent Nigerian political structure. Three years later in 1963, Lagos population was put at 1,136,154 people (Balogun et al. 1999). In 1967, having been conferred with the status of a state, Lagos became a larger entity with five regions namely, Lagos, Epe, Ikeja, Ikorodu and Badagry Divisions. During the Local Government reform of 1976, the five regions were further divided into eight Administrative Divisions, namely: Lagos Island, Mainland, Mushin, Somolu, Ikeja, Ikorodu, Epe and Badagry. In 1989, the Local Government Areas in Lagos grew to twelve with the addition of Eti-Osa, Ojo, Ibeju-Lekki and Agege to the existing ones. By 1991 when the federal capital was formally moved to Abuja, Lagos had fifteen Local Government Areas.

But by 1996, Lagos grew to twenty Local Government Areas namely Ikeja, Ajeromi-Ifelodun, Alimoso, Amuwo-Odofin, Apapa, Eti-Osa, Ifako-Ijaye, Agege, Ojo, Badagry, Kosofe, Lagos Island, Lagos Mainland, Oshodi-Isolo, Shomolu, Epe, Ikorodu, Mushin, Ibeju-Lekki and Surulere. The twenty (20) Local Government Area structures remain till today the substantively and legally recognized administrative structures in the state. However, thirty-seven development areas have been added to increase the local administrative units to a total of fifty-seven. Sixteen of the twenty LGAs are categorized formally as Lagos Metropolitan Areas (Megacity Region), while Badagry, Epe, Ibeju-Lekki and Ikorodu are often viewed to some extent as suburban or rural areas. The metropolitan area (LMA) constitutes about 80% of the entire state at any point in time. The Lagos Metropolitan Area (LMA) fondly referred to as the Lagos Megacity Region (LMR) forms the study area for this book.

2.4 Historical Accounts of Lagos Settlements

The history of Lagos is like the general history of other Yoruba settlements whose progenitors were originally from Ile-Ife in the present Osun State Western Nigeria. However, the rise of Lagos is the most dramatic in the entire Western Nigerian region. Of course, the history of Lagos dates back to the ancient era of the Yoruba and Bini Kingdoms. Some controversy actually characterizes the historical rendition of Lagos provenance as there are two dialectical but somehow convergent stories of the evolution of Lagos. The two contentious historical points of view are Yoruba-Awori and Edo-Bini versions. The Yoruba-Awori version seems to be more popularly and more convincingly accepted (Adefuye et al. 1987; Lawal 1994; Balogun et al. 1999). The reason for this is not far to seek. Besides the linguistic evidence which proves clearly the Aworis true claim, the Edo-Bini story anchored on military conquest is infinitely remote in authenticity as Bini itself has its origin from Ile-Ife. The Yoruba-Awori historical account of the origin of Lagos canvasses the fact that one Ogunfere, a famous hunter, entered Lagos through the Northern region of the state on a hunting expedition from Ile-Ife and after several successful expeditions decided to create an abode in Idumagbo an Awori neighborhood in the present Lagos Mainland LGA. From Idumagbo, Ogunfere and his large family members began a gradual occupation of the Northern Lagos region. Perhaps for many physical reasons, the earlier settlers were unable to expand the frontier of their settlement to the coastal areas which were heavily river-rine and inhabited by wild animals like alligators and pythons. For these reasons, the Idumagbo settlers therefore dedicated Lagos coastal forest areas to farming and hunting activities.

On the other hand, the Bini version of Lagos evolution argues that Lagos was a war-seized land where Oba Erediauwa of Bini kingdom in the present-day Edo State of Nigeria used to have his war arsenals and permanently used by the King warriors as a war camp. This line of account seems to be too tenuous to believe as there is only little evidence aside from the historic relics of the Royal Kingship of Lagos to support Benin theory. If at all there was any scintilla of credence in the Bini theory of Lagos evolution, it was that the conquest by the Bini warlords was largely incomplete and unsuccessful. It was not sufficient to lay claim to the colonization of a place without successfully inhabiting the area. Till date, there was no relatively homogenous Bini family in Lagos. Perhaps, the only major claim to Lagos by the Bini people was the controversial name EKO given to Lagos by the indigenous population. While EKO according to the Bini means war settlement, Awori sees EKO as a corrupted word for Oko meaning farm which reflects the fact that Lagos Island area was being used as farm by Ogunfere and his descendants then. This is very different from the Bini account of Eko as armory war camp. The Aworis are the most visible and most populous of the indigenes today in Lagos, and the Ogu people of Badagry whose history is traced to the Republic of Benin are also very distinct settlers occupying the Western flank of Lagos.

By the turn of the fourteenth century, Lagos had become an established settlement with potential for population growth and spatial expansion. This coincided with the time of risky expedition by the Europeans, especially the Portuguese who made their first contact with Lagos in the fifteenth century. The main interest of the Europeans then was the purchase of slaves for use as labors in Sugar plantations in North America and Europe. Lagos rose into fame on the crest of slave trade and was regarded as the most important slave trade market in the whole West African subregion. But after the Berlin Treaty in 1851, slave trade was declared an illegal activity that must be halted, and later in 1851, when the British who later colonized Nigeria, banished King Dosumu to Epetedo for his non-compliance with the Treaty on the Abolition of the Slave Trade in the continent, Lagos assumed another role as the seat of colonial administration. By 1914 when it became more imminent that the Lagos Colony, the Northern and Southern protectorates were certainly being prepared to unite into a single entity, Lagos also emerged as the de facto first capital of Nigeria. The prominence enjoyed by Lagos was due to the fact that the colonial administrators had realized the vantage position that Lagos occupied within the contexts of administrative, economic, demographic and strategic realities of the country.

The coastal location of Lagos must have also influenced its role as a choice of the colonial masters. The location gives Lagos convivial climatic conditions similar to those experienced in Europe, and the settlement is accessible through the sea and the land; the development that had led to the influx of people to the state right from the earlier period of Lagos life. The modern Lagos settlement is composed of more other people besides the Awori and Ogu. By 1967, when the state of Lagos was created by the Military Government, the spatial extent of the emergent state became wider including Ijebu communities of Ikorodu, and Ijede as well as Ikeja areas. Immigration into Lagos over time has also influenced the ethnic composition of the settlement as even the Awori has long been overnumbered by the non-indigenes of fairly long historical antecedents. Studies have confirmed that the Yoruba from other parts of Western region are the dominant ethnic group in the contemporary Lagos settlement (Odumosu 2004). The Igbo people of the Eastern Nigeria and Edo people of Bini origin and Hausa from the North have substantial presence in Lagos today.

2.5 Lagos Economic and Regional Development

As stated earlier, Lagos is undoubtedly the most urbanized and most economically developed area of Nigeria and perhaps the entire West African subregion. Lagos State has remained at the fore front of economic, social and political development in Nigeria since the precolonial time till the present days. It played prominent role in linking the country sides to the coastal ports during the slave trade enterprise that spanned almost eight centuries in Africa. And by the time slavery finally ceased in the late nineteenth century, Lagos naturally became the seat of colonial rule from where the British colonial administrators administered the rest of the country from 1914 to 1960. As the seat of power during this time, most developmental efforts were concentrated in Lagos, and more than any factor, this was the major contributor to the rise of Lagos as the economic nerve center of the country. Lagos has been the focus of industrial concentration for decades. This rapid industrialization has its route in the post-independent regional policies embarked upon by both the federal and regional governments of the time. At the time of independence in 1960 with Lagos as the capital city of Nigeria, a number of industrial estates were conceptualized and developed making the state the most industrialized in the entire West African subregion. As today, Lagos in all modesty is a highly urbanized and industrialized city virtually distinct from other parts of the country. By the leadership in economic and industrial activities, Lagos had played and is still playing a vital role in the development of Nigeria and generates about 60% of the value added tax (VAT) obtained in the country.

Lagos has contributed so enormously from basic and non-basic city functions it generates. Broadly speaking, the economic activities in Lagos are divided into two: formal sector and informal sector. The formal sector economic activities are those that spring up from governments and other organized institutions, while those of the informal sector are economic concerns that individuals outside the formal sector create. Until 1991, when the seat of power was taken to Abuja from Lagos, most of the federal government offices and parastatals found their locations in Lagos. Important economic concerns such as the Nigerian Port Authority (NPA), Murtala Mohammed Airport (MMA) at Ikeja, the Federal Secretariat at Ikoyi, the Central Bank of Nigeria (CBN), just to name a few were located in Lagos. Besides this formal presence, several industrial estates were established at Apapa, Ikeja, Ilupeju, Isolo, Amuwo and Gbagada. These industries engage in the production of products ranging from textiles, tobacco, tea, beverages, paints, building materials, soft drinks, brewery, to automobile products (Balogun et al. 1999). All these industrial productions are results of long period of regional planning that have characterized the region (Fig. 2.4 indicates the regional and land use development plan of Lagos State).

The private sector has its share of economic contribution to the development of Lagos. Virtually, all serious banks and financial institutions up till now have their headquarters in Lagos. Some of these banks which survived after recapitalization policy between 1999 and 2007 include Intercontinental, First City Monument Bank, Stanbic, Eko, Zenith, Union, United Bank of Africa, Wema, First Bank, Guaranty Trust Bank, and others, numbering about twenty-five. We also have other microfinance banks as well as insurance companies all with their head offices in Lagos. Besides, there is a huge aggregation or localization of manufacturing companies in Lagos. It has been estimated that over 50% of the industrial companies in Nigeria are located and sited in Lagos State. Apart from the medium and large-scale industrial conglomerates and government concerns small-scale industries and individuals businesses are engaged by Nigerians and other non-Nigerian entrepreneurs to make money. Many traders are found in Idumota, Trade Fair along Badagry-Mile 2 road, Oshodi and other parts of the metropolis. Several markets are also provided in the state to keep the residents economically active; hence, such markets as Ojuwoye, Oyingbo, Aswani, Alaba, Alade, Ayobo and Mile 12 agricultural product markets are sources of economic activities.

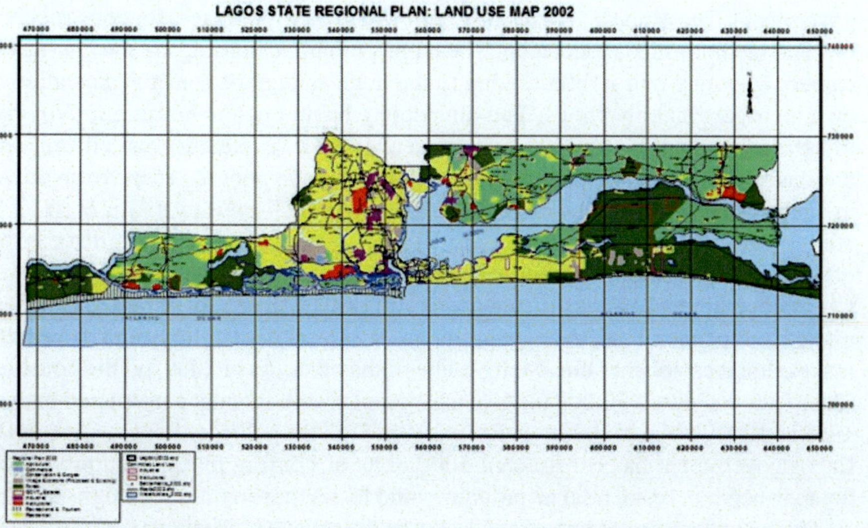

Fig. 2.4 Regional plan and land use map of Lagos (Lagos Ministry of Urban and Physical Planning; Aliu 2012)

Usually, the predominant economic activities in Lagos as an urban center are in secondary and tertiary realms. Except in Ikorodu, Epe and Badagry areas of Lagos, agriculture has no place in the vocation of the people of Lagos and this shows its extensive urban nature (Odumosu 2004). Most of the populations are traders and civil servants. A number of small-scale industries also characterize Lagos State informal sectors. These outfits include plastic, apparel, metal, furniture, woodwork, jewelry, carpets and rugs, footwear, electrical, welding, cutlery, and hand tools industries. They provide employments for many residents of the state and revenue for government in terms of taxes. Lagos also has a lot of educational institutions such as Lagos State University, Lagos State Polytechnic, Adeniran Ogunsanya College of Education, University of Lagos, Administrative Staff College of Nigeria, French Village, Nigerian Institute of Journalism and a host of others. Few of these institutions only have residential apartments exclusively built for their employees while majority of them allow their employees to source for accommodation by themselves. The concentration of economic activities in Lagos increases the demand for housing of diverse nature that reflects the socioeconomic characteristics of the city dwellers.

2.6 Housing Development in Lagos

Housing development in Lagos Metropolitan Area has two sources (Aliu and Ajala 2015; Aluko 2000). The first is the public housing market which consists of properties built for and sold to Nigerian citizens by the governments including state and federal government. These houses are usually built where there are spaces for construction of low and medium-income housing. The targets of public housing are the low-income earners who may find it difficult due to the huge amount of housing expenditure to own their personal dwellings. The philosophy behind public housing in Nigeria is to use the program to improve homeownership and elevate Nigerian citizens from the shackles of poverty and penury hence assisting the poor to escape from poverty as many homeowners convert their property to rental housing (Aliu et al. 2018; Aliu 2020, 2023). Lagos remains one of the states in Nigeria with a long history of public property development and estate buildings. Right from the colonial time, Lagos government has constructed and is still constructing a lot of public residential estates by the federal and state governments. Every regime (military and democratic) makes sure it establishes one public estate or the other. As of 2009, public housing in Lagos stood at about 50,000 units consisting of dwelling units constructed between 1989 and 2009 (Aliu et al. 2018). Recently through the policy of Rent to Own (RTO), Lagos government has constructed 5000 units of housing in 12 locations to boost homeownership, residential affordability and lessen poverty among Lagosians.

The second source of housing in Lagos is the private housing market. This sector consists of two players namely the individuals who build houses and real properties for personal occupation and rent in the city and the organized property developers who build and sell housing units and real estate to ordinary willing persons at a commercial rate. Lagos is dominated by the low socioeconomic residents who majorly work in the informal sectors of the city. These people gradually build their houses either for personal occupation or for rent or for both in what has been characterized as incremental self-help housing (Aliu et al. 2018). In fact, an average Nigerian sees urban housing as a means of raising revenue, and they seek to build one in their life span. Of course, the rich also build houses, especially for their own occupation. While housing from incremental sources may have some elements of informality for lack of official entitlement to the land on which they are constructed, those from the rich are mostly backed up by some official formalizations. The informal housing rental market is the largest, the least qualitative and the cheapest housing in Lagos. In many situations, it relapses into slums due to lack of building maintenance, poor neighborhood quality and lack of access to land ownership. Most of the informal housing does not have title deeds or certificates of occupancy (C of O). However, due to the volatility of land market in Lagos, eviction and dispossession due to lack of title deeds have been less applied on the informal housing owners.

A large swath of the megacity is under the informal housing market and with variegated quality and prices. Unlike the informal housing, the organized private property is more decent and more formalized but of less quantity. The main underlining philosophy of private housing either by the individuals or by the developers is to make profit. Hence, the private housing market is profit driven, unlike the public housing market that seeks to just make beak-even and support the common Nigerian in his drive to own a house (Aliu 2023). The goal of the private housing is to use housing to make economic gain. However, while the informal housing provides affordable accommodation for the low-income groups, the private estates constructed by the organized private developers who build houses for profit enterprises are for the medium- and the high-income urban residents. In truth, the contribution of organized housing sector to the private housing in Lagos is less than 10%. Incidentally, this book covers the private housing market consisting of houses produced by the individuals only excluding those provided by the organized property developers. Hence, residential estates by the organized developers are excluded from consideration. The choice of this segment of the housing market in Lagos was based on the fact that it consists of the majority of housing in Lagos Metropolitan Area, and it consists of clusters of different socioeconomic status (SES) residents. Of course, the dwelling units from the private housing market largely produce the nature of residential quality and quantity observed in Lagos Metropolitan Area (see Fig. 2.5).

2.7 The Nature of Urban Private Housing Market in Lagos

Urban private housing dominates Lagos metropolitan housing markets even though there are pockets of public estates located within the central area of the megacity. The public estates accommodate less than 10 percents of the Lagos residents. Urban private housing in Lagos defines the city spatial residential patterns and land use with some elements of sluminization and informalities (see Aliu et al. 2021). Urban private housing market accounts for over 80% of the residential apartments in Lagos megacity. Lagos urban private housing market displays profound polarization in terms of quality and values (Aliu and Ajala 2014; Aliu 2023). This polarization can be traced to the different sources of housing development in the city. As shown in Fig. 2.6, spatially Lagos urban housing market has three segments differentiated by residential and room density[1] (Aliu and Ajala 2014; Aluko 2000). This residential structure simply reflects spatial dimensions of residential and physical land uses as canvassed by the urban morphological models of Burgess (1925), Hoyt (1939), Harris and Ullman (1945). The first residential market area in Metropolitan Lagos is the low residential density (LRD) area which consists of the neighborhoods that are designed and characterized by few number of housing units per acre, lower room density and houses that are of high quality and prices. This area is obviously the place for the highly rich Lagosians who rent or purchase houses for personal occupation. The

[1] Density as a measure of the degree to which an area is filled or occupied is a controversial concept. However, in the context of housing development and urban planning policy, residential density refers to the quantity of dwelling units per acre of lot size in an area. It is the ratio of all occupants or dwelling units in a building to the lot size of the building. Of course, the term also lends itself to two subterms, namely gross residential density which measures the total dwelling units per acre in a given area including all types of land uses such as streets, sidewalks, public spaces and net residential density which measures the number of dwelling units per acre of an area devoted to residential purposes excluding walkways, open spaces and other non-residential uses. A related concept to residential density is room density which is a term often used to describe the number of occupants per room. The higher the ratio of occupants to a room, the higher the level of residential congestion of an apartment. Both residential density and room density are measures of housing quality and overcrowding.

Fig. 2.5 Aerial views of Metropolitan Lagos residential neighborhoods. *Source* Open source data

LRD neighborhoods are well planned and exhibit exquisite properties with accessibility. Such areas include Ikoyi, Victoria Island, Lekki Peninsula and some areas in Ikeja and Ilupeju industrial neighborhoods. In terms of security, this area though relies heavily on formal security apparatus such as the state police but also relies on privately organized security agencies. The residential buildings are often surrounded by perimeter fences, Close Circuit Television (CCTV) and heavily constructed iron gates. These gates are manned by well-trained and armed security personnel from

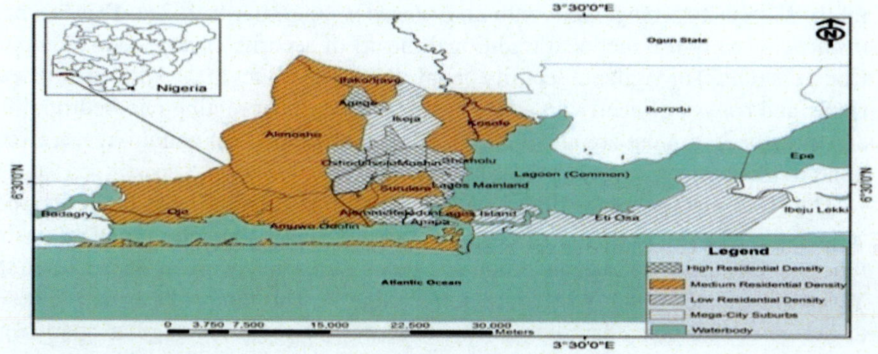

Fig. 2.6 Lagos residential density areas. *Source* Aliu (2016)

organized security outfits. Residential values of dwellings in the LRD are very high and come with formal land use charges and value added taxes. One-bedroom flat and three-bedroom flat go for N650,000 and N2,120,000 per annum, respectively. Land costs about N331,614 per m^2 in this area of Lagos.

The second segmented market area is the medium residential density (MRD) neighborhood which consists of somewhat planned areas with good dwellings, not very dense houses and environment that is very convivial to live. The residential density and the room density of MRD areas are higher than the LRD. The residents are usually civil servants and private workers with medium incomes. This area is populated by the middle working-class residents who are fairly well paid and live in a mix of flats and tenement residences. The MRD area includes Maryland, Surulere, Yaba, Apapa and Oregun in Ikeja. In terms of security, these neighborhoods are secured by the police and some organized security personnel who may not be licensed armed weapon carriers. Residential values of MRD housing units are moderately high with little add-on taxes. The costs of renting one-bedroom flat and three-bedroom flat are about N200,000 and N1,500,000 per annum, respectively. The cost of land is about N250,000 per m^2.

The last segmented residential neighborhoods in the urban private housing market of Lagos is the high residential density area (HRD) which consists of poorly planned neighborhoods with dense residential buildings per acre, high population, high room density, poor-quality properties, poor environment and low-value houses. This neighborhood parades the highest possible levels of residential density and occupancy. The HRD neighborhoods are populated by the least rich residents who majorly live in one-room apartment residences (see Aliu 2012; Aliu and Ajala 2014). This area is also dominated by informal housing with no formal tenure and informal security. Housing here does not have perimeter fencing and are usually built on smaller plot size. The HRD areas include Lagos Island, Lagos Mainland, Mushin, Isolo, Ejigbo, Orile, Ijeshatedo, Ajegunle, Ojota, Agege, Ilasa and Oshodi. Although there are several police stations within the neighborhoods, they are not well equipped and funded to operate more efficiently. The informal neighborhoods often resort to informal security arrangement with no licensed weapons (Aliu 2023). This is where residents usually use the local traditional means of security such as Odua People's Congress (OPC) or vigilante security people. Housing values in the HRD are the least costly and consist of nearly no add-on taxes. The costs of renting one-bedroom flat and three-bedroom flat are about N320,000 and N950,000 per annum, respectively. Land property costs about N140,714 per m^2.

The HRD market area is dominated by traditional housing types often regarded as face-me-I face-you (FMIFY) or vernacular housing types. The FMIFY housing type is a reflection of the general housing types across many towns and cities in the Yoruba-dominated South Western region of Nigeria. This kind of housing is devised to accommodate many families in two rows of one-room rectangular apartments facing one another with general spaces for corridors, toilets, joint kitchens, joint baths, joint toilets and joint verandas. Apart from saving physical space, the face-me-I-face-you housing types in the Lagos HRD area also save cost. Most of the residential services like water, energy or light, central corridors, gates or entrances, toilets, kitchens and baths are jointly shared by all the residents living in the house as a whole. Residential and room densities are usually high. Of course, this kind of apartment is a reflection of the socioeconomic conditions of the residents who are generally of low-status workers.

2.8 Summary

Lagos is an old settlement that rose to prominence during the Portuguese explorations in the fifteenth century. It was the epicenter of slavery trade in West African subregion, the Crown Colony in 1851 and subsequently became the capital city of the emergent Nigerian nation in 1914 under the British colonial governance. At the Nigeria's attainment of independence in 1960, Lagos transformed to the seat of power and center of economic trade. Naturally, the city is a much-endowed settlement with livable climate and a natural port that lent to further development in its economic domination. Lagos Metropolitan Area which is a combination of several communities with its hub at the Lagos Island is a progressively cosmopolitan region with diverse ethnic groups and foreign citizens. The housing and physical development of Lagos megacity is very complex and intriguing so also the land use systems of the city.

References

Abegunde MAA (1987) Aspects of the physical environment of Lagos State. In: Adefuye A, Babatunde A, Osuntokun J (eds) History of the people of Lagos. Lantern Books Ltd, Lagos

Adefuye A, Agiri B, Oshuntokun J (eds) (1987) History of the people of Lagos. Lantern Books Ltd., Nigeria, Lagos

Aliu IR, Ajala OA. (2014) Intra-city polarization, residential type and attribute importance: a discrete choice study of Lagos. Habitat Int 42(2):11–20 https://doi.org/10.1016/j.habitatint.2013.10.002

Aliu IR, Ajala OA (2015) Residential polarization in an african megacity: an exploratory study of Lagos. S Afr Geogr J 97(3):264–286. https://doi.org/10.1080/03736245.2014.977810

Aliu IR (2016) Marginal land use and value characterizations in Lagos: untangling the drivers and implications for sustainability. J Environ Dev Sustain 18(2):1615–1634 https://doi.org/10.1007/s10668-015-9706-2

Aliu IR, Towry-Coker L, Odumosu T (2018) Housing policy debacle in Sub-Saharan Africa: an appraisal of three housing programmes in Lagos Nigeria. Afr Geogr Rev 37(3), 241–256. https://doi.org/10.1080/19376812.2017.1284005

Aliu IR (2020) Energy efficiency in postpaid-prepaid metered homes: analyzing effects of socioeconomic, housing and metering factors in Lagos, Nigeria. Energ Effi 13(5):853–869 https://doi.org/10.1007/s12053-020-09850-y

Aliu IR (2023) Urban property markets and security risk: explaining how neighborhood security shapes urban rental housing prices in Ojo Lagos, Nigeria. Property Manag 41(3):404–430

Aliu IR (2012) Spatial patterns of residential quality and housing preferences in selected local government areas of Lagos. A PhD thesis Obafemi Awolowo University Ile-Ife Nigeria, p 254

Aliu IR, Akoteyon IS, & Soladoye O (2021) Living on the margins: socio-spatial characterization of residential and water deprivations in Lagos informal communities, Nigeria. Habitat Int 107: 102293https://doi.org/10.1016/j.habitatint.2020.102293

Aluko EO (2000) Urban market segmentation and house values in metropolitan Lagos. Niger Geogr J 3&4:148–157

Balogun YO, Odumosu OJ, Ojo OA (1999) (eds) Lagos in maps. Pumark, Lagos

Burgess EW (1925) The growth of the city: an introduction to a research project. In: Parks RE, Burgess E, Mckenzie RD (eds) The city. Chicago University Press, Chicago, pp 44–62

Harris CD, Ullman EL (1945) The nature of cities. Annals of the American Academy of Political and Social Sciences, pp 7–11

Hoyt H (1939) The structure and growth of residential neighborhood in American cities. The United States Federal Housing Administration, Washington, D.C.

Jeje LK (1978) Aspects of the geomorphology of Nigeria. In: Oguntoyinbo JS, Areola OO, Filani M (1978) (eds) A Geography of Nigerian Development. Heinemann, Ibadan, pp 17–44

Lawal K (1994) Urban transition in Africa: aspects of urbanization and change in Lagos. Pumark Nigeria Limited, Lagos

Mabogunje AL (1968) Urbanization in Nigeria. University of London Press, London

Odumosu JO (2004) Catalo-reactant of development: urbanization through the ages—an inaugural lecture. March 2004, Lagos State University, Ojo, Lagos

Peil M (1994) African urban society. University Press, Birmingham, Birmingham

Peil M (1991) Lagos: the people are the city. London, Belhaven

National Population Commission (2006) Nigerian population census. Abuja, Nigeria

United Nations Habitat (2008). State of african cities. Nairobi, Kenya: united Nations Human Settlements Programme. Retrieved from https://www.unhabitat.org

Chapter 3
Residential Quality and Housing Preference Theories

Abstract Housing as a complex sociophysical process has lent itself to a number of theories, concepts and models. These theories and models are essential frameworks for understanding the underlying constructs in housing issues. Theory itself is a framework often invoked to explain and understand the intricate interconnected issues, variables and indicators that link the problem variables to independent variables. The importance is to throw more light to the connections among the various variables in a phenomenon. In the same vein, the theories of housing including the concept of housing, residential quality, housing preferences and choices, as well as those that lie at the intersection of urbanization and housing, help to create comprehension of the housing complexity. Explanation of housing quality and residential choices is predicated upon the theory of urban spatial structure, Herbert's Residential Choice Decision (RCD) Theory and McFadden Random Utility (MRU) Theory.

Keywords Housing theory · Residential quality · Housing preference · Residential choice decision theory · Random utility theory

This chapter deals with the theoretical frameworks and review of housing preference models that are of direct relevance to housing quality and residential preference. It is divided into two broad subsections. Firstly, existing theories in housing such as the meaning of housing, residential quality, housing need, housing preference and models of the spatial pattern of residential neighborhoods are treated. Secondly, the theoretical basis for residential choice decision making is also provided. This section of the book therefore presents the major theoretical framework employed in the empirical analysis of residential quality and housing preferences exhibited in Lagos urban private housing markets.

© The Author(s), under exclusive license to Springer Nature Switzerland AG 2024
I. R. Aliu, *Urban Private Housing in Nigeria*, The Urban Book Series,
https://doi.org/10.1007/978-3-031-47432-3_3

3.1 Existing Housing Theories

3.1.1 Meaning of Housing

There is no one catch-all universal definition of housing in the literature. This is because the issue of shelter has proved to be highly subjective and sometimes extremely dynamic. In a reiteration of this fact, Onokerhoraye (1984: 216) opines that:

> The perception of housing as a human requirement has been changing over the years. In the past housing was looked upon primarily as a physical phenomenon which offered mere protection against uncontrolled elements and other forms of intrusion…In recent years, the conception of housing has changed remarkably, apart from the protection it offers, housing is viewed in its wider socioeconomic context. Housing may serve as a workplace for families, it can be used for recreational activities, generate income, a symbol of achievement and provide a storage space for man's valuable possessions.

Over the years, the three broad perspectives from which housing as a concept has been popularly discussed are physical, sociocultural and economic viewpoints. The variability of the meaning of housing reflects the rationale for individual predilections and preferences. Beyer (1965) defines housing as a highly complex product which is a bulky, durable and permanent product that has a fixed location, being used in the place where it is built. Once built it tends to remain in existence for many years. But housing is more than a complex product. It is both an economic and a social process. This definition apparently emphasizes the underlying processes involved in housing with a subtle reference to its physical nature. The only problem with the definition is that it does not elaborate on what the nature of these economic and social processes may look like. Turner (1976) expresses a similar view but from a clearer perspective as he defines housing as: "both the stock of dwelling units and the process by which that stock is maintained. It is also entirely reasonable to speak about human and social values of housing action and housing processes."

The definition as given by Turner stresses the value of housing from the point of its actions and values rather than the complexity of its physical presence. His definition gives a clearer picture of housing from the value man himself attaches to it. He also underscores the processes through which housing has evolved. Of course, the flaw in the definition is its uncontemplative silence on the economic implication of social and housing processes. Burns and Grebbler (1977) in advancing the scope of the definition see housing as a means of achieving other services besides shelter such as indoor cooking, sanitary and storage facilities, or the assurance of privacy and rest or the provision of space for recreation and children's education. Although this definition takes into consideration a lot of other issues such as the place of family as the predominant consumption unit of housing, it fails to pay attention to the socioeconomic factors as important determinants in housing acquisition. However, it firmly establishes the utility components and invariably the features that influence housing preferences. Housing as an institution is the theme curiously canvassed by Rapoport (1969) who defines a house as an institution not just a structure created for a complex set of purposes. Because building is a cultural phenomenon, its form and organization are greatly influenced by the cultural milieu to which it belongs. This definition is particularly noteworthy for one reason: It takes an unprecedented provision for the position of cultural phenomenon in housing design and construction. It awakens our consciousness to the physical variation in the shape, type, size and nature of housing in different civilizations. However, the definition suffers a terrible weakness in that it offers no idea about the influence of social as well as economic processes on the cultural milieu. Mabogunje et al. (1978) define housing as an organic entity that provides for man's biological needs, such as clean air, water and food, his psychological needs such as satisfaction, contentment, prestige, privacy, choice, freedom and security for his life and property, and also for his social needs such as interaction with others, human development and cultural activities. The view by Mabogunje et al. (1978) that housing is a means to achieve certain level of comforts in life establishes a strong basis for the variation in preferences from the utility point.

One definition which can be regarded as all embracing and all encompassing (for it takes into consideration, the physical, sociocultural and economic attributes of housing) has been given by Bourne (1981) who asserts that housing is a physical entity, a social artifact, an economic good, a capital stock and a status symbol. As a physical entity, unit or structure, housing provides shelter to its occupants, and as an economic good or commodity, it is a consumable good which is traded or exchanged in a market (Bourne 1981). Buttressing Bourne's view Adams (1986) succinctly avers that housing is economically a major speculative investment, a store of wealth and a vivid symbol of material achievement. Rapoport (2001) defines housing as a system of settings within which a certain system of activities takes place; and hence, housing is more than the dwelling—the neighborhood and its environmental quality profiles—become important. In this definition, the role of environmental quality consisting of location and neighborhood is given a prominent place in housing. This is particularly gratifying in that housing cannot be well understood when it is isolated from the environmental quality component, and this makes this particular definition a highly satisfactory one and relevant to the view that the residential quality components are strong issues in housing preference formation process. In a rather synthetic manner, Lee (2005) views a house as built environment where a person can develop his or her identity, where human activities and social relationships start to be structured and where the most important experiences occur. Ajala and Adelodun (2007) define housing as the provision of shelter for individuals, and it comprises all the ancillary services and community facilities which are necessary for human well-being.

In this treatise, housing is taken conceptually as a physical structure and a social process by which shelter is provided, in convivial environment, with basic facilities, and at a location in which demand and supply come into terms and choices are made. Housing as a physical structure connotes residential buildings, their designs, material qualities, their arrangements in space and their ecological interactions with the physical environment, and as a social structure, it connotes a set of residence-based activities, their characters, social qualities and their socioeconomic interactions in space with the immediate communities and wide society. These definitions of housing adequately reflect the underlying factors that influence housing quality, preferences and choices.

3.1.2 Residential Quality

Defining residential quality has been very challenging to housing scholars, generally perhaps, for the inherent multiplicity of its perception by different peoples of the world. There are divergent opinions by scholars on what housing quality entails; while some argue on the basis of availability of internal facilities within the house, others favor environmental variables such as public facilities available within the neighborhood; hence, both internal and external attributes of housing are crucial to the explanation of residential quality (Ajala and Adelodun 2007). However, a number of scholars have conceived residential quality as minimum livable conditions of a residential dwelling in terms of structural design, dimension of space and environmental suitability (Mabogunje et al. 1978; Sumka 1979). In addition, residential quality emphasizes structural solidity and durability, basic services provision, unfettered accessibility, security of tenure, security, choice and reduction of crowdedness (Premius 2001; World Bank 1993; Agbola 2005). Theoretically, housing possesses three physical quality dimensions: location, structural and neighborhood quality (Goodwin 1977; Sumka 1979; Ndulo 1985; Can 1991; Arimah 1992; Aluko 2000; Rapoport 2001). The structural quality reflects the intrinsic values of houses, the location quality reflects the positional attributes of dwelling and the neighborhood quality reflects the extrinsic values of the neighborhood where houses are located. Studies have shown that the residential quality determines housing values or prices (Goodwin 1977; Ndulo 1985; Arimah 1992; Aluko 2000; Ajala and Adelodun 2007).

However, residential quality is very controversial and has been shown to be unique to different races (Mabogunje et al. 1978). There is no universal residential standard that is acceptable to all societies of the world. Geographical and ethnographic peculiarities define more often the type of housing quality and standard that prevail within a particular sociocultural setting (Rapoport 2001). What determines the residential quality as well as preferences of the individual is certainly the socioeconomic status in the society. Obviously, there is a link between residential quality and economic power or poverty (see Dewilde and De Keulenaer 2003). In most developing countries including Nigeria, lack of economic strength or poverty has undermined the quality of housing available to people, whom majority are poor. The environmental and dwelling attributes are influenced by socioeconomic indices which also determine the individual preferences. In another way, the quality of dwellings provided, in a place or region, depends on the socioeconomic status of the builders. In poor societies where people struggle to have property, the structural and neighborhood facilities of houses are hugely compromised, and since most renters make do with what is available, these forms of housing are taken by the city dwellers that are less economically privileged (Aliu and Adebayo 2010). Given the socioeconomic and cultural reasons, housing often displays not only intermarket variations but intramarket differentiation in quality. As there are differences in housing quality from one city to the other or one country to the other, there are also differences in quality from one neighborhood to the other. Residential quality therefore can be perceived along varying geographical scales: global, regional and local. *In this treatise, residential quality is viewed as the structural as well as the neighborhood attributes of dwellings in a specific location.*

3.1.3 Housing Need and Housing Demand

A key issue in residential quality and housing choice decision making is the concept of housing need. Generally speaking, housing need is an essentially prescriptive concept used to denote the inadequacy of existing housing provision and allocation when compared with a commonly accepted but socially normative assumption such as quality of opportunity (Grimes 1976). Housing need is a concept that addresses both the issues of adequate supply of decent housing and the realization of the equity objective that deals with the fair distribution of housing among the population. Ordinarily, the idea of housing need is anchored to the total requirement for shelter regardless of the ability of households to pay for it (Grimes 1976; Anusionwu 1982). In his contribution, Needleman (1964) defines housing need as the extent to which the quantity and quality of existing accommodation falls short of that required to provide each household or person in the population irrespective of ability to pay or of particular personal preferences with accommodation of a specified minimum standard. This seems to tally with the opinion of Onibokun (1982) when he defines housing need from the perspective of a planner as essentially the extent to which existing accommodation fails to meet demand in standards.

The common preoccupation of the two definitions as given above is the idea of a minimum standard. But the standards which determine habitability are generally subjective and may officially be set arbitrarily. This may be in terms of hygiene, quality of structure, occupancy rate and minimum privacy, space requirement, overcrowding among others (Grimes 1976; Mabogunje et al. 1978; Wakely et al. 1976; Lewin 1981; Anusionwu 1982; Mafico 1994). In quality terms therefore, housing need can otherwise be expressed as the difference between the total number of households and the number of dwellings that are habitable (Anusionwu 1982), although this counters the belief that demography and population growth must be factored into projection of housing needs. Primarily housing need can be seen as the expression of five fundamental desires: normative need, felt need, expressed need, comparative need and demand need. However in the literature, it has been pervasively argued that the housing need approach as either a policy tool or a means of assessing the magnitude of housing problem has little or no relevance. Reasons for this are given as follows: Firstly, the fact that it is often difficult to define a minimum standard of housing provision with precision. Secondly, the lack of consensus as to what standard should be. And finally, the fact that even when a standard is agreed upon, the concept of housing need reveals numerous housing deficiencies that cannot be met with available resources. Thus, the standard becomes so hopelessly difficult to meet that it is meaningless and conveys no idea of priorities as a basis for understanding preferences. And in view of these obvious difficulties concerning the use of housing need concept as a tool for explaining housing preferences, there is a general shift to the concept of effective demand which differs a bit from the housing need concept, but obviously more realistic and meaningful. This is because effective demand determines the level of residential quality and housing preferences by the individual.

Grimes (1976, p. 62) defines effective housing demand as the number of dwellings that can be afforded by families through unsubsidized loans from credit institutions. This definition reveals the fact that the concept of effective demand is anchored to affordability, unlike the principle of housing need that pays no attention to the financial ability of households to pay for their respective dwellings. However, the definition of housing demand is too limited and unsubstantiated when related to those to whom the housing is required. Needleman (1964, p. 18) in his opinion submits that effective housing demand represents the accommodation for which people are able and willing to pay. This definition prescribes the condition under which housing could be attained. A demand profile based on the ability to pay for diverse types of housing is then made. By and large, this definition takes no account of personal or social considerations that cannot be fulfilled because of lack of money. Adams (1986) maintains that if the concept of housing demand is well grasped, it seems to depict the set of housing wants and needs of the population based on its size, composition, tastes and resources, but there is actually more flavor and texture to housing demand than the simple aggregate count of households. The assertion of Adams here, especially the last clause of his observation, is primarily targeted at debunking, the confusion between housing need and housing demand. Previous works have shown that besides demographic changes, effective housing demand is largely influenced by migration, regional potentials, changes in income and employment (Harris and Todaro 1970; Anusionwu 1982), and in the urban milieu by a variety of social, legal and organizational as well as administrative factors (Lewin 1981). This also depends on the economic strength and social class of the residents. In Lagos as in many other developing countries globalizing cities the residents are majorly poor with low level of economic capacity and demand.

In the perception of effective housing demand concept, there are tangible objective elements and less concrete but nonetheless important subjective considerations. Lewin (1981) in view of this asserts that effective housing demand is determined by objective conditions such as a household's income, the share of income available for housing-income rent ratio-urban growth and construction rate, age and status of rural migrants, availability of rented accommodation and its location, physical standard and security of tenure. In addition, it is also influenced by the household's payment propensity, the place of housing on the list of priorities, housing traditions or customs and the attitude of migrants toward their urban sojourn. However, effective housing demand varies from country to country because of varying land values and construction cost, it is dependent on the changes in the economy at large and for the fact that housing is not a homogenous product, the price of housing thus, like the housing demand is influenced by the attributes of location, size, type, condition, age and facilities of the house. *Housing need in this treatise therefore represents the household housing requirements in terms of quality and quantity given his/her sociodemographic status while housing demand is the type and quality of housing that a resident can assess based on his ability to pay.*

3.1.4 Housing Preference

Housing preference has been defined from diverse points of view; however, it is usual to define housing preference as a predisposition of an individual to some neighborhood and structural attributes of a residential building. Housing preferences are predilections for a particular set of attributes of housing products within the context of underlying tastes which exist independently of constraints (Maclennan, 1977). Given the orientation of Maclennan definition, it is therefore presumed that housing preferences are predicated upon tastes which can vary according to the individual socioeconomic attributes and lifestyles. According to Kardes (1999), preferences are evaluative judgements concerning two or more objects and are based on comparisons of attributes or features of the objects. In this way, housing preferences are assumed to be based on attributes of housing and attitudes of renters or buyers. Within the extant literature, two categories of preference theory have dominated contemporary studies on housing: attitudinal-behavioral models and rational-economic choice models. Most of the studies in housing preferences have been situated in one or both of these theoretical frameworks (see Maclennan 1977; Megbolugbe 1989; Arimah 1997; Wang and Li 2004; Hoong and Foong 2006).

Attitudinal-behavioral models: Attitudinal-behavioral models are a suite of doctrines predicated on the fact that housing preferences are a decision-making process. These models propagate the belief that home seekers possess and express basic pattern of behaviors that describe, evaluate and advocate action with respect to some extrinsic and intrinsic attributes of a house, and these guide their decision-making process (Maclennan 1977). The fact is that consumers form attitude from their perception of the attributes of home around them and over time establish their preferences on these attributes. Such housing attributes like the external design, internal design, kitchen, bath, toilets, room space and the general appearance of the surrounding are criteria for the formation of attitude that influence preferences. The housing preference attitudes are formed also from past experiences, and whenever the opportunity comes to seek for residence, the individual acts accordingly. The underlying principles in these models hold the fact that home seekers are social beings that always want the outcomes of their search to reflect their psychological orientations and preferences. The proponents of behavioral school of thought argue that individuals would behave in a natural pattern that is predictable and, with regards to housing preference, in a way to depict some hidden tendencies that capture their social and economic aspirations. Several works that tend toward attitudinal models of housing preference favor the use of stated approach to study housing preferences (Earnhart 2002; Walker et al. 2002; Wang and Li 2004). However, there are two critical limitations in behavioral models that need to be examined cautiously. The first is that man's behavior can hardly be predicted and secondly that what controls preferences cannot be wholly expressed physically. The unpredictability assumption imposes a weakness of inconsistency. This weakness makes preference studies using the stated approach very susceptible to inaccuracies and poor estimations of aspirations and choices. Abstract factors, such as perceptions, tastes, attitudes, diverse agency relationships, aspirations and beliefs, direct the individual behavior and also his preferences. One cannot therefore less agree with some critics who have noted that what the behaviorists of housing market analysis in fact have done is to produce an experimental guide to the analysis of housing, where preferences that are based on mere market transactions and utility maximizing have largely failed (see Monk et al. 1991; Kauko 2006). The behavioral models are therefore a reaction to the economic models of housing preferences which canvass the hedonic implication of consumers' choices.

Rational-economic choice models: The proponents of rational choice models canvass the mode of explanation that sees housing preferences as products of rational thought process. It is assumed that man is a rational economic being who would take actions based upon some economic realities and not just on sheer emotions. Rational choice models have enjoyed a long tradition in the study of housing preferences especially among the urban economists. They gained ascendancy in sundry research because their assumptions seem reasonable and because they provide a potentially powerful set of tools to unravel the complexities of choice decision making. Although rational models of housing preference begin with similar assumptions as behavioral—that consumers are goal directed, gain seekers—rational choice theories emphasize that these goal directed actors operate in strategic or interdependent manner. It is perhaps interesting to note that the rational choice proponents make use of revealed preference approach in their research to unravel the underlying determinants of housing preference.

The impression given by these models is that it is the economic strength that gives a plausible prediction of housing decision making by the individuals. Economic models thrive on the employment of hedonic analyses in the explanation of housing preferences as seen in many previous works (Maclennan 1977; Megbolugbe 1989; Arimah 1997; Hoong and Foong 2006). A commendable fact about the economic rational choice models is that it establishes preference decision on effective demand and therefore underscores the relevance of socioeconomic status in choice-making process. However, economic models of housing preference have been criticized widely. For instance, Maclennan (1977) pointed out black boxes in housing choice analysis, not indicating how housing attributes enter the individual's utility function and the lack of spatial consideration in preference conceptualization. Subsequently, Maclennan and Tu (1996) argued that housing economics focuses too much on the aggregate level analysis of the housing market, as it has neglected the micro-level processes of household decision making in relation to consumption, and that there is much to be learned from other models especially those used by spatial analysts and planners. Several other scholars have directed their tirades against the rational preference models criticizing the underlying assumptions of the proponents and asking for the justification for their exclusive application in housing choice inquiries (the most recent ones are Kauko 2006; Tayyaran and Khan 2007). *Summarily, in this book, housing preference is taken as the predilection and internalized attitudes formed by an individual for a dwelling unit based on its structural and neighborhood attributes.*

3.1.5 Theory of Urban Residential Spatial Pattern

Since urban areas are dominated by the private housing market, urban spatial structures are equally determined by the nature of urban housing. Usually, housing and neighborhood attributes give the city its most visible physical structure, as the nature of residential buildings often to a greater extent determines the shape of the city (Muth 1969; Sada 1975; Pritchard 1976; Drakakis-Smith 1981; Brueckner and Colwell 1983). The residential pattern of urban centers is usually influenced by a lot of factors including the prevailing policies on land use control and land tenure system as well as the socioeconomic development prevailing at the time. Since the spatial pattern of residential attributes might influence the prices of housing, it could also influence preference and choice behavior. An understanding of the spatial pattern of the city helps in expanding the knowledge of housing preference dynamics as a social process influenced by the contending forces of demand and supply that characterize the urban housing market. Attempts at understanding the role that buildings and dwellings played in the city structure date back to the early decades of the nineteenth century. The first efforts at unraveling how residential quality shapes city physical structure were made by a set of social research scholars in America between the 1920s and 1940s. Known collectively as the Chicago school of thought, three important studies conducted by Ernest Watson Burgess (1886–1966), Homer Hoyt (1895–1984) and Edward Louis Ullman (1912–1976) and Chauncey Dennison Harris (1914–2003) made radical and unprecedented propositions of the city structure that later came to be regarded as the foundation of empirical analysis of the city arrangement. The city structure has been expressed in a set of theories which can be regarded as the models of urban spatial structure. These three classical models of urban spatial structure, as displayed in Fig. 2.1, are: (I) The Concentric Zone Theory by Burgess (1925), (II) the Sector Theory by Homer Hoyt (1939) and (III) The Multiple Nuclei Theory by Harris and Ullman (1945).

The first model of urban structure which was predicated on some logical and systematic study of the city residential neighborhoods was put forward by Burgess (1925). This theory is called the Concentric Model of the city structure. According to Burgess (1925), the city is spatially characterized by land uses that are circular, zonal and monotonous. His idea of the city is a complex medley of human ecological habitat, whose arrangement, hierarchies and orderings have socioeconomic, demographic and environmental dimensions. The Burgess theory of city growth presupposes the urban land use pattern arranged around a single activity-propelling center that is centrally located. The theory postulates a zonal arrangement of specific land uses around the city core (see Fig. 3.1a). Accordingly, the first zone of the Burgess model is the Central Business District (CBD) which forms the focus of commercial, social and industrial activities. The second zone is the zone of transition. This is where the poor workers dwell, and it is characterized by residential buildings that are suffering from utter decay, precarious dirt and despicable congestion (Ayeni 1979). The third circle signifies the zone of independent workmen's and second immigrant's homes. Instead of one-room apartments as often seen in the transition zone, we have two flat houses in this area. It is also called the Deutschland Ghetto. The fourth zone is the part of the city characterized by high-income residences and single-family dwelling units. The fifth zone in the Burgess concentric zone model represents the zone of commuters. This is the last outermost circle where buildings are in forms of detached bungalows located at lines of rapid transport transit and the choice neighborhood of the city rich. The Burgess theory of city growth as summarized above is no doubt an outstanding depiction of the modern city structure. It throws more light on our understanding of the intricate spatial distribution of the land uses in the city including housing and allows our clear view of the relationship inherent in such distribution. This description aids our understanding of the underlying factors—neighborhood and structural—that shape housing choices and residential mobility. In fact, the greatest contribution of the theory is the postulation of the Central Business District (CBD) concept, which represents the core city area where activities are focused and housing is of poorest quality. Even though the overriding theme of a circuitous zonal disposition of city land use in an objective appraisal is based on invasion and succession, the operation of the urban rent mechanism was implicit as it underlies the process of that invasion and succession of urban land uses (Ayeni 1979).

Another model that explicitly explains the spatial dimension of urban residential quality—neighborhood and structural—pattern as basis for spatial behavior in home choices in the city is the sector model propounded originally by Hoyt (1939) after a re-examination of the work of Burgess for possible improvement. The study by Hoyt (1939) is significantly at variance with the ideas put forward by Burgess especially his hypothesis of zonal land uses (see Fig. 3.1b). The sector model is predicated upon the earlier works by Hurd (1924) who described urban expansion as "axial growth, pushing out from the center along transportation lines." Homer Hoyt framed his theory of city growth, arguing that a particular kind of urban land use locates and remains in a particular sector of the city. For instance, industries tend to locate and situate according to him in one sector, high-class residential buildings in an opposite sector and working-class housing in the intermediate sectors. This model later became the model for the estate construction in both developed and emerging countries of the developing world. Hoyt's sector theory, otherwise known as the wedge theory, was based on a research conducted in some American cities into residential rent patterns. The sector model accounts for the importance of transportation routes on the growth

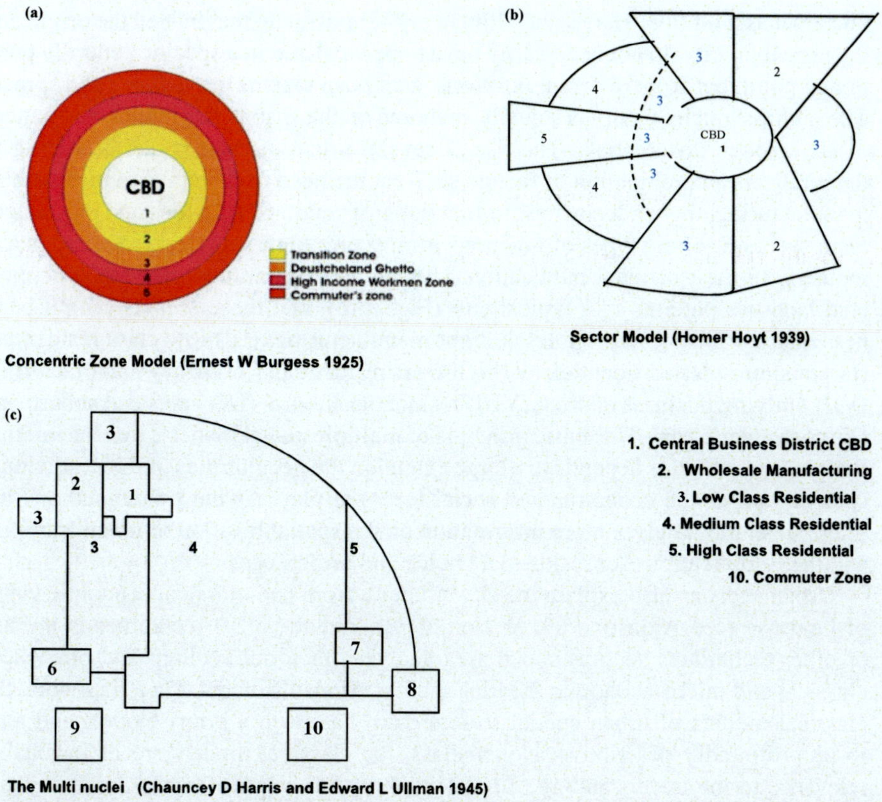

Fig. 3.1 Urban spatial pattern theories

of an urban area. Homer Hoyt maintains that expansion along a specific axis of transport usually takes the form of similar types of land use, which are in agreement to a pattern of sectors rather than the set of circles as canvassed by Burgess earlier. The sector model like the Burgess' concentric theory makes provision for the place of the CBD as the hub of the city activities. Perhaps better than Burgess's hypothesis, Hoyt's sector model of the urban spatial pattern seems to depict the most realistic constructs underlying housing preference behavior in the city.

Besides these two classical models of spatial structure of urban neighborhoods, another attempt was made by two eminent geographers namely Chauncey D. Harris and Edward L. Ullman in 1945. The duo in a well-received treatise published their research work which depicts the city growth and urban physical structure as resulting from multiple foci of opportunities and consequently termed their model as multinuclei model of urban spatial pattern. Having examined the inherent weaknesses in the earlier models by Burgess and Hoyt, especially the assumption that the city growth takes its provenance from a particular location called the CBD which is centrally located, the multiple nuclei theory was mooted to confront such seeming groundless universal assumption. Harris and Ullman (1945) postulate that indeed the origin and the growth of city do not necessarily have to be localized in a specific centrally positioned point, but from different positions, a city can take its provenance and spread. The multiple nuclei theory is actually anchored on the spatial distribution and pattern of city growth differentials. The rise of several urban discrete nuclei according to them reflects a combination of factors such as: the need of certain activities such as manufacturing, the tendency toward functional specialized activities and the antagonism between certain types of functions for instance high-class residence and heavy industry. In their original publication, Ullman and Harris identified ten differentiated land use patterns in a typical city (Fig. 3.1c), and these are: (I) central business district (CBD), (II) wholesale light manufacturing, (III) low-class residential, (IV) medium-class residential, (V) high-class residential, (VI) heavy manufacturing, (VII) outlying business district, (VIII) residential suburb, (IX) industrial suburb and (X) commuter's zone. The basic principle of multiple nuclei model is that the internal morphology of cities depends to a large extent on the peculiarities of their individual sites as well as the economic and social forces at play. As put by the authors, the multinuclei model gives more information on the spatial location of urban activities and their implications for residential choice and preferences.

Urban analysts also explain the city structure from neo-classical economic views of land use (see Alonso 1964; Wilson 1970). Ayeni (1979) recommends the use of other techniques such as social area analysis, factorial ecology and other neo-classical and micro-economic theories such as Alonso's model. On a final note, the classical models of urban spatial structure are based on a priori models and tend to be profoundly descriptive. Nonetheless, the classical models are of invaluable relevance to the understanding of residential quality and preference dynamics in a rapidly changing urban environment like Lagos. While Burgess model has limited application to the Lagos city morphology including residential structure, the multiple nuclei model of Harris and Ullman has most relevance to the understanding of Lagos city spatial patterns and residential organization. Lagos has many points of economic activity and growth. It is one city that demonstrates multiple growth centers and not necessarily one growth center. There are therefore multiple CBDs across the metropolis, and these serve to underscore the import of multiple nuclei principles as propounded by the two eminent urban geographers.

3.2 Theoretical Basis—*Residential Choice Decision Theory*

Urban residents' decisions on residential quality and housing preferences are typically predicated on residential choice decision theory (RCD) as propounded by Herbert (1972) but modified by McFadden (1977) and Carter (1982). While Herbert's work provides "a priori" explanation of residential mobility and housing preference formation, McFadden's theoretical exposition provides an operational framework for estimating housing preference decision making using random utility theory (RUT). Residential location models generally reflect the view that the decision to change residence is a response to mismatch between household preferences and housing unit characteristics (Carter 1982; Long 1988). Flaming and Griffith (1984) provide insights about the causal issues in residential preference and location. Upon realizing this mismatch, the household begins to search for a new unit and ultimately selects the unit that best suits its needs and budget. The pool of alternative units known to household is largely shaped by household characteristics and knowledge of available vacancies. But housing unit characteristics are a function of structural, location and neighborhood quality. The neighborhood attributes often play immense role in the decision to move to a new residence, and this finds basis in earlier theories of city structure and urban spatial growth.

The major urban ecological models as propounded by Burgess (1925), Hoyt (1939) and Harris and Ullman (1945) and perhaps urban land use theory by Alonso (1964) and spatial interaction models by Wilson (1970) serve to remind us of the structure of the city as basis for constant flux in residential predilections by the urban residents. Each of these theories attempts to depict the world of the city fabric graphically in order to establish some empirical regularity in the arrangement of land uses and the underlying processes that led to the spatial patterns of housing conditions observed within the city neighborhood. Although they are old idealizations of city structure in advanced economies, the ecological models inform of the dynamics that control the attitudes and spatial behavior of urban residents generally. These bodies of work are often regarded as Chicago school of thought and they inaugurated the classical theory of urban spatial structure. While Burgess argues that urban structure displays circuitous pattern around a center called Central Business District from where development radiates spirally outwards and around which there is a transition zone characterized by decrepit and filth housing by the low-wage labors, Hoyt proposes a radial structure of the city where development takes place along transport routes in a sectoral form around a CBD, and Harris and Ullman propose a theory of urban structure where development springs from different points of opportunities and extends around different multinuclei creating different rental patterns. The inherent weaknesses of these models have been over flogged in urban studies; nonetheless, they remain relevant foundations to anchor discourses in urban spatial organization. Based perhaps on the ecological models of urban structure, contemporary theoretical ideas on how the city conditions influence residential choices have been expounded as a process. The spatial organization of economic activities gives the rationale for individual residential choices and predilections which become more apparent during residential change or search (Farley 1993). Of course, Clark and Onaka (1983) have reduced reasons for changing residence to two: voluntarily induced and involuntarily induced or forced factors. What constitutes the involuntarily induced factors are the negative externalities such as deteriorating environmental conditions including the neighborhood and residential conditions or attributes. In the same vein, the voluntarily induced factors are socioeconomic factors which are composed of income, occupation, lifestyle and stage in lifecycle. While some of these are determinants of housing choices, the environmental factors are purely criteria that give signals to the home seeker on the location that it is to him a preferred place.

Both residential change and preference are a multiple decision-making optimization process. The choice of residential status comes from change in neighborhood and dwelling characteristics or what Herbert (1972) has characterized as "external considerations" on the one hand and change in the economic status, lifestyle and family status or what has been characterized as "internal considerations" on the other. Research has shown that even when models of housing preference can typically explain the link between household and dwelling characteristics from the perspective of the household, this link can also be explicated through the kind of housing unit, location, neighborhood, racial or ethnic composition (Farley 1993; Rosenbaum 1996). Of course, a deplorable change in the environment and dwelling qualities, that is "*place utilities,*" constitute normally environmental stress and lack of improvement in economic well-being constitutes a need stress.

Both of these forms of stress will determine whether an individual would begin the process of relocation to a better place and residence or not. Except incapacitated by cost, the household may decide to look for a new home, and success in this endeavor depends on information about vacancies and expectations of place utility. The residential location decision model has an important connection with preference studies in the sense that the same issues that form basis for relocation are the criteria for the choice of new dwelling units. Herbert's RLD model is adopted with a huge modification in this book, as it provides basis for understanding the various housing attributes criteria and socioeconomic factors that influence individual housing predilections and choices. It is adopted in form of Multi-Attribute Residential Preference framework (MARP) to explain the underlying factors responsible for variations in housing preferences in Lagos. In extending the residential location decision model, the external considerations are framed in the context of six factors neighborhood prestige, convenience, and location on one hand and dwelling use value, design and cost on the other. These six residential characteristics serve as forces that drive residential preferences. Again the internal considerations are viewed from socioeconomic status and stage in lifecycle.

The Multi-Attribute Residential Preference (MARP) model heavily draws upon Multi-Attribute Utility Theory (MAUT) which is based on multiple criteria and objectives (Edwards 1977; Barron and Barrett 1996; Triantaphyllou 2000; Figueira et al. 2004; Linkov et al. 2004; Sylvia et al. 2010). This stems from the assumption that housing preference reflects the interaction between multiple residential criteria and household characteristics. Actually, MAUT is a generic name for a medley of decision-making models including Analytical Hierarchy Process (AHP), Simple Multi-Attribute Rating Techniques (SMART), Group Decision-Making model (GDM), Generalized Means Model (GMM) and others like Out Ranking Methods (ORM) often called the French method (Barron and Barret 1996; Sylvia et al. 2010). Theoretically, as indicated in Fig. 3.2 and explained earlier, housing possesses two attributes or quality dimensions: structural (intrinsic) and location-neighborhood (extrinsic).

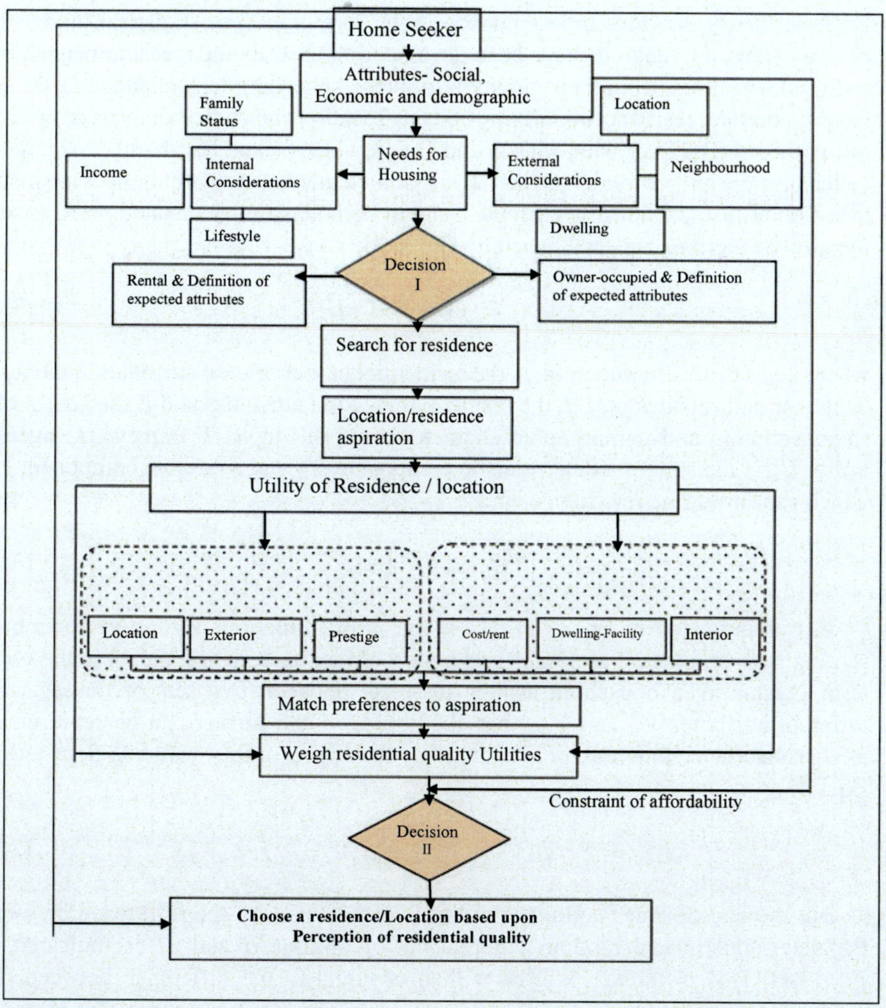

Fig. 3.2 Multi-attribute residential preference framework MARP (Author's Impression)

The fact is that dwellings are expected to possess *dwelling facility*, *design* and *cost* qualities. And besides, they are also expected to possess *prestige*, *convenience* and *location* qualities (see Wang and Li 2004; Cirman 2006). These six latent variables, as conceptualized in this study, consist of many other alternative explanatory variables. The argument is that these multiple residential quality variables interact with socioeconomic and demographic variables of residents to determine housing preferences. The MARP model builds on the *thesis that, when forming their residential preferences, home seekers weigh up the attributes of houses (including neighborhood conditions and location) and their own socioeconomic peculiarities*, the same assumption underlying the RLC model as propounded by McFadden (1977).

Because theory provides little guidance in the formulation of statistical models of choice behaviors, methods have been developed to abstract the measurement of the utility of dwellings from their quality attributes. According to McFadden (1977), a basic theoretical construct underlying housing location and choice analysis is random utility theory (RUT) or what Mason and Quigley (1990) and Earnhart (2002; 2001) called discrete choice model (DCM). It is assumed that housing preferences are made based on utilities of housing attributes, and in both revealed and stated preferences, the utility functions are established by Eq. (3.1):

$$U_{ij} = f(N, S, L, E), \tag{3.1}$$

where U_{ij} is the utility function, N the residential neighborhood attributes, S the residential structural attributes, L the residential location attributes and E the household socioeconomic and demographic characteristics. But in RUT framework, overall utility U_{ij} is the sum of a deterministic component V_{ij} and a random component e_{ij}, which can further be rewritten as in Eq. (3.2):

$$U_{ij} = V_{ij} + e_{ij.} \tag{3.2}$$

Just as indicated in Eq. (3.1), U_{ij} is the utility function, V_{ij} the vector representing both residential attributes and household characteristics and e_{ij} is the error term. Assuming a household aspires to select between two sets of houses with different attributes V_{ij} and V_{nj}, then the choice of the former can be represented as a probabilistic function, $\varkappa_{n(i)}$ which has the higher utility value as depicted in Eq. (3.3).

$$\chi_{n(i)} = Prob\big(V_{ij} + e_{ij} \geq V_{nj} + e_{nj} : j \in K_j\big). \tag{3.3}$$

But the choice that maximizes utility is determined by the difference between the deterministic and random components of options *ij* and *nj* as indicated in Eq. (3.4). This difference is greater than or equal to the difference between the random components.

$$\chi_{n(i)} = Prob\big(V_{ij} - V_{nj}\big) > e_{nj} - e_{ij.} \tag{3.4}$$

If the random components are identically and independently distributed, that is GUMBELL IID distributed with scale parameter μ, then the probability that the individuals j chooses dwelling unit i rather than n, $\varkappa_{n(i)}$ is of the logit form in Eq. (3.5):

$$\text{Hence } \chi_{n(i)} = \exp\big(\mu V_{ij}\big)/\Sigma \exp\big(\mu V_{nj}\big). \tag{3.5}$$

Usually in multinomial models μ which depicts the distribution of random components of choice attributes is normalized to 1.0. The estimated parameters of vector β are unique up to the scale factor μ (see Earnhart 2002). The probability of choosing a particular residence is conditioned on the systematic utilities of the alternatives which themselves are functions of the independent variables. In practice, the functions are usually depicted in form of linear format as presented in Eq. (3.6):

$$V_{ij} = \beta_o + \beta_1 \chi_1 + \beta_2 \chi_2 + \beta_3 \chi_3 + \ldots \beta_n \chi_n + e_{ij}, \tag{3.6}$$

where $\beta_o, \beta_1, \beta_2, \beta_3, \beta_n$ are parameters representing the utility weights of the variables; X_1, X_2, X_3, X_n are variables representing residential and household attributes; and e_{ij} is the error term which is randomly distributed.

The discrete choice model presented in Eq. (3.6) can be used with multinomial model to extract useful parameters which can be interpreted as utilities for residential attributes, given that the error term e_{ij} is randomly distributed and independent of irrelevant alternatives IIA. For the model to meet the rigorous assumption of being independent of what McFadden term Irrelevant Alternatives IIA however, further assumption that the home seeker would first select the neighborhood of his choice and then the house of preference must be made. This leads naturally to nested logit model (see McFadden 1973, 1977). The multinomial model for utility function is often represented as the probability of household selecting a home or a home feature within a location in standard form as put in Eq. (3.7):

$$Prob(Y = m|X_i) = \exp\ V_{ij}/\Sigma \exp\ V_{iJ}. \tag{3.7}$$

Housing preference formation is a complex decision-making process which requires an understanding of models of behavioral pattern. The discrete choice models are more popular in transport and marketing studies (Ben-Akiva and Lerman 1985; Ben-Akiva and Morikawa 1990), and it was extended to geographic studies by scholars of behavioral leaning (Wrigley 1985). Some problems that often crop up in housing preference studies border on whether to use revealed or stated approach or both. There is no consensus yet as to the more appropriate approach for the measurement and analysis of residential preferences between revealed and stated models, as both models are riddled with severe limitations some of which have been documented in previous studies (see Earnhart 2002; Walker et al. 2002; Wang and Li 2004; Tayyaran and Khan 2007). Both the revealed and stated approaches are used in this study in order to benefit from their strengths and minimize the risk of their weaknesses (Earnhart 2001, 2002; Tayyaran and Khan 2007). The stated and revealed preference methods aim at estimating an indirect utility function with housing attributes and are premised upon the assumption that the individual household can freely search over urban space for the housing alternatives that best suit its preferences and budget constraints given the household characteristics (Timmermans et al. 1994; Earnhart 2002; Wang and Li 2004).

However, the two models differ in their data collection procedures and in their underlying assumptions about decision-making process. Revealed preference is based on observational choice data which could be interpreted in terms of utility maximizing behavior. It involves the selection of one observation per respondent. On the contrary, stated preference establishes utility function based on hypothetical alternatives. Conventionally, stated approach requires each respondent to make several choices or evaluations. For revealed discrete choice model, a direct employment of multinomial logit to establish utility function for choices is easier to handle, since a dependent categorical variable can take on any number of independent continuous or categorical variables, but for stated discrete choice model, there are little operational difficulties in constructing unbiased choice alternatives (see Timmermans et al. 1994). However, according to Earnhart (2002), it is logical to assume that home seekers would normally choose based on feasible housing types available in the market and limited choice alternatives using fractional factorial design, instead of the full factorial design.

3.3 Research Hypotheses

Given the theoretical framework and objectives of this book, four hypotheses are put up for validation, and these are:

Hypothesis I
Ho1: *There is no significant correlation between the preferred dwelling attributes and socioeconomic characteristics of residents.*

Ha1: *There is significant correlation between the preferred dwelling attributes and socioeconomic characteristics of residents.*

The basis for the first hypothesis stems from the fact that there is a perceived association between the residential quality and socioeconomic status of the individual in any given society. Since housing is often viewed as a bundle of consumption which reflects complexity and heterogeneity, it is expected that what individuals have will depend largely on their economic and social status in the society (see Rosenbaum 1996; Cirman 2006).

Hypothesis II
Ho2: *The residential quality variables that shape housing choice formation could not be explained by few variables.*

Ha2: *The residential quality variables that shape housing choice formation could be explained by few variables.*

The second hypothesis is premised upon the notion that in most cases home seekers actually combine few residential quality variables to make decisions on residential choice. This must certainly have informed the thought of scholars who employ stated approach to housing preferences (see Timmermans et al. 1996; Walker et al. 2002; Earnhart 2002; Wang and Li 2004).

Hypothesis III
Ho3: *Socioeconomic and lifecycle variables are not significant predictors of housing preferences.*

Ha3: *Socioeconomic and lifecycle variables are significant predictors of housing preferences.*

Hypothesis three directly emanates from the first hypothesis, and the assumption is that the level of housing preferences in terms of housing type, location and tenure as well as other residential attributes is directly related to and hence determined by the socioeconomic status of the individual. This assumption finds rationale in several previous studies (see Cho 1997; Arimah 1997; Wang and Li 2004; Gibler et al. 2009; Opoku and Abdul-Muhmin 2010).

Hypothesis IV
Ho4: *There is no significant variation in the preferred residential quality variables within the residential density areas of Lagos.*

Ha4: *There is a significant variation in the preferred residential quality variables within the residential density areas of Lagos.*

The rationale for hypothesis four stems from the space-time construct of geography which often suggests the existence of spatial differentiation and the assumption that in many cases, home seekers do not perceive the structural and neighborhood quality components equally in the three residential density areas (see Rosenbaum 1996; Timmermans et al. 1996; Wang and Li 2004; Clark et al. 2006). Having discussed the theoretical basis of this research, it is normal to veer into the literature review.

3.4 Summary

This chapter on housing theories and concepts has established the theoretical background to residential quality and housing preferences generally. The definitional aspect gives information on the canonical meanings of housing, residential quality, housing preference, housing demand and housing need. These concepts are key concepts in housing studies that need to be well understood, and within the context of this book, a critical justification has been done to them. The theories of housing preferences and choices are equally important for establishing the theoretical path to housing markets dynamics in Lagos and Nigeria as a whole. The ideas of revealed and stated housing preferences are given in order to enlighten readers on the major housing preference models. These models are core issues in the study of housing choices and therefore require full comprehension.

References

Adams JS (1986) Housing markets in the twilight of materialism. Prof Geogr 38(3):233–237

Agbola T (2005) Nigerian housing debacle, an inaugural lecture Dept. of Urban and Regional planning University of Ibadan, Nigeria

Ajala OA, Adelodun OA (2007) Determinants of housing quality in Ibadan North Local Government Area of North Western Nigeria. Baselius Res 8(2):72–84

Aliu IR, Adebayo A (2010) Evaluating the influence of residential quality on urban residents' wellbeing: the case of Lagos Nigeria. Int J Acad Res 2(6):400–410

Alonso W (1964) Location and land use: towards a general theory of land rent. Harvard University Press, Cambridge MA

Aluko EO (2000) Urban market segmentation and house values in metropolitan Lagos. Niger Geogr J 3&4:148–157

Anusionwu EC (1982) Low cost housing in Nigeria: problems and new perspectives. Niger J Econ Soc Stud 24(3):299–316

Arimah B (1992) Variations in housing values in a Nigerian City: the case of Ibadan. Malays J Trop Geogr 23(1):1–12

Arimah BC (1997) The determinants of housing tenure choice in Ibadan Nigeria. Urban Stud 31(4):105–124

Ayeni B (1979) Concepts and techniques in urban analysis. Croom Helm, London

Barron FH, Barrett BE (1996) The efficacy of SMARTER (simple multi-attribute rating techniques extended to ranking). Acta Psychol 93:23–36

Ben-Akiva M, Lerman SR (1985) Discrete choice analysis: theory and application to travel demand. MIT press, Cambridge

Ben-Akiva M, Morikawa T (1990) Estimation of travels demand model from multiple data sources. In: Koshi M (ed) Transportation and traffic theory. Elsevier Publication, New York, pp 461–476

Beyer GH (1965) Housing and society. Macmillan, London

Bourne L (1981) The geography of housing. Macmillan Press, New York

Brueckner JK, Colwell PF (1983) A spatial model of housing attributes: theory and evidence. Land Econ 59:58–69. https://doi.org/10.2307/3145876

Burgess EW (1925) The growth of the city: an introduction to a research project. In: Parks RE, Burgess E, Mckenzie RD (eds) The city. Chicago University Press, Chicago, pp, 44–62

Burns LS, Grebbler L (1977) The housing of nations. Macmillan Press, London

Can A (1991) The measurement of neighborhood dynamics in urban housing prices. J Urban Econ 1:254–272

Carter H (1982) The study of urban geography, 3rd edn. Arnold, London

Cho C (1997) Joint choice of tenure and dwelling type: a multinomial logit analysis for the city of Chongju. Urban Stud 34(9):1459–1473

Cirman A (2006) Housing tenure preferences in the post-privatization period: the case of Slovenia. Hous Stud 21(1):113–134

Clark WAV, Onaka JL (1983) Lifecycle and housing adjustment as explanations of residential mobility. Urban Stud 20:47–57

Clark WAC, Deurloo M, Dieleman F (2006) Residential mobility and neighborhood outcomes. Hous Stud 21(3):323–342

Dewilde C, De Keulenaer F (2003) Housing and poverty: the missing link. Eur J Hous Policy 3(2):127–153

Drakakis-Smith D (1981) Urbanization, housing and the development process. Croom Helm, London

Earnhart D (2001) Combining revealed and stated preference methods to value environmental amenities at residential locations. Land Econ 77(1):12–29

Earnhart D (2002) Combining revealed and stated data to examine housing decisions using discrete choice analysis. J Urban Econ 51:143–169

Edwards W (1977) How to use multi-attribute utility measurement for social decision making. IEEE Trans Syst Man Cybern 7:326–340

Farley R (1993) Neighborhood preferences and aspirations among Blacks and Whites. In: Kingsley GT, Turner MA (eds) Housing markets and residential mobility. Urban Institute, Washington D.C., pp 161–191

Figueira J, Greco S, Ehrgott M (eds) (2004) Multiple criteria decision analysis: state of the art surveys. Springer, New York

Flaming HK, Griffith WI (1984) Causal modeling as a guide to housing preference research: a theoretical note. Hous Stud 11(2):108–111

Gibler KM, Taltavul P, Casado-Diaz JM, Casado-Diaz AM, Rodriguez V (2009) Examining retirement housing preferences among international retirees' migrants. Int Real Estate Rev 12(1):1–22

Goodwin AS (1977) Measuring the values of housing quality—a note J. Reg Sci 17(1):107–115

Grimes OF (1976) Housing for the low income urban families. John Hopkins University Press, Baltimore

Harris CD, Ullman EL (1945) The nature of cities. Annals of the American Academy of Political and Social Sciences, pp 7–11

Harris JC, Todaro MP (1970) Migration, unemployment and development. Am Econ Rev LX:139–149

Herbert DT (1972) Urban geography: a social perspective. Newton Abbot, London

Hoong CC, Foong WK (2006) Influence of school accessibility on housing values. J Reg Plann Develop 132(3):120–129

Hoyt H (1939) The structure and growth of residential neighborhood in American cities. The United States Federal Housing Administration, Washington, D.C.

Hurd R (1924) Principles of city land values. New York

Kardes FR (1999) Consumer behavior and management decision making. Addison Willey, London

Kauko T (2006) Expression of housing consumer preferences: proposition for a research agenda. Hous Theory Soc 23(2):92–108

Lee H (2005) Influence of lifestyles on housing preferences of multifamily housing residents. PhD dissertation submitted to The Virginia State University, USA

Lewin AC (1981) Housing cooperatives in developing countries: a manual for self-help in low-cost housing schemes. Wiley, New York

Linkov I, Varghese A, Jamil S, Seager TP, Kiker G, Bridges T (2004) Multi-criteria decision analysis: a framework for structuring remedial decisions at the contaminated sites. In: Linkov I, Ramadan AB (eds) Comparative risk assessment and environmental decision making. Springer, New York, pp 15–54

Long L (1988) Migration and residential mobility in the United States. Russell Sage, New York

Mabogunje AL, Hardoy JE, Misra RP (1978) Shelter provision in developing countries. Scientific Committee on Problems of the Environment SCOPE. Wiley, New York

Maclennan D (1977) Information, space and the measurement of housing preferences and demand. Scott J Polit Econ 24(2):97–115

Maclennan D, Tu Y (1996) Economic perspectives on the structure of local housing systems. Hous Stud 11(3):387–406

Mafico CJC (1994) Urban low income housing in Zimbabwe. Averbury Australia, Sydney

Mason C, Quigley JM (1990) Comparing the performance of discrete choice and hedonic models. In: Fischer MM, Njikamp P, Papageorglou (eds) Spatial choices and processes. Holland, Elsevier, pp 219–246

McFadden D (1973) Conditional logit analysis of qualitative choice behavior. In: Zarembca PZ (ed) Frontiers in econometrics. Academic Press, New York

McFadden D (1977) Modeling the choice of residential location. Cowles Foundation Discussion Paper No 477, Yale University Connecticut, pp 1–34

Megbolugbe IF (1989) A hedonic index model: the housing market of Jos. Urban Studies 26:486–494

Monk S, Pearce B, Whitehead C (1991) Planning, land supply and house prices—a literature review. Land economy monograph 21. University of Cambridge, Cambridge
Muth RF (1969) Cities and housing: the spatial pattern of urban residential land use. University of Chicago press, Chicago
Ndulo M (1985) The determinants of urban housing value: the evidence from Zambia. Malays J Trop Geogr 12:31–36
Needleman L (1964) The economies of housing. Staples Press, London
Onibokun A (1982) Housing needs and responses: a planner's viewpoint. J Niger Inst Town Plan 2:1–2
Onokerhoraye GA (1984) Social services in Nigeria: an introduction. Kegan Paul, New York
Opoku RA, Abdul-Muhmin AG (2010) Housing preferences and attribute importance among low-income consumers in Saudi Arabia. Habitat Int 34:219–227
Premius H (2001) Poverty and housing in the netherlands: a plea for tenure-neutral public policy. Hous Stud 16(3):277–289
Pritchard RM (1976) Housing and the spatial structure of the city. Cambridge Press, London
Rapoport A (1969) House form and culture. Prentice Hall, New Jersey
Rapoport A (2001) Theory, culture and housing. Hous Theory Soc 17:145–165
Rosenbaum J (1996) The influence of race on Hispanic housing choices in New York City 1978–1987. Urban Aff Rev 32(2):217–243
Sada PO (1975) Urban housing and spatial pattern of modernization in Benin City. Niger Geogr J 18(1):39–55
Sumka HJ (1979) Measuring the quality of housing: an econometric analysis of tax appraisal records. Land Econ 53:293–309
Sylvia J, Henny C, Roland G (eds) (2010) Methodology for research into housing preferences and choices. Springer, New York
Tayyaran MR, Khan MA (2007) Telecommuting and residential location decisions: combined stated and revealed preferences model. Can J Civ Eng 34:1324–1333
Timmermans H, Molin E, van Nootwijk L (1994) Housing choice processes: stated versus revealed modeling approaches. Nether J Hous Built Environ 9(3):215–227
Timmermans H, van Nootwijk L, Oppewal L, van der Waerden P (1996) Modeling constrained choice behavior in regulated housing markets by means of discrete choice experiments and universal logit models: an application to the residential choice behavior of divorcees. Environ Plan A 28:1095–1112
Triantaphyllou E (2000) Multi-criteria decision making methods: a comparative study. Kluwer Academic Publishers, Dordrecht
Turner JFC (1976) Housing by people: towards autonomy in building environment. Marion Boyards, London
Wakely PL, Schmetzer H, Mumtaz BK (1976) Urban housing strategies. Pitman Publishing, Bath
Walker B, Marsh A, Wardman M, Niner P (2002) Modelling tenant choices in the public rented sector: a stated preference approach. Urban Stud 39(4):665–688
Wang D, Li S-M (2004) Housing preferences in a transitional housing system: the case of Beijing, China. Environ Plan A 36:69–87
World Bank (1993) Housing: enabling markets to work a policy paper. International Bank for Reconstruction and Development IBRD, New York
Wrigley N (1985) Categorical data analysis for geographers and environmental scientists. Longman, New York
Wilson AG (1970) Entropy in urban and regional planning. London, Pion Publications

Chapter 4
Empirical Perspectives on Residential Quality and Housing Preferences

Abstract The major focus of existing bodies of literature has been the explanation of the specific housing characteristics, tenure, location and prices associated with the socioeconomic peculiarities of individuals and groups within the urban setting. In doing these, attempts are not directly focused on the complexity of housing choice decision-making process engendered by the intricate polarization of urban residential markets but on understudying the relation between personality and domiciles. Of course, housing choice in a polarized residential market is a complex decision-making process involving two interrelated perceptive issues: quality of home and affordability both of which are underlined by household socioeconomic peculiarities. Residential quality splits into structural and neighborhood-location attributes of dwellings, while housing affordability splits into economic status of home renters and the prevailing prices of property within the housing submarkets. However, for the purpose of simplification, review of empirical studies involving housing preferences in this book is pursued along three broad perspectives: urban market segmentation or polarization, environmental attachment and housing preferences, residential quality, socioeconomic dynamics and housing preferences and empirical modeling of housing preferences.

Keywords Residential polarization · Housing choice determinants · Structural quality · Neighborhood quality · Locational quality · Housing preference determinants · Housing choice modeling

4.1 Spatial Polarization, Environmental Attachment and Housing Preferences

Urban housing markets often display spatial segmentation which is the outcome of housing qualities and prices in different areas or residential neighborhoods of the city. Housing, like all other physical phenomena, has spatial dimensions and also possesses attributes that provide sociopsychological needs of individuals and families (Mabogunje et al. 1978; McGray and Weber 1991). Urban residential segmentation

© The Author(s), under exclusive license to Springer Nature Switzerland AG 2024

I. R. Aliu, *Urban Private Housing in Nigeria*, The Urban Book Series,
https://doi.org/10.1007/978-3-031-47432-3_4

reflects in residents' housing preference and satisfaction with the specific characteristics of the housing environment. It is also associated with the socioeconomic needs of urban residents and the influence of the perception of spatial and cultural norms in housing decision making (McGray and Weber 1991). Hence, housing preferences are attributed to environmental attachment and geography of locations or places or neighborhoods where residential dwellings are situated. This urban residential segmentation or polarization reflects the imperative of a strong theme of geography–space which in the words of Tuan (1974) is synonymous with "place having spirit, sense and personality." The personality of place is a composite of natural endowments and the modifications wrought by successive generations of human beings. A sense of place describes the innate picturesque idea that individuals have for a particular place and it could be either aesthetics or moral. Because of the formlessness of space, it wears the toga of spirit place. Yi-Fu Tuan further divides space into two, perhaps based on personality trait: place as public symbol having high image of sacredness, formality, monumental architecture, public square, ideal city and place as field of care- having low image of park, home, street corner, neighborhood, market, and town. The aggregation of all these traits predisposes man to develop a stereotypical attachment to a particular place or location (Tuan 1974). According to Harvey (1969), space has three attributes relative, absolute and relational attributes. Although space is a natural phenomenon, its conception and perception are quite different from person to person and culture to culture. In all of its attributes, space cannot be rationalized as a phenomenon having fixity and infinity of existence. Space is required for a variety of reasons: social interaction, shelter construction and economic opportunities. Therefore, in all human endeavors including housing, space and environmental quality form central issues in choices decision making and future life considerations.

Some housing researchers have studied housing preferences of home buyers and discovered that the perception of the neighborhood and environmental conditions of where dwellings are located play some roles in housing preference formation (Clark 1991; Adair et al. 2000; Wang and Li 2004; Gbakeji and Ojeifo 2009; Sanni and Akinyemi 2009). When people talk of their homes, they refer both to the features of their houses and to the wider neighborhood and the environment. In a study of housing preference, Clark (1991) outlined some neighborhood and location stressor variables that could form criteria for housing choices as consisting of size and facilities of dwelling units, access to work, proximity to friends and relatives, kind of people living in the neighborhood and environmental quality with respect to pollution. The study shows how neighborhood conditions could determine future housing tenure of residents. The author employed regression analytic method to predict that these variables could cause the initial desire to embark on residential mobility that manifests itself in locational change. Clark's study however does not include certain relevant variables like stage in family cycle, lifestyles or household size.

A study of the housing preferences in Belfast Ireland by Adair et al. (2000) indicated that neighborhood accessibility is significant in shaping residential preferences of urban residents. The study that was primarily designed to establish a link between accessibility and housing prices discovers that more accessible areas of the city receive more locational choices and higher property values than the less accessible areas. The conclusion of the authors was that the higher rental values observed in the study area were due to high number of people that are seeking for residential homes in the areas with good road networks and in locations that are close to main roads. In a more recent study, Wang and Li (2004) considered housing preferences from the neighborhood and residential type perspectives. In their study, the authors employed the stated preference modeling approach to analyze the factors that determine housing preferences and choices among Chinese people of Beijing. Using conjoint analytical method, the researchers discovered that neighborhood variables are more important than dwelling or house variables in the choice of housing in China. This work is extremely useful for understanding the housing preferences in developing countries like Nigeria. However, the variables used were too few and unsuitable to the Nigerian situation. Studies have linked the quality of residential neighborhood, housing choices and crimes. An expansive study by Tital et al. (2006) found exciting connections between the neighborhood socioeconomic characteristics and the level of crimes being perpetrated within an area indicating that there are more crimes in mixed neighborhoods than in fairly homogenous areas.

Gbakeji and Ojeifo (2009) revealed the preferences of urban residents for dwelling unit, neighborhood quality and social setting of the neighborhood in Warri, Nigeria. Simple weighted means were employed to rank and interpret levels of preference for these dwelling attributes. However, there are fundamental drawbacks in this work: The methodology is questionable as it is very doubtful if respondents can effectively rank 25 localities simultaneously, and besides, variables employed to depict neighborhood and dwelling quality are too composite. As remarked by Galster (1979), geographic rankings are not better than hypothetical perception of aspirations which can hardly be taken as preferences. Strangely enough, this study does not identify the determinants of neighborhood and dwelling preferences. Sanni and Akinyemi (2009) studied district and housing preferences in Ibadan, Nigeria. The study examines the determinants of households' residential district preferences within the metropolitan city of Ibadan. Variables considered as determinants, based on households' survey and used for appraisal in this study include quality of the environment in terms of good layout, availability of infrastructural facilities like good roads, water supply, quietness, peace and adequate security; sociocultural activities; accessibility to place of work; mere chance like occupying the only vacant place; security of land ownership; and affinity to place of birth and need to live close to relatives. The authors found that different categories of residential density districts of the city had distinct set of households' residential districts preferences peculiar to them and broad generalizations for the whole city could be erroneous. Aside from establishing link between housing preference and neighborhood quality, studies have also shown the influence of location on housing preferences (Daniels 1975; Kauko 2006; Kasten 2007; Dufty 2007). Kauko (2006) in an explorative study reported evidence on residential location preferences, tastes and intentions of consumers in Randstad, Holland, using open interviews with experts who were real estate and planning professionals, and therefore familiar with the variety of consumer preferences. The results show that, for the majority of housing consumers, the functionality and spaciousness of the house itself matter more than location, and that tangible factors carry more weight than intangible ones when it comes to evaluating the physical surroundings.

These findings from Holland further evince the fact that among the location factors the more intangible, aesthetical-symbolic factors have taken over from the traditional, technical-functional tangible factors, due to a general shift in Western consumer cultures, from a more constrained housing market to the present situation in which factors related to consumer choice and product variety are playing a more substantial role. The relevance of this study to the present research is its unusual emphasis on the role of aesthetics in housing consumer preferences. Whether Lagosians will exhibit this behavioral tendency remains an interesting thing to find out. A genre of scholars have concentrated on the modeling of housing choices and preferences in order to provide evidences that could form bases for urban housing planning (Earnhart 2002; Tayyaran and Khan 2007). In a study of Fairfield in Connecticut USA, Earnhart (2002) made use of the RP and SP data to estimate the benefits and value of environmental amenities that are associated with residential locations. He noted that properly structured SP and RP data could provide almost the same useful results. The influence of telecommuting on residential preferences was the focus of a study conducted in Ottawa, Canada, by Tayyaran and Khan (2007). Just like the Earnhart (2002) study, the Canadian researchers made use of both SP and RP data for their study, and they found that indeed the residential location, decisions are made by considering the telecommuting of households in the region.

Clark et al. (2006) investigated the role of neighborhood and dwelling attributes on housing mobility and choice in Netherlands. Specifically, the study was carried out to provide a behavioral enrichment to hedonic models which factor neighborhood into the house price and to examine across a set of objective measures of how individuals behave when they change houses. In this study, neighborhood quality was defined by two variables: socioeconomic status and environmental quality. On the whole, the study provides evidence to support the way in which neighborhood quality works independently and with dwelling quality in the residential choice process. Employing both descriptive and multivariate logit techniques, the researchers found that neighborhood quality played more role than the dwelling quality in determining residential choices among the Dutch. The attributes used to depict neighborhood and dwelling units are apparently too composite. Further studies have indicated stronger perception of location in housing choices. A study by Kasten (2007) showed the inherent relationship between housing preferences and location. The study actually addresses the housing predilection of middle-class families living in the city of Rotterdam, with the aim of explaining the reason for the seeming disconnect between urban families and the suburbs. The author actually found three interrelated sets of housing preference behavior among residents in the city.

First, Kasten (2007) noted that families express clearly the time-geographical reasons for urban living. In particular, the location of work provides a strong incentive to seek housing in the same city. Second, social embeddings are a strong reason for staying. Understanding housing preferences requires the conceptualization of families as social networks. Third, the interviewees define themselves as true urbanites and sturdy families who reject the suburbs as a suitable place in which to live.

However, the relevance of this study to the Lagos situation is only questioned by the disappearance of the middle class since the 1990s and the absolute lack of quantitative analysis. On the same issue of location, Dufty (2007) explored the potential locational preferences of housing assistance recipients for rural regions in New South Wales, Australia. In particular, it investigates whether rural public housing tenants are likely to become more mobile or locationally flexible with greater locational choice and to analyze how "economically rational" these locational preferences would be. The study finds that while a majority of tenants indicated a preparedness to become locationally flexible, this preference was not influenced predominantly by economically rational factors. Dufty (2007) also noted that likewise, at a regional scale, a majority of tenants indicated a preference for rural areas, with their discourses exhibiting country-minded attitudes and a strong attachment to place. The study concludes with the reflection that the use of choice as a policy tool of government is unlikely to produce the economically rational, locationally flexible responses that policymakers pursue as means of addressing regional disadvantage. Instead, the author asserts that such governmental processes are likely to be hindered by other non-economic factors that remain as strong influences in how individuals come to their locational preference.

4.2 Residential Quality, Housing Preferences and Socioeconomic Dynamics

Besides neighborhood attachment and environmental attractions, housing preferences and choices are also predicated upon dwelling attributes and socioeconomic characteristics of households. A number of studies have provided evidence to support the idea that housing preferences are directly related to housing characteristics and this has been confirmed with their construction of hedonic price indices on housing features (Borukhov et al. 1978; GilderBloom 1980; Megbolugbe 1989; Ekanem 1995; Ajala and Adelodun 2007). For instance, Borukhov et al. (1978) investigated housing prices and preferences in Tel Aviv, Israel. The study is predicated upon the prices of a sample of apartments offered for sale in the metropolitan areas of Tel Aviv. Employing the hedonic approach of multiple regression analysis, price indices were obtained for large number of characteristics of the apartments, the neighborhood and location in the metropolitan area. It was found that a premium is paid for characteristics which facilitate maintenance and features that serve as indicators for social components of the neighbors and their attitudes. In Megbolugbe (1989), using hedonic regression methodology allocated prices to some housing attributes such as number of rooms, road conditions, clean street, and distance from the Central Business Districts (CBD) to determine the level of preferences among the residents of the area. He however discovered that the housing attributes of residents were dictated by their affordability. He further observed that the locational factors, for instance, distance from the CBD, and conditions of the streets were significant indicators of housing values much as the attributes of dwelling such as room space and internal structural attributes. Ekanem (1995) took a comparative study of the determinants of housing values in Minnesota, USA, and Surulere in Lagos, Nigeria. The aim was to explore the locational similarity between the two localities in terms of housing market characteristics in order to establish some correlations in the housing values between the two cities. Using hedonic regression, the author fitted prices for different housing attributes. In his submission, the author argued that though housing values are not perfectly the same in the two localities, there are reasons to believe the Minnesota study could serve the housing market condition in Lagos positively.

The role played by socioeconomic and demographic variables of consumers in housing preference formation has attracted the attention of a number of scholars (Galster 1979; Krivo 1986; Timmermans et al. 1994; Arimah 1997; Li 2000; Li and Li 2006). Galster (1979) analyzed the level of preferences among black and white population in America using the bid-rent approach. He discovered that the blacks had distinct preferences for houses in some districts and neighborhoods that are dominated by the non-whites. From the study, he observed that the blacks also showed more interest in new property and larger units than whites' counterparts in St. Louis. The study concluded that the level of confidence in the differences was moderately statistically significant, and no consistent interracial differences were observed in preferences for neighborhood attributes or dwelling quality. This is one of the many racial dimensions of residential segregation studies which have dominated housing choices in North American communities (Daniels 1975; Clark 1991; Skaburskis 1996; Wachter and Megbolugbe 1992; Clark and Dielemann 1996). Krivo (1986) examined the determinants of homeownership pattern of New York city dwellers using data from census over a decade. He found out that apart from the demographic variable of households the metropolitan status of location also influenced the tenure type or homeownership. Turnbull et al. (1991) investigated the joint influence of income and housing prices on location choices and found out that the two actually have significant impact on housing decision making among urban households. The way marital status determines home choices has been well illustrated in the Netherlands (Timmermans et al. 1996). Using discrete choice experiment, the authors modeled housing choices of divorcees and discovered that they actually exhibit a more complex residential behavior than other groups of households. The choices of divorcee homes vary according to their peculiar socioeconomic conditions as well as their household sizes.

Buchel and Hoesli (1995) analyzed the rent difference for the tenants of subsidized units and unsubsidized units in Geneva, Switzerland. The existence of any pecuniary disadvantage for the owner of a subsidized unit is investigated by considering his rental revenue. It is found that there exists a premium between an unsubsidized and a subsidized unit when using the amount paid by the tenant as the dependent variable. Also, the study found that the subsidy system in Geneva had an influence on the pricing of each characteristic of a unit. Furthermore, it is found that when using rental revenue as the dependent variable, both subsamples can be used in a single hedonic equation. Thus, the researchers found that owners of subsidized units are not at a disadvantage due to the granting of a subsidy. In a similar study of the

Chinese urban population, Huang (2003) conducted a study using a multilevel data covering the entire country survey into rental choices in private, bureau (public), and work unit housing choices. Using multinomial logit regression model, the results showed that housing choices of renters vary according to age, income and work type. The study further indicated that residential quality varies among the households depending on housing choices-public, work unit and private or others with the best being work unit housing followed by public housing. Arimah (1997) in a study of the determinants of housing tenure choices estimated housing tenure choice models for the Ibadan housing market in Nigeria. The empirical analysis, based on logistic and hedonic regression models, reveals that the key determinants of the probability of homeownership are: income, the investment motive for home ownership, number of children in the house, gender of the head of household, stage in family lifecycle, length of stay in the city and access to land on the basis of ethnic qualification. He further noted that access to institutional sources of housing finance is selective and, as such, has not been effective in enhancing home ownership across the city.

Cho (1997) explored the variables that influence choices in the Chonju housing market in Korea. A joint model of tenure and dwelling type is estimated within the multinomial logit framework. The logit model of housing choice is fitted to the whole sample and to two subsamples, which are categorized on the basis of neighborhood quality. According to the author, empirical results do not exhibit a uniform pattern over the three sample cases. In the case of the whole sample, housing choice is influenced by the age, educational level and occupation of household head, a dummy of school-age children, and the ratio of housing price to household income. The Korean study also revealed that for the households located in the high-quality neighborhoods, the age, educational level and occupation of household head, and the housing price to income ratio appear significant. In the second subgroup, which comprises the households choosing a poor-quality neighborhood, the age and occupation, a dummy of school-age children and the housing price to income ratio appear to be the responsible variables. Huang and Clark (2002) examined the influence of sociodemographic factors in housing choice dynamics for Chinese cities. Employing data from a national survey of housing in China and a multilevel modeling technique, the study revealed the housing tenure choice in transitional urban China where households have been granted limited freedom of choice in the housing market since the housing reforms of 1988. The researchers observed that both market mechanisms and institutional forces affect households' tenure choice in urban China. While the authors discovered that some socioeconomic factors such as age, household size, household income and housing price have similar effects on tenure choice as in the West, they also observed that others such as the number of workers and marital status have rather different effects. In addition, factors characterizing institutional relationships among the state, work units and households, such as *hukou*, job rank and work unit rank, still play important roles in tenure choice. The study concludes that tenure choices among socialist, transitional and market economies differ in the country.

Some scholars have conducted studies on the interactions between migration and housing choices (Bourassa 1994; Clark et al. 1997). Clark et al. (1997) presented a new dimension to housing preference studies with a focus on migration, mobility and housing tenure choice using the concept of the life course in providing an enriched analysis of the context within which housing choices are made and of the demographic and economic variables which are critical determinants of the decisions to move and to change tenures. The availability of panel series data for the USA and Germany allows cross-national comparisons of the migration and tenure choice processes. The binational, comparative study discovers that there are substantial differences in the rates of mobility and the rates of moves of households from the rental sector to ownership, especially for couples, but the results confirm the overall similarities in the mobility and tenure choice processes despite the differing government commitments to housing policy. The study shows that it is primarily couples and families who make the transition to ownership and that income and number of earners are important in both contexts, and German households have even higher incomes before they make the transition to ownership. At the same time, the tax benefits in Germany have also made it possible for families with relatively lower incomes to move to the ownership sector. Li (2000) investigated the influence of households' characteristics on housing tenure in the Chinese city of Guangzhou using multilevel logit model. The researcher divided the Chinese housing by tenure into four—the open market housing, work unit housing, housing bureau housing and the resettlement housing. Results from the Guangzhou study indicate that those who are in the subsidized housing have lower socioeconomic status than those residents that occupy the open market housing. These results are perhaps due to the new orientation in the Chinese economy where communism is being jettisoned for free market economy and the housing market is under the control of the price mechanism. The study by Warren and Bell (2000) in Australia revealed the intricate nature of housing choices of people with mental challenges. An exploratory study that categorized treatments into three categories, the place, other consumers and a normal life was an investigation of the housing desires of post-psychiatric patients. The study found out that the outpatients desired to live a normal life and in homes away from where they could easily be noticed as former psychiatric patients.

In a similar study, Gibler et al. (2009) examined the characteristics, attitudes and preferences about retirement housing among immigrant retirees currently living in traditional housing in a retirement destination in Alicante, Spain. Using results from a survey of German and British retirees living in the region, the researchers found through logistic regression that preference for retirement housing is associated with aging and gaining access to in-home support services. The conclusion arrived at by the study was that as a growing number of proportion of aging residents in many countries are undertaking late-life moves, their preferences would definitely have influence on destination housing markets. Lee (2005) conducted a research into the housing preferences of households in multiunit dwelling structures in Virginia, USA. The focus of that study was the cross-examination of preferences in the context of households lifestyles. He discovered that the blacks housing preferences of households in the city reflect their lifestyles. He employed cluster and discriminant analysis to unravel the preference behavior of respondents in the study area. Residential choices are also influenced by the perception of schools for children for households. Li and Li (2006) studied homeownership in Guangzhou city of China. Using a longitudinal data, the authors established the transition from renting to owning among the city residents. They found out that age and education attributes of residents are significant predictors of homeownership. Change in marital status was also found to be of tremendous influence in changing housing tenure in China. They observed that work unit and state housing still affect household tenure choice and behavior in the study area. Cirman (2006) examined housing preferences in Slovenia, one of the Eastern European countries just experiencing some level of economic liberty and social freedom in the twilight of the twentieth century. The core of the study is the analysis of tenure dimensions of housing preferences having noted in previous studies that majority of the people in Slovenia own houses compared to a small group of renters. In the study under review, the approach used was to infer the tenure preference from the positions respondents took on certain characteristics of the different tenure forms and confront these positions with household characteristics. Using factor analytic framework and structural equations, the findings from this study show that housing tenure preferences that favored owner-occupation in Slovenia are strongly influenced by household characteristics, house use value, financial attractiveness, and lack of availability of vacant rental housing.

In a study of the underlying determinants of housing quality in Ibadan Northern region, Ajala and Adelodun (2007) found out that indeed the quality of housing available to individual residents has strong association with their socioeconomic attributes. Using both neighborhood and dwelling features, the scholars concluded that the dwelling features are obviously the most correlated housing quality indicators with socioeconomic attributes of residents which also include both demographic and economic indicators. The housing features identified by this study are of tremendous importance in understanding residential quality and choice dynamics of urban residents in developing countries. Garcia and Hernandez (2007) reported the simultaneous individual choices in Spain as regards housing and urban location decisions, taking into account certain unobserved heterogeneity exhibited by individuals. The authors employed multinomial logit models to depict household decisions considering four different options: homeownership according to the type of urbanization of the neighborhood: high-level urban property, medium/inferior-level urban property and rural property and renting. Controlling for sample selection, the results confirm that both housing tenure and urban location, in addition to the unobserved heterogeneity of individuals in this context, could modify appreciably housing demand estimates for both owners and renters. Berenyi and Szabo (2009) conducted an inquiry into the influence of inner-city neighborhoods on the housing preferences in Budapest city capital of Hungary. The study found out that the real estate prices increased in all parts of the inner city but the highest prices were found in the traditional neighborhoods of the city. The researchers also observed that the social structure of the city had changed with younger residents and more educated individuals having more representation and the location was seen as the most important factor influencing housing choices in Budapest. The residents' views of the inner city of Budapest are sharply divided between the old and the young population.

Studies have shown that the age of households' heads is an important factor that influences housing preferences. A study of the housing preferences of elderly people was carried out by Choi and Kang (2010). Their study examined preferences of elderly retirees in a small town of Silver estate in California, USA, using structural equation and factor analytical models. The results of the study showed that the elderly people prefer houses that are suitable for the old who for senility would not have anything to do with dwellings located in faraway to activity places and abhor dwellings that are large size and far from their relations. A more recent study by Fong and Chan (2011) examined residential patterns among religious groups in Canada and found out that religion per se does not influence residential segregation but the religious institution to which the residents belong. The study discovered that four religious institutions, namely institutional orientation of religious services, subcultural identity, religious identity and racial discrimination are responsible for residential segregation behaviors exhibited in the metropolitan areas of Canada. The researchers found out that it is these religious institutional behaviors that are related to the residential segregation observed among the religious groups. This seems to be in support of the fact that religious institutions do shape social structures and processes. While this assertion is partly true in many instances, especially in the multicultural cities, it is less noticeable in the less developed countries like Nigeria.

4.3 Modeling of Housing Preferences

In the scholarship of housing preference, empirical studies have generally focused on how to explain factors influencing housing preference formation. There are two patterns of empirical literature that dominate residential preference studies: hedonic and discrete choice. First, a generation of housing literature exists which focuses on the interpretation of housing demand and preferences using the implicit hedonic price functions as popularized by Kain and Quigley (1970) and Rosen (1974) to estimate utilities of housing features through linear regressions (see Aminu 1977; Maclennan 1977; Galster 1979; Borukhov et al. 1978; Megbolugbe 1989; Ekanem 1995; Arimah 1992), and second, a substantial number of literature follows a methodological framework that makes use of discrete choice utility model which estimates housing preference as a probabilistic framework of utility estimation using logits and analytical frameworks other than OLS (see Arimah 1997; Clark et al. 1997; Cho 1997; Cirman 2006; Karsten 2007; Dufty 2007; Opoku and Abdul-Muhmin 2010; Fong and Chan 2011).

Empirical modeling of housing preferences has been generally pursued along two lines. The first modeling method uses demand utility maximization function based on the housing attributes and prices. This methodological technique operationalizes preferences by observing actual housing consumption patterns. It revealed preference approach (RP) to housing preferences. The RP model estimates housing preferences from actual choices of consumers. The RP or demand utility maximization modeling of housing preferences follows the hedonic price approach popularized by Rosen (1974), which is predicated upon the fact that each housing attribute carries with it a specific utility and price as well as trade-off. Hence, a consumer selects a house by equating its marginal utility with the house attributed marginal price (Taylor 2008). Revealed choice/preference models are either discrete choice models, where the dependent variable(s) represent individual choices, and the goal of the estimation (i.e., the betas, part-worth utilities) is the propensities to make that choice, or hedonic models of the housing market, where the dependent variable is a proxy for property value—usually transaction price, and the betas constitute shadow prices of each independent characteristic of the regression. The hedonic model is a variant of linear regression model in which housing price is regressed on a number of independent housing characteristics. The hedonic methodological framework analyzes preferences by examining coefficients of the various components comprising the housing package after the unit's price has been regressed on them in the form of a hedonic index (Daniels 1975; Galster 1979; Megbolugbe 1989; Ekanem 1995; Arimah 1997; Aluko 2000). The hedonic model assumes that the observed choices of consumers represent points of tangency between the level sets of continuously differentiable utility functions with nonlinear but observable market prices for the attributes of goods. The assumption is that an individual unit of the good could contain any combination of its underlying attributes. Consumers implicitly select from among every conceivable configuration of the complex good those which simultaneously maximize profit and utility. In hedonic medium, choice sets do not yield discrete parameters of consumers' utility functions because the choices are the outcomes of an optimization process over a continuous set of alternative subjects to budget constraints. However, the RP model has some critical drawbacks. Recent studies have confirmed that the beta coefficients yielded by the OLS regression model with multiple variables are often incorrect, suffer from multicollinearity and could be misleading in explaining categorical dependent variables (Earnhart 2002; Walker et al. 2002).

The second method, on the other hand, employs discrete choice model based on the assumption that preferences can be measured from the choices made by the individual from a range of alternative housing attributes (Wang and Li 2004). This methodological approach uses interview of households directly in order to uncover what features of housing they hypothetically would like to consume. It is stated preference approach (SP) to housing preferences. The discrete choice model presumes probabilistic consumer decision process. The goods in the consumer choice sets are treated as discrete and indivisible and no underlying assumption about the price function is made. It is believed that consumers simply choose the good that yields the highest utility from a set of discrete alternatives. Utility function of the choice made is often composed of two components: a deterministic and a stochastic component. In order to estimate the parameters of the deterministic component, there is a need to make strong assumption about the distribution of the stochastic component. This methodology has been used by many researchers who analyze preferences through logit models of conjoint, logistic and probit regression (Cho 1997; Wang and Li 2004). Multinomial regression has become the most popular of these logit regression models because it allows the use of multileveled dependent variables. Mixed logit has also received a lot of considerations from urban housing modelers (Garcia and Hernandez 2007) and studies using structural equation models are also substantial (Cirman 2004, 2006; Choi and Kang 2010). However, the SP model possesses profound weaknesses. Of course, the SP approach has been criticized for being experimentally dependent, employing too few variables, considering hypothetical choice alternatives and may not capture real choices of consumers due to information loss (Timmermans et al. 1994; Earnhart 2002). Generally, in addition to the two main modeling methods, housing preferences are sometimes explained by combining the SP and RP methods (see Earnhart 2002; Tayyaran and Khan 2007), using descriptive statistics such as percentages, mean, coefficient of variation (Warren and Bell 2000; O Connel et al. 2006) and the multivariate techniques of Multi-Attribute Utility Techniques (MAUT) and factor analytic procedures like principal component analysis (PCA) which employs factor/component loading index (Cirman 2006; Li and Li 2006; Choi and Kang 2010; Opoku and Abdul-Muhmin 2010). This current study, however, has a special predilection for a combination of SP, RP, MAUT and PCA methods, perhaps because of their robust and apposite depiction of the real issues in housing preference measurement and spatial dimensions of choices.

4.4 Summary

In summary, existing studies have thrown lights on the fact that (i) neighborhood external attributes such as security, sanitation, recreational parks, drainage, ethnic constituents, (ii) location attributes such as closeness to workplace and to CBD, accessibility to public transport and (iii) structural quality components of dwellings such as number of rooms, room space, kitchen and baths are important criteria for housing preference decisions and (iv) socioeconomic characteristics of households such as ratio of housing price to household income, education, occupation, age and marital status are crucial determinants. Indeed, the literature review does not only establish the context to appreciate issues in housing preferences, but it also provides a clearer orientation for the current study. However, from the reviewed literature, three important gaps have been noted; the first observation is that most of the studies on housing preferences are centered on advanced economies with socioeconomic and cultural peculiarities different from that of Africa, the second observation is that there is extremely few housing preference research that has combined revealed and stated methods and the third observation is that studies on housing preferences based on quality variations within the residential density areas and the manners in which prospective consumers trade off housing characteristics during housing preference formation have not been explicitly explained. Perhaps, these areas represent significant gaps that require further investigation.

The review of previous studies on housing quality and preferences from diverse background has revealed the frontier of knowledge and gaps that remain to be filled in housing study. The literature has provided us with a number of important information on housing preferences. It has explicitly exposed the scope of empirical and theoretical efforts in housing preference studies. It has also provided the framework for the explanation of intricate issues in housing preferences from empirical, conceptual and theoretical perspectives. The rich literature has given us the advantage of seeing the goal of this book and the methodology for achieving it. From the review, it is obvious however that an analysis of the pattern of residential quality and housing preferences remains an important aspect that would need to be explained in understanding the housing preference dynamics of urban dwellers. Besides, some of the previous arguments and counterarguments on the factors that explain housing choices of urban residents in complex societies like Lagos megacity need to be revisited. While previous studies have identified varying factors in housing choices, there is little knowledge in existing studies about the ways these factors are combined by housing consumers in choosing their homes. The burden of explaining the choice formation process requires for more heuristic methodologies that can further explicate behavioral patterns of renters. The next chapter of this book therefore dwells on the methods employed in achieving its goals and objectives.

References

Adair A, Mcgreal S, Smyth A, Cooper J, Ryley T (2000) House prices and accessibility: the testing of relationships within the Belfast urban area. Hous Stud 15(5):699–716

Ajala OA, Adelodun OA (2007) Determinants of housing quality in Ibadan North Local Government Area of North Western Nigeria. Baselius Res 8(2):72–84

Aluko EO (2000) Urban market segmentation and house values in metropolitan Lagos. Niger Geogr J 3&4:148–157

Aminu FA (1977) The social and cultural bases for housing preferences in Ibadan Nigeria. PhD thesis, University of Michigan, USA Microfilms International, 30(3), p 1701

Arimah B (1992) Variations in housing values in a Nigerian City: the case of Ibadan. Malays J Trop Geogr 23(1):1–12

Arimah BC (1997) The determinants of housing tenure choice in Ibadan Nigeria. Urban Stud 31(4):105–124

Berenyi E, Szabo B (2009) Housing preferences and the image of the inner city neighbourhood in Budapest. Hung Geograph Bull 58(3):201–214

Borukhov E, Ginsberg Y, Werczberger E (1978) Housing prices and housing preferences in Israel. Urban Stud 15:187–200

Bourassa SC (1994) Immigration and housing tenure choice in Australia. J Hous Res 5:117–137

Buchel S, Hoesli M (1995) A hedonic analysis of rent and rental revenue in the subsidized and unsubsidized housing sector in Geneva. Urban Stud 32(7):1199–1213

Cho C (1997) Joint choice of tenure and dwelling type: a multinomial Logit analysis for the city of Chongju. Urban Stud 34(9):1459–1473

Choi S-H, Kang M (2010) An analysis on elderly housing preference using structural equation model: focusing on Silver Town Int J Urban Sci 14(3):254–263

Cirman A (2004) Housing tenure preferences in society with marginal rental sectors: the case of Slovenia, A paper delivered at the conference on adequate and affordable housing for all, 24–26 June, Toronto, Canada

Cirman A (2006) Housing tenure preferences in the post-privatization period: the case of Slovenia. Hous Stud 21(1):113–134

Clark WAV (1991) Residential preferences and neighborhood racial segregation: a test of the Schelling model. Demography 28(1):1–19

Clark WAV, Dielemann FM (1996) Households and housing: choices and outcomes in the housing market. Centre for Urban policy Research Rutgers University, Rutgers New Jersey
Clark WAC, Derloo MC, Dieleman FM (1997) Entry to home-ownership in Germany: some comparisons with the United States of America. Urban Stud 34(1):7–19
Clark WAC, Deurloo M, Dieleman F (2006) Residential mobility and neighborhood outcomes. Hous Stud 21(3):323–342
Daniels C (1975) The influence of racial segregation on housing prices. J Urban Econ 2:105–122
Dufty R (2007) Governing through locational choice: the locational preferences of rural public housing tenants in south western New South Wales, Australia. Hous Theory Soc 24(3):183–206
Earnhart D (2002) Combining revealed and stated data to examine housing decisions using discrete choice analysis. J Urban Econ 51:143–169
Ekanem FN (1995) Determinants of the price of homes in a suburban area of Washington D.C. compared with those in a suburban area of Lagos, Nigeria. Niger J Econ Soc Stud 37(1):1–11
Fong E, Chan E (2011) Residential patterns among religious groups in Canadian cities. City Commun 10(4):393–412
Galster G (1979) Interracial variations in housing preferences. Reg Sci 9:1–17
Garcia JAB, Hernandez JER (2007) Housing and urban location decision in Spain: an econometric analysis with unobserved heterogeneity. Urban Stud 44(9):1657–1676
Gbakeji OJ, Ojeifo OM (2009) Aspects of residential and neighborhood preferences in the warri metropolis delta state Nigeria. Stud Home Commun Sci 1(2):121–126
Gibler KM, Taltavul lP, Casado-Diaz JM, Casado-Diaz AM, Rodriguez V (2009) Examining retirement housing preferences among international retirees' migrants. Int Real Estate Rev 12(1):1–12
GilderBloom JI (1980) Socio economic influences on rental for US urban housing. Am J Econ Sociol 48(3):273–291
Harvey D (1969) Explanation in geography. Edward Arnold, London, London
Huang Y (2003) Renters' housing behavior in transitional Urban China. Hous Stud 18(1):103–126
Huang Y, Clark WAV (2002) Housing tenure in transitional Urban China: a multilevel analysis. Urban Stud 39(1):3–7
Kain JF, Quigley JM (1970) Measuring the value of house quality. J Am Stat Assoc 65(330):532–548
Karsten L (2007) Housing as a way of life: towards an understanding of middle class families' preference for an urban residential location. Hous Stud 22(1):83–98
Kauko T (2006) Expression of housing consumer preferences: proposition for a research agenda. Hous Theory Soc 23(2):92–108
Krivo JL (1986) Home ownership differences between Hispanics and Anglos in the United States. J Soc Soc Probl 33(4):319–333
Lee H (2005) Influence of lifestyles on housing preferences of multifamily housing residents. PhD dissertation submitted to The Virginia State University, USA
Li S-M (2000) The housing market and tenure decisions in Chinese cities: a multivariate analysis of the case of Guangzhou. Hous Stud 15(1):213–236
Li S-M, Li Limei (2006) Life course and housing tenure change in urban China: a study of Guangzhou. Hous Stud 21(5):653–670
Mabogunje AL, Hardoy JE, Misra RP (1978) *Shelter Provision in Developing Countries.* Scientific Committee on Problems of the Environment SCOPE. John Wiley, New York
Maclennan D (1977) Information, space and the measurement of housing preferences and demand. Scott J Political Econ 24(2):97–115
McGray J, Weber M (1991) Perception boundaries: A proposed socio-psychological framework for housing adequacy. J Hous Soc 18(1):49–61
Megbolugbe IF (1989) A hedonic index model: the housing market of Jos. Urban Stud 26:486–494
O Connel M, Rosenheck R, Kasprov W, Frisman L (2006) An examination of fulfilled housing preferences and quality of life among homeless persons with mental illness and substance use disorder. J Behav Health Serv Res 33(3):354–366

Opoku RA, Abdul-Muhmin AG (2010) Housing preferences and attribute importance among low-income consumers in Saudi Arabia. Habitat Int 34:219–227

Rosen S (1974) Hedonic prices and implicit markets: product differentiation in pure competition. J Political Econ 82:34–55

Sanni L, Akinyemi, F (2009) Determinants of household Residential districts preferences within metropolitan city of Ibadan, Nigeria. J Hum Ecol 25(2):137–141

Skaburskis A (1996) Race and tenure in Toronto. Urban Stud 33(2):223–252

Taylor LO (2008) Theoretical foundations and empirical developments in hedonic modeling. In: Baranziniet A et al (eds) Hedonic methods in housing markets. Springer, New York, pp 15–38

Tayyaran MR, Khan MA (2007) Telecommuting and residential location decisions: combined stated and revealed preferences model. Can J Civil Eng 34:1324–1333

Timmermans H, Molin E, van Nootwijk L (1994) Housing choice processes: stated versus revealed modeling approaches. Neth J Hous Built Environ 9(3):215–227

Timmermans H, van Nootwijk L, Oppewal L, van der Waerden P (1996) Modeling constrained choice behavior in regulated housing markets by means of discrete choice experiments and universal logit models: an application to the residential choice behavior of divorcees. Environment and Planning A 28:1095–1112

Tita EG, Petras T L, Greenbaum RT (2006) Crime and residential choice: a neighborhood level analysis of the impact of crime on housing prices. J Quant Criminol 22:299–317

Tuan Y-F (1974) Space and place: humanistic perspective. Prog Hum Geogr 6:233–246

Turnbull GK, Glascock JL, Sirmans CS (1991) Uncertain income and housing price and location choice. J Reg Sci 31(4):417–433

Wachter SM, Megbolugbe IF (1992) Racial and ethnic disparities in homeownership. Housing Policy Debate 3:333–370

Walker B, Marsh A, Wardman M, Niner P (2002) Modelling tenant choices in the public rented sector: a stated preference approach. Urban Stud 39(4):665–688

Wang D, Li S-M (2004) Housing preferences in a transitional housing system: the case of Beijing China. Environ Plann A 36:69–87

Warren R, Bell P (2000) An exploratory investigation into the housing preferences of consumers of mental health services. Aust N Z J Mental Health Nurs 9:195–202

Chapter 5
Methods for Assessing Residential Quality and Housing Preferences in Lagos

Abstract This chapter dwells on the types and sources of data, research design, methods of data collection, estimation of models and measures of variables and analytical techniques adopted for the study of residential quality and housing preferences in Lagos. The strategies for housing preference analysis are heuristic in nature, as it involves with direct revealed choices and the explanation of the conjoint experimental design used in the stated choices. The chapter gives information on the model specification and model estimation. The variables used are explained, and the different statistical techniques employed are also enunciated. Further, information on the statistical tools for testing the set hypotheses in the book is elaborated upon.

Keywords Housing preference analysis · Housing preference methods · Revealed preference data · Stated preference data · Conjoint experimental design · Housing preference modeling

5.1 Nature and Sources of Housing Quality and Preference Data

The data used in the study can be categorized into two: *primary data and secondary data.* However, for many reasons and in contrast with studies from advanced economies that make use of census data (for instance, Cho 1997; Cirman 2006), this study relied absolutely on primary data from field survey. The 2006 national census in Nigeria does not take into consideration comprehensive and crucial information on housing preferences and residential quality that could be of profound benefit to this study. In the absence of such organized secondary data from census tracts, the primary data, (which are in revealed and stated forms), were drawn from the field survey carried out in the study area. Depending on the quality of the research survey, primary data are actually far better than secondary data in matters of housing quality and value survey (Arimah 1992; Ekanem 1995). The information that was obtained from this source includes location, structural and neighborhood attributes of houses as well as the characteristics of respondents. The instrument of data collection for

© The Author(s), under exclusive license to Springer Nature Switzerland AG 2024

I. R. Aliu, *Urban Private Housing in Nigeria*, The Urban Book Series,
https://doi.org/10.1007/978-3-031-47432-3_5

the study is the questionnaire. A set of structured questionnaires was employed to elicit information on the perception of the respondents on a number of environmental and structural quality and preference issues in housing. Since the study employed both stated and revealed data, the questionnaire was designed to contain multiple residential quality and preference questions. The questionnaire is divided into three sections: Section A contains the revealed preference and residential quality data, Section B contains the stated housing preference and residential quality data and Section C contains the household characteristics survey. The background secondary data on housing quality in Lagos were obtained from the National Bureau of Statistics (NBS) Abuja; information on electoral wards and localities was derived from the Independent National Electoral Commission (INEC), while the maps were collected from the National Population Commission (NPC) at Eric Moore in Lagos Nigeria.

5.2 Research Design and Methods of Data Collection

This study employed both descriptive cross-sectional survey and experimental designs. The methods used in this study followed the general methodological approaches as employed by Earnhart (2002), Wang and Li (2004), Walker et al. (2002), Tayyaran and Khan (2007). As a quantitative discrete choice research, the methods of data collection for the study reflect two approaches, namely stated approach and revealed approach. The revealed data covered actual housing choices that had been made by individuals, while the stated data covered the hypothetical housing choices that individuals would prefer based on their attributes and socioeconomic status.

5.2.1 Strategy for Collecting Revealed Housing Preference Data-Observed Choices

For the collection of revealed data, the questionnaire was designed to know the conditions of the residence when the respondent first decided to take it. The questions are therefore structured in such a way as to reveal the residential quality components that actually attracted the residents to their present dwelling units. These data were used to achieve objectives one, two, three and partly four. Within the revealed model framework, choices are made with respect to the utilities derivable from the residential attributes (Timmermans et al. 1994, 1996; Earnhart 2002). Section A of the questionnaire addresses the revealed data. The section is broken into three subsections: location/neighborhood attributes, structural attributes and cost constraints. The structuring of this section was to measure three housing preference areas, namely location/neighborhood preference, house type preference and tenure type preference. In all twenty residential quality questions were considered under revealed preference section. In order to establish trade-offs between housing attributes and prices, control of other variables is important. Unlike Earnhart (2002), who decided to measure the unmeasured aspect of housing by setting hedonic price equation on the housing structural and neighborhood attributes, this study does not bother about the hedonic price implications of choices.

5.2.2 *Strategy for Collecting Stated Housing Preference Data-Conjoint Design*

While the revealed data were obtained from real choices, the stated data were derived from hypothesized choices constructed according to the principles of statistical experiments. From the housing choice alternatives, respondents were asked to choose one alternative, and the preference/choice utility function can then be estimated with the multinomial logit models (see Timmermans et al. 1994; Earnhart 2002; Markley 2011). The statistical design made use of a conjoint experimentation. Naturally, there are two methods to achieve this end; the orthogonal design which becomes imperative when there are similar attribute levels within one choice dimension and the uniform design which is used whenever there is more than one choice dimension (Timmermans et al. 1994; Wang and Li 2004). Of course, we imagined that households would actually in practice, and contrary to Wang and Li (2004), make residential choices in a sequential manner by first choosing location/neighborhood and later the dwelling type of choice. In this case, the orthogonal design was deemed a more appropriate method. However, the fractional factorial design was also used since we could hardly put across for respondents' consideration all the full profiles emanating from the experiment. Data from this approach were used to achieve objective four and partly five. The stated preference questionnaire was generally structured in form of profiles consisting of hypothetical combination of different residential attributes for a number of housing scenarios. Ordinarily, 30 profiles were generated through the conjoint experiment, and out of these, 6 choice sets were presented to the respondents for consideration. Based on the level of exposure of target respondents to this kind of interview, it was actually believed that the respondents would find these six choices more manageable than being given the whole profiles at once, and this agrees with general practice for fractional factorial design (Earnhart 2002; Wang and Li 2004; Sylvia et al. 2010). These profiles were put in choice sets in the questionnaire, and each respondent was asked to choose one option out of the six choices.

However, a single questionnaire containing questions on both the revealed and stated variables was administered on the same set of respondents. This was to facilitate comparison of results using stated and revealed methods (Earnhart 2001, 2002; Tayyaran and Khan 2007). However, a weakness of this method is the limitation posed by less number of choices to be made by respondents for as stated by Earnhart (2002) the more the choices the more the results mimic appropriately the actual situation. This weakness was addressed by using eight residential quality variables that were found to be essential to housing choices in the study area.

5.2.3 *Sampling Techniques (Sample Size and Administration of Questionnaires)*

The population for this survey consists of the entire household units in Lagos state. Twelve LGAs constituted the sampling sites and these form 60% of the whole sampling frame. According to National Population Commission NPC (2006), Lagos has a population of 9,013,534 and 2,497,419 households (CBN/NBS, 2006). It was estimated that the 12 LGAs had 4,968,786 people with 570,550 households (see Table 5.1).

As presented in Table 5.1, this study is limited to the Greater Lagos Metropolitan Areas or the usually called the megacity region. The study area covers approximately 548.4 km^2, a total population of 4,968,876 residents and approximately 9061 people per km^2. Using the statistic recommended by Salant and Dillman (1994), Krejcie and Morgan (1970), and Saroj (1981), the sample size for the survey was estimated to be about 1500 respondents consisting of the household heads, and this meets the expected minimum number of respondents given 2.5% precision. The sample size was determined by the model in Eq. (5.1):

$$S = Q * (1 + Q/n)^{-1} \text{ and } Q = \left(1.96^2 * (p * 1 - p)/e^2\right), \quad (5.1)$$

Table 5.1 Selected study areas of Lagos by population distribution (12 LGAs)

S/N	Local government area	Population	Land area (km^2)	Density (persons/km^2)
1	Agege	459,939	11.2	41,071
2	Ajeromi-Ifelodun	684,105	12.3	55,474
3	Amuwo-Odofin	318,166	134.6	2364
4	Apapa	217,362	26.7	8153
5	Eti-Osa	287,785	192.3	1496
6	Ikeja	313,196	46.2	6785
7	Lagos Island	209,437	8.7	24,182
8	Lagos Mainland	317,720	19.2	16,322
9	Mushin	633,009	17.5	36,213
10	Oshodi-Isolo	621,509	44.8	13,886
11	Shomolu	402,673	11.6	34,862
12	Surulere	503,975	23.0	21,912
Total	12	4,968,876	548.4	9060.68

Source National Population Commission NPC 2006

where S = sample size, n = households population, e = precision level or 2.5%, 1.96 = t value at 95% p = highest expected sampling coverage 60%, $1 - p$ = least expected sampling coverage 40%.

The survey employed multistage sampling approach involving stratified random sampling method and systematic random procedure. These sampling methods were employed for two reasons: for their cost effectiveness and appropriateness in setting the path for the application of discrete choice models (King 1969; Hammond and McCullagh 1974; Saroj 1981; Kanaroglou 1994). The twelve Local Government Areas were chosen based on the population (see Appendix A). The LGAs are arranged into three residential density clusters, namely low residential density (LRD), medium residential density (MRD) and high residential density area (HRD). Since each of these residential density areas contains numerous communities, one can only select some of the communities for survey. Hence, 56 neighborhoods/wards out of 157 neighborhoods/wards, based on the LGA population, were used for the survey (see Appendices A and B). The EA maps provided a guide for the selection of streets within the neighborhoods. The neighborhoods were also selected on the residential density basis. Therefore, ten neighborhoods were selected in the low residential density areas (LRD-10), eighteen neighborhoods in the medium residential density areas (MRD-18) and twenty-eight neighborhoods in the high residential density areas (HRD-28). A comprehensive house list was prepared to know the actual houses that were to be selected for sampling. Since this is a stratified sampling, picking a singular sampling interval kth for the whole sample would be inappropriate; hence, a sampling interval of 4 was used for each stratum or each residential density area. The administration of questionnaires began randomly with the 2nd house on a chosen street in the neighborhood. However, the total number of questionnaires administered in each LGA was proportional to the number of neighborhoods chosen in ratio 5:9:14 (LRD I = 270; MRD II = 486; HRD III = 729). The copies of the questionnaires were administered randomly on the respondents that were household heads and currently occupying a property either rented or personally owned. One respondent per chosen house was interviewed. The residential quality and housing preference survey was conducted in 6 months.

5.3 Measures of Variables and Specification of Models

5.3.1 Residential Quality Variables for Revealed Preference

Taking cue from housing preference literature, especially Timmermans et al. (1996), Earnhart (2002), Wang and Li (2004), Yates and Machay (2006), Cirman (2006) and Tayyaran and Khan (2007), revealed preference data in this study were measured by twenty residential quality variables, and these are presented in Table 5.2. The residential quality variables were all discrete categorical nominal variables with two or three alternative levels. However, all the categorical discrete variables were coded using the logit $k - 1$ format. As indicated in Table 5.2, the twenty quality variables were made of location, neighborhood and structural quality attributes of dwellings in light of previous studies. These are the attributes of dwellings that Lagos residents were found to be associated with given their capabilities, needs and aspirations.

Table 5.2 Residential quality variables used for revealed choices

SN	Residential quality	Residential attribute	Coding description
1	Metro location	City core/outer city/suburbs	Residential district of preference; mutually exclusive coding
2	Security	Police/private	Security provision as found in a location; 1 category applies, 0 if otherwise
3	Proximity to market	0–4 km/5+ km	Distance to market; 1 if category applies, 0 if otherwise
4	Accessibility	Highly accessible/limited accessibility	Accessibility to public transport; 1 if category applies; 0 if otherwise
5	Layout	Well planned/poorly planned	Orderliness as defined by residential layout; 1 if category applies, 0 if otherwise
6	Social relations	0–4 km/5+ km	Defined as closeness to friends and relations; 1 if category applies, 0 if otherwise
7	Proximity to work	0–4 km/5+ km and more	Distance of workplace to place of residence; 1 if category applies, 0 if otherwise
8	Proximity to hospital	0–4 km/5+ km	Closeness to public hospital; 1 if category applies, 0 if otherwise
9	Proximity to school	0–4 km/5+ km	Closeness to public schools; 1 if category applies, 0 if otherwise
10	Proximity to worship	0–4 km/5+ km	Closeness to a place of worship; 1 if category applies, 0 if otherwise
11	Exterior quality	Good/poor	Exterior quality of house; 1 if category applies, 0 if otherwise
12	House type	Duplex/flat/multiunit rooming	Housing type; mutually exclusive coding
13	Room number	1–2 rooms/3+ rooms	Number of rooms; 1 if category applies, 0 if otherwise
14	Room space	3×3 m^2/3×4 m^2	Room space dimensions; 1 if category applies, 0 if otherwise
15	Water	Pipe-borne/borehole/open well/vendor	Water facility; 1 if category applies, 0 if otherwise
16	Toilet/bath	2 toilets and 2 baths/1 toilet and 1 bath	Sanitary condition; 1 if category applies, 0 if otherwise
17	Kitchen	Tiled and separate/un-tiled and separate	The presence of tile in kitchen; 1 if category applies, 0 if otherwise
18	Interior quality	Good/poor	Interior quality of house; 1 if category applies, 0 if otherwise
19	Tenure	Owner-occupied/renter	Tenure of preference; 1 if category applies, 0 if otherwise
20	ARENT	N200000 and below/ N201000-400000/N401000-800000	Annual house rent; mutually exclusive coding

5.3.2 Residential Quality Variables for Stated Preference

According to Earnhart (2002) and Wang and Li (2004), to model housing preferences using stated approach, we need to engage few attributes/variables to produce manageable orthogonal profiles. Hence, as presented in Table 5.3, nine residential quality variables were used for generating stated preference data. The variables used in stated choice profiles are location, accessibility, Living Convenience, prestige, number of rooms, housing type, Room Design, Dwelling Facility and finally price. These variables are chosen from and tally with the revealed data sets. Table 5.3 shows the attributes used and their levels. From previous studies, these nine variables were found to be common residential quality variables of preference, although they were modified to suit local realities in Lagos (see Earnhart 2002; Wang and Li 2004). Seven attributes consisting of three attribute levels and two variables consisting of two attribute levels give a total of 1372 possible combinations ($2^2 * 7^3$). Using orthogonal fractional factorial design, 30 profiles (27 main profiles and 3 holdouts) were generated. The 30 profiles were reduced into six choice sets, and the respondents had to make a choice from the six choice sets. That means each choice sets went to about 250 respondents. Table 5.4 represents an example of the choice sets used for the study. In addition, twenty-five other residential quality variables are also used to determine future housing expectations and needs of respondents. They are only different from the variables used for experimental stated data, in the sense that they are to be rated and not choice alternatives. The intent behind this was to use the information to perform the SMART analyses for the study. All the residential attributes that require rating were coded using a Likert scale of 0–6, for unimportant, less important, important and extremely important, respectively.

5.3.3 Household Characteristics Variables

The attributes of the households are crucial to residential quality and housing preference explanation. The individual preferences for environmental and dwelling attributes are influenced by lifecycle and socioeconomic indices of households (Rosenbaum 1996; Li 2000; Li and Li 2006; Wang and Li 2004). There are fourteen (14) socioeconomic and demographic variables used in this study: (1) demographic variables are represented by gender (GEN), age (AGE), marital status (MAR), household size (HHS), number of children (CHD), religion REL), ethnic origin (ETH), length of stay (LEN), children above 18 yrs (CHD18); (2) socioeconomic variables are represented by education (EDU), occupation (OCC), income (INC) and (3) experiential variables represented by years worked (EXP) and years spent in Lagos (FAM).

Table 5.3 Residential attributes used in stated preference and their levels

SN	Residential quality	Level of attribute	Attribute levels $N = 25$
1	**Neighborhood** Metro location	(1) City core, (2) Outer city core, (3) City suburb	*3*
2	Accessibility to transport	(1) Limited accessibility to public transport, (2) Reasonable accessibility to public transport, (3) High accessibility to public transport	*3*
3	Living convenience/ closeness to market	(1) 1 km to market or shopping mall, (2) 2–4 km to market or shopping mall, (3) 5 km and above to market or shopping mall	*3*
4	Prestige/ security	(1) Police station within the neighborhood, (2) Private security within the neighborhood, (3) Private security/ police within the neighborhood	*3*
5	**Structural** Dwelling rooms	(1) 1 room housing unit, (2) 2–4 rooms housing unit, (3) 5 rooms and more housing unit	*3*
6	Type/housing type	(1) Multifamily unit rooming house built one or more than one floor, (2) Flat detached housing unit on one floor, (3) Maisonette/duplex house	3
7	Water/water supply	(1) Potable water/borehole, (2) Well water/water vendors	2
8	Design/room space	(1) Small parlor/large room, (2) Large parlor/small room	2
9	Price/rent	(1) NGN100–200K, (2) NGN201–400K, (3) NGN401–800K	3

Table 5.4 Typical conjoint housing choice set

House 1	(Rooming multiunit)
Location	City core
Accessibility	Limited
Proximity to public utility	Market within 2–4 km
Security	Private security
Number of rooms	1–2 RMs
Room design	Small rooms
Water	Well
Price/rent	NGN100–200K
Your choice	☐

5.3.4 Dependent and Independent Variables

By design the dependent variables are five in number divided broadly into two: contextual variables—housing choice profiles and metropolitan characteristics and individual characteristic variables—marital status, age and income. In the revealed model, the three individual variables, that is, marital, age and income groups and a contextual variable that is metropolitan characteristics were used as dependent variables as the purpose was to see the change in housing quality choices across the marital status, age and income groups and across metropolitan areas. In the stated model, the housing choice profiles were employed as dependent variables. These five variables were coded using logit format $k - 1$. The independent variables are the remaining residential quality attributes already indicated in Sects. 5.3.1 and 5.3.2. The dependent and independent variables were used to estimate preference models explained in Sect. 5.3.5.

5.3.5 Specification of Models

(a) Estimation of Revealed Preference Data

Based on the assumptions enunciated in the theoretical section and the hypotheses stated earlier in this study, especially hypotheses 3 and 4, nine models were separately estimated using multinomial logit regression on revealed data. The first four models were fitted on the housing quality data only. The models estimated the relative effects of residential quality on housing type choices. A set of five logit models were also estimated based on the interactions between socioeconomic and residential quality variables. These models estimated the influential residential quality factors driving housing choice formation of different households based upon marital status, age, income and metropolitan characteristics. The general model for estimating each of the MNL models for the revealed data is given by Eq. (5.2):

$$\Pr(Y) = \exp V_{ij} / \Sigma \exp V_{ij} = \beta_o + \beta_n \chi_n + e_n, \tag{5.2}$$

where $\Pr(Y)$ = probability of household choosing a house type; β_o = alternative specific constant coefficient; β_n = coefficient for housing and household characteristics; e_n = random error value.

(b) Estimation of Stated Preference Data

Four models were fitted on stated data only. The models measure the influential factors driving housing preference formation across residential density areas. The general equation for estimating the MNL models for stated preference is given in Eq. (5.3):

$$\Pr(Y) = \exp V_{ij} / \Sigma \exp V_{ij} = \lambda_o + \lambda_n \chi_n + \mu_n, \tag{5.3}$$

where Pr(Y) = probability of household choosing a housing choice; λ_o = alternative specific constant coefficient; λ_n = coefficient for housing and household characteristics; μ_n = random error value.

5.4 Analytical Techniques

5.4.1 Univariate and Bivariate Analysis

Data analysis in this book followed three analytical paths-univariate-bivariate, multivariate and SMART analyses. The first analytical path involved the use of *Descriptive Statistical* techniques such as mean, standard deviation, coefficient of variation, cross-tabulation and percentage frequency distribution. These are univariate analytical methods that were used to describe and summarize residential and household data. The Pearson correlation technique was used to establish association between pairs of household and residential quality variables. The bivariate correlation results were used to test the first hypothesis in the study.

5.4.2 Multivariate Analysis

Multivariate analysis was performed in this study using three statistical tools: Principal Component Analysis (PCA), Analysis of Variance (ANOVA) and discrete multinomial logit regression (MNL). The PCA technique is a multivariate statistical technique that has as its objectives to take p variables $\boldsymbol{\omega}_s$ (standardized original variables) and to find linear combination of these to produce indices Z_s that are orthogonal (Hardy and Bryan, 2006; Robinson 1998). PCA is a data reduction technique which was used in this study to reduce many variables on location, neighborhood and structural characteristics of dwellings in the study area to a few important components and thus explain level of contribution to total variation observed in the data. According to literature, a total variance of 70.0% is sufficient (Robinson 1998). This follows a successful use by Ajala (2004) in Osun State Nigeria, Cirman (2006), in his housing preference study of Slovenia and Choi and Kang (2010) in their study of housing preferences in Silver estate California, United States of America. The PCA results were used to test the second hypothesis in the study. The second multivariate technique employed in this research is the Analysis of Variance. The ANOVA model was used to determine the inter-residential density area variation in residential quality and housing preferences. Results from the ANOVA model were handy in the validation and explanation of the veracity of the fourth hypotheses in the study. The third multivariate analytical technique used in this study is the discrete multinomial logit (MNL). This is a standard technique for preference analysis; much more preferred to ordinary least square regression OLS, for its accurate estimation of coefficients and predictive capability of categorical data. In this study, multinomial logit model was employed to predict renter preferences for residential quality—neighborhood and structural—as well as the determinants of housing preferences in the study area. The betas produced by multinomial model are more accurate and show marginal increases in probabilities of a buyer/renter to choose a particular housing choice compared to the reference alternative. The use of logit procedure follows earlier works by Timmermans et al. (1996), Rosenbaum (1996), Cho (1997), Li (2000), Walker et al. (2002), Wang and Li (2004). The results from the logit analysis provided evidence to test the third and the fourth hypotheses. The standard multinomial logit model is stated in Eq. (5.4); thus:

$$\text{Prob}(Y = m|x_i) = \exp(\phi \chi_i \beta_m) / \Sigma \exp(\phi \chi_i \beta_j). \tag{5.4}$$

The symbol ϕ is an unidentified scale parameter, inversely proportional to the standard deviation of the error term and usually in multinomial models normalized to unity (Earnhart 2002; Tayyaran and Khan 2007). The data are presumed to reflect a random variable e_i that is independently and Identically GUMBEL Distributed (IID). The multinomial model uses maximum likelihood method to estimate some parameters such as coefficient β_i, odd ratio exp β_i, Wald/t-ratio and Rho-square ρ^2 that are very important for the explanation of housing preferences and their determinants. The exp β_i as an intuitively meaningful parameter was used to explain the probability of a respondent choosing a dwelling or residential quality indicator as against the reference category, Wald test was used to determine the significance of housing and household variables, the coefficient β_i tells how much the logit increases for a unit increase in the independent variable, McFadden ρ^2 provides the test of fit of logit regression model as deduced from the likelihood ratio and Chi-square χ^2 statistics (Walker et al. 2002; Jerry 2007).

5.4.3 *SMART Analysis*

The Simple Multi-Attribute Rating Technique (SMART), which is otherwise called Compositional Model, is a variant of Multi-Attribute Utility Theory (MAUT) that functions on the Weighted Algebraic Mean (WAM) to determine the utility values of housing attributes (Timmermans et al. 1994; Edwards 1977). The SMART framework is the simplest form of the MAUT methods that operates on ranking. The ranking value χ_j of alternative a_{ij} is obtained as the weighted algebraic mean of the utility values associated with the alternative, as given in Eq. (5.5):

$$\chi_j = \sum w_i a_{ij} / \sum w_i, \tag{5.5}$$

where χ_j represents ranking value of a variable; w represents weight of alternative, a represents alternative score and $j = 1, 2 \ldots n$.

The SMART model also provides a simple method to assess weights for each of the residential attribute criteria in order to reflect its relative importance to the home preference decision (see Edwards 1977). First, the criteria are ranked in order of importance and scores are assigned to the criteria from 1 being the least to 10 being the highest criterion. Scores are assigned to reflect the attribute relative importance. The final weights are obtained by normalizing the sum of the scores to one. However, as Edwards and Barron (1994) pointed out, the comparison of the importance of attributes is meaningless if it does not reflect the range of the utility values of the alternatives as well. Hence, the utility values of alternatives are to be provided in determining the level of preferences of the housing attributes.

The SMART is used in this study following through eight processes:

(i) **Identify the decision maker**: Lagos households
(ii) **State the decision issues**: Seeking for desirable homes according to needs and affordability
(iii) **Choices to be made**: Lagos households often make three housing choices
    (a) Multiunit housing
    (b) Flat unit
    (c) Duplex housing unit
(iv) **Value dimensions**: In making housing choices, households emphasize three values:
    (a) Neighborhood quality
    (b) Structural quality
    (c) Cost/price
(v) **Ranking of value dimensions and scores**:
    (a) Max. Neighborhood
    (b) Max. Structural quality
    (c) Min. Cost/rent
(vi) **Determine the probability for each option of the value dimensions: Multiunit/Flat/Duplex**
    (a) Neighborhood
    (b) Structural quality
    (c) Cost
(vii) **Estimation of utilities for choices**
(viii) **Ranking of choice alternative according to utilities.**

The only weakness of the SMART and generally the MAUT frameworks is the subjectivity of the ranking and scoring values allocated to choice alternatives. This weakness is however attenuated or remediated in this study by using the mean of the rankings by the respondents instead of arbitrary values. The SMART model estimates housing preference structures by recording separately and explicitly the way home seekers evaluate residential features and by determining the relative importance of each feature. The scores are aggregated using the linear additive rule. The underlying assumption of MAUT procedure which stipulates that the data be taken at dimensionless level is well observed. However, the SMART framework as devised by Edwards (1977) is to be used in this study for its simplicity and appropriateness in depicting the manner in which residential variables are traded off during home search. Given the nature of inquiry envisaged in this study, the research design for the analysis of data is, therefore, a multistage one (see Fig. 5.1).

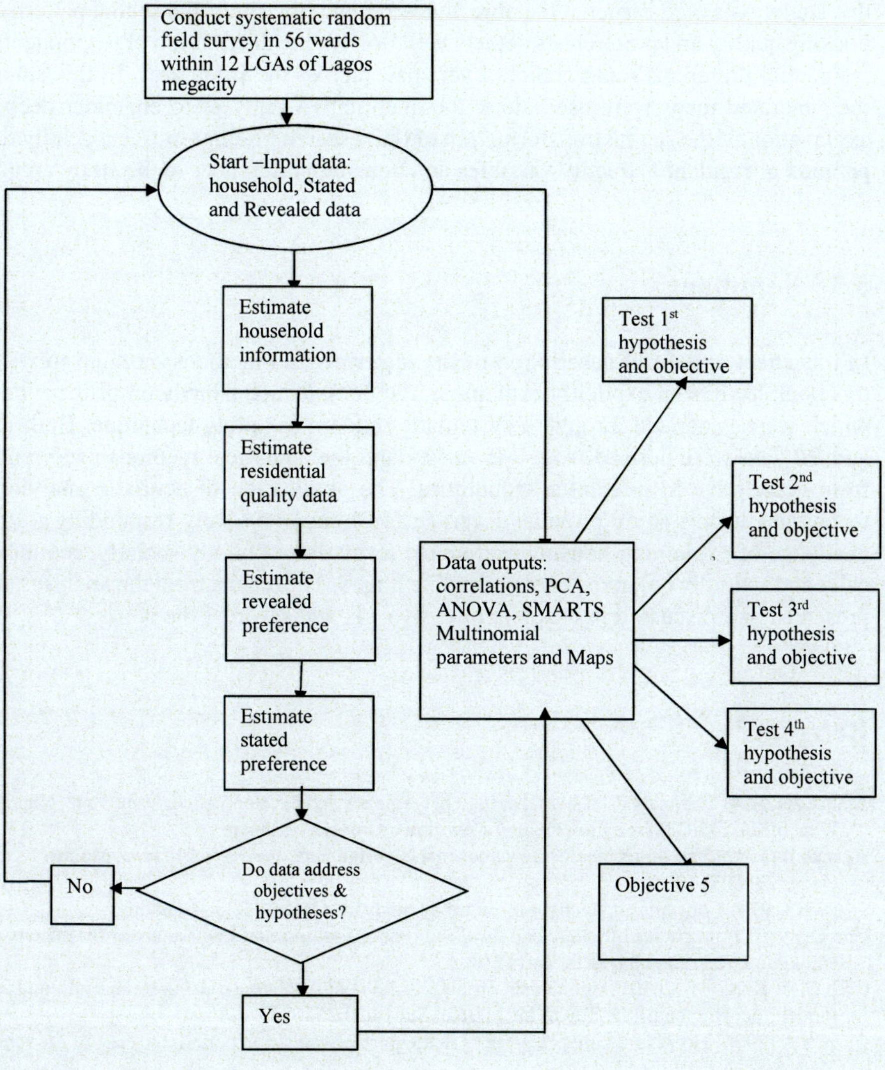

Fig. 5.1 Flowchart of methodological design

5.4.4 *Residential Quality and Housing Preference Mapping*

The mapping of residential quality and housing preferences in this study was done using the PCA method. This method makes use of PCA Eigenvector scores of the residential quality variables on the LGAs, that is, variables versus geographic area matrices (see Ayeni 1979; Robinson 1998; Neumann 1997; Hardy and Bryan 2006). These scores are thereafter decomposed into four groups depending on the values. The groups are coded as high, medium, low and very low-value areas. This mapping can be performed with many graphical packages but the Arc GIS 9.0 package was used in this study. As stated earlier at the objective section of the study, the spatial pattern of housing quality and preferences depicts variations in the distribution of respondents' residential preferences and choices over space across the study area. In this study, the generated maps were used along the quantitative analyses to engender deeper explanation of the spatial transformation of the research findings most especially the patterns of residential quality variables and housing preferences in the study area.

5.5 Summary

In this chapter, the full description of the materials and methods required to write this book have been explicitly explained. The book leaned heavily on primary data which were generated through a systematic random sampling technique. Both RP and SP data were derived from this survey and the analytical methods used range from descriptive to inferential techniques. The application of heuristic analytical techniques in this study provides leverage for comprehensively responding to the challenge of explaining housing preference formation in highly socially, economically and spatially polarized economies like Lagos. The results from the analyses are presented and discussed in chapters four, five, six and seven of the book.

References

Ajala OA (2004) The analysis of spatial pattern of resources and development in Osun State, Nigeria. Unpublished PhD dissertation Obafemi Awolowo University, Ile-Ife

Arimah B (1992) Variations in housing values in a Nigerian City: the case of Ibadan. Malays J Trop Geogr 23(1):1–12

Ayeni B (1979) Concepts and techniques in urban analysis. Croom Helm, London

Cho C (1997) Joint choice of tenure and dwelling type: a multinomial Logit analysis for the city of Chongju. Urban Stud 34(9):1459–1473

Choi S-H, Kang M (2010) An analysis on elderly housing preference using structural equation model: focusing on Silver Town. Int J Urban Sci 14(3):254–263

Cirman A (2006) Housing tenure preferences in the post-privatization period: the case of Slovenia. Hous Stud 21(1):113–134

Earnhart D (2001) Combining revealed and stated preference methods to value environmental amenities at residential locations. Land Econ 77(1):12–29

Earnhart D (2002) Combining revealed and stated data to examine housing decisions using discrete choice analysis. J Urban Econ 51:143–169

Edwards W (1977) How to use multi-attribute utility measurement for social decision making. IEEE Trans Syst Man Cybern 7:326–340

Edwards W, Barron FH (1994) SMARTS and SMARTER: improved simple methods for multi-attribute utility measurements. Organ Behav Hum Decis Process 60:306–325

Ekanem FN (1995) Determinants of the price of homes in a suburban area of Washington D.C. compared with those in a suburban area of Lagos, Nigeria. Niger J Econ Soc Stud 37(1):1–11

Hammond P, McCullagh PS (1974) Quantitative techniques in geography. Oxford University Press, London

Jerry A (2007) The geography of opportunity: race and housing choice in Metropolitan America, edited by Xavier de Souza Briggs. 2005. Series: James A. Joaszhnson Metro Series. Brookings Institution Press, Washington, p 353 (reviewed) J Reg Sci 47(2):405–407

Hardy M, Bryan A (eds) (2006) Handbook on data analysis. SAGE, London

Kanaroglou SP (1994) Methods and techniques: sampling and discrete choice analysis. Prof Geogr 46(3):359–358

King JL (1969) Statistical analysis in geography. Prentice-Hall, London

Krejcie RV, Morgan DW (1970) Determining sample size for research activities. Educ Psychol Measur 30:607–610

Li S-M (2000) The housing market and tenure decisions in Chinese cities: a multivariate analysis of the case of Guangzhou. Hous Stud 15(1):213–236

Li S-M, Li L (2006) Life course and housing tenure change in urban China: a study of Guangzhou. Hous Stud 21(5):653–670

Markley S (2011) Spatially-oriented discrete choice predictions: a case study of French supermarket preferences. http://www.bentley.edu/csbigs/vol1-1/markley.pdf:pp26-46. Accessed on 23rd Feb 2012

Neumann WL (1997) Social research methods. Routledge, London

Robinson MG (1998) Methods and techniques in human geography. Wiley, New York

Rosenbaum J (1996) The influence of race on Hispanic housing choices in New York City 1978–1987. Urban Aff Rev 32(2):217–243

Salant P, Dillman DA (1994) How to conduct your own survey. Wiley, New York

Saroj KP (1981) Statistical techniques: a basic approach to geography. McGraw Hill, New Delhi

Sylvia J, Henny C, Roland G (eds) (2010) Methodology for research into housing preferences and choices. Springer, New York

Tayyaran MR, Khan MA (2007) Telecommuting and residential location decisions: combined stated and revealed preferences model. Can J Civ Eng 34:1324–1333

Timmermans H, Molin E, van Nootwijk L (1994) Housing choice processes: stated versus revealed modeling approaches. Netherl J Hous Built Environ 9(3):215–227

Timmermans H, van Nootwijk L, Oppewal L, van der Waerden P (1996) Modeling constrained choice behavior in regulated housing markets by means of discrete choice experiments and universal logit models: an application to the residential choice behavior of divorcees. Environ Plan A 28:1095–1112

Walker B, Marsh A, Wardman M, Niner P (2002) Modelling tenant choices in the public rented sector: a stated preference approach. Urban Stud 39(4):665–688

Wang D, Li S-M (2004) Housing preferences in a transitional housing system: the case of Beijing China. Environ Plan A 36:69–87

Yates J, Machay DF (2006) Discrete choice modeling of urban housing markets: a critical review and application. Urban Stud 43(3):559–581

Chapter 6
Lagos Households' Sociodemographic and Housing Characteristics

Abstract Analyses performed in this chapter are grouped into six sections which include demographic characteristics, socioeconomic characteristics, experiential and familiarity, residential quality and revealed choices, households' characteristics and residential quality and summary. The respondents' background information provides the basis for understanding the observed behavioral patterns. First of all, the socioeconomic and demographic characteristics of the sampled households are provided and later in the chapter the attributes of their dwelling units using simple descriptive statistics and bivariate correlation analysis are presented.

Keywords Lagos household characteristics · Demographic characteristics · Socioeconomic characteristics · Residential characteristics · Private residential markets

The previous chapters have considered the research problem, objectives, overview of theoretical background and methodology of this book in detail, the preoccupation of this chapter, however, is the presentation and explanation of results of data after analysis. The chapter on methodology has indicated that 1500 respondents served as the sample size for the study. However, questionnaires from 15 respondents could not be accommodated due to incomplete responses and the inability to retrieve them, leaving us with exactly 1485 questionnaires upon which the analyses in the book are based. The retrieval rate is therefore 99%, which is almost the same as the initially estimated sample. The analysis in this chapter is divided into six sections which include demographic characteristics, socioeconomic characteristics, experiential and familiarity, residential quality and revealed choices, households' characteristics and residential quality and summary. The respondents' background information provides the basis for understanding the observed behavioral patterns (Krivo 1986; Rosenbaum 1995, 1996; Neumann 1997). First of all, the socioeconomic and demographic characteristics of the sampled households are provided and later in the chapter the attributes of their dwelling units using simple descriptive statistics and bivariate correlation analysis are presented.

© The Author(s), under exclusive license to Springer Nature Switzerland AG 2024

I. R. Aliu, *Urban Private Housing in Nigeria*, The Urban Book Series,
https://doi.org/10.1007/978-3-031-47432-3_6

6.1 Demographic Characteristics of Households

Seven variables are used to summarize the demographic characteristics of the respondents. These demographic variables are gender, marital status, age, household size, number of children, number of children above 18 years and ethnicity. Table 6.1 shows the summary of the demographic variables of households interviewed. According to the table, the gender distribution of the heads of households reveals that exactly 77.6% are males and 22.4% are females. Further analysis indicates the same pattern along the residential zones although as indicated in Fig. 6.1 variations along the residential density areas are not significant especially when viewed from the Chi-square χ^2 value of 0.07 at *p* > *0.05 confidence levels.* Explanation for the domination by males can be rendered from the fact that more men are readily and favorably disposed to the filling of the questionnaires than do the women when dealing with study on residential choices as it is traditionally the responsibility of men to provide shelter for their respective families. Except in separated or widowed households hardly can one find a situation where the responsibility of paying for accommodation is shouldered by the female folks.

Besides gender home choice decisions and residential quality preferences are influenced by marital status. Marital status of households is categorized into three, namely single, married and widowed/divorced. The married in Nigeria like in all other African countries could be polygamy or monogamy depending on the number of women a male respondent has. In this study, there is no separation between the two. The same Table 6.1 shows that the proportion of the respondents that are married is 90%, while the single is 6.7% and the widowed is 3.3%. In all three density areas, the pattern is the same with the majority of the respondents being married and the intergroup independence as depicted by Chi-square χ^2 value of 20.97, is significant at $p < 0.01$. Another important household's demographic variable observed in the study is age. While some studies used the numerical age of respondents, in this study age is a discrete variable categorized into three: 21–40 years being young households, 41–60 years being middle aged and 61 years and above being old household heads. On account of age distribution, 42% are between ages 21 years and 40 years, 53.9% between 41 years and 60 years while the remaining 4.1% are old people above 61 years of age. There is a significant intergroup independence as shown by χ^2 value of 21.658 at $p < 0.01$. The implication of this age distribution pattern for housing quality and preferences in the study area is that we are likely going to witness choices that are made based upon well informed and realistic reasons as the sample is made majorly of the adults. Closely related to marital status and age is the number of children in each household. Information as contained in Table 6.1 indicates that the overall mean number of children per household is approximately 3 children. Perhaps, one reason that may be adduced for the low number of children per household in the study area is that Nigerians for cultural reasons are not readily disposed to giving the actual number of children they have. There is a suspicion that the households deliberately underreported their total number of children for cultural reasons.

Table 6.1 Demographic characteristics of households

Household characteristic	Total sample ARD (*N* = 1485) %	LRD subsample (*N* = 270) %	MRD subsample (*N* = 486) %	HRD subsample (*N* = 729) %	Test of intergroup independence χ^2
Gender					
Male	1152(77.6)	209(14.1)	376(25.3)	567(38.2)	0.072 $p <$ 0.996
Female	333(22.4)	61(4.0)	110(7.5)	162(10.9)	
Marital status					
Married	1337(90.0)	247(16.6)	457(30.8)	633(42.6)	20.97 $p <$ 0.000
Single	100(6.7)	19(1.3)	21(1.4)	59(4.0)	
Widowed	48(3.3)	4(0.3)	9(0.6)	36(2.4)	
Age					
20–40	624(42.0)	107(7.2)	174(11.7)	343(23.2)	21.658 $p <$ 0.001
41–60	800(53.9)	157(10.6)	287(19.3)	356(24.0)	
61 and above	61(4.1)	6(0.4)	25(1.7)	30(2.0)	
Household size					
1–2	117(7.9)	35(2.3)	17(1.1)	65(4.4)	114.804 $p <$ 0.000
3–6	1143(77.0)	222(14.9)	331(22.3)	589(39.7)	
7 and above	225(15.1)	13(0.9)	138(9.3)	74(4.9)	
Children > 18 yrs					
1–3	578(38.9)	95(6.4)	213(14.3)	270(18.2)	7.762 $p <$ 0.101
4–7	27(1.8)	6(0.4)	7(0.5)	13(0.9)	
None	880(59.3)	169(11.4)	266(17.8)	445(30.0)	
Children (mean)	2.62	2.38	2.86	2.55	
Ethnicity					
Yoruba	829(55.8)	126(8.5)	238(16.0)	465(31.3)	51.20 $p <$ 0.000
Others in Nigeria	610(41.1)	125(8.4)	238(16.0)	248(16.7)	
Others outside Nigeria	46(3.1)	19(1.3)	10(0.7)	16(1.1)	

A much better measure of household composition therefore would seem to be the household size. The household variable is categorized into three those households that have 1–2 members, those that have 3–6 members and those that have 7 persons and more. On the basis of household size, the study discovers that the households with 1–2 persons constitute 7.9%, those with 3–6 persons constitute 77% while the remaining 15.1% are those with 7 persons and more. This implies a preponderance of households with 3–6 persons per housing unit. Depending upon the nature of residential unit being occupied variously by these households, the room density may

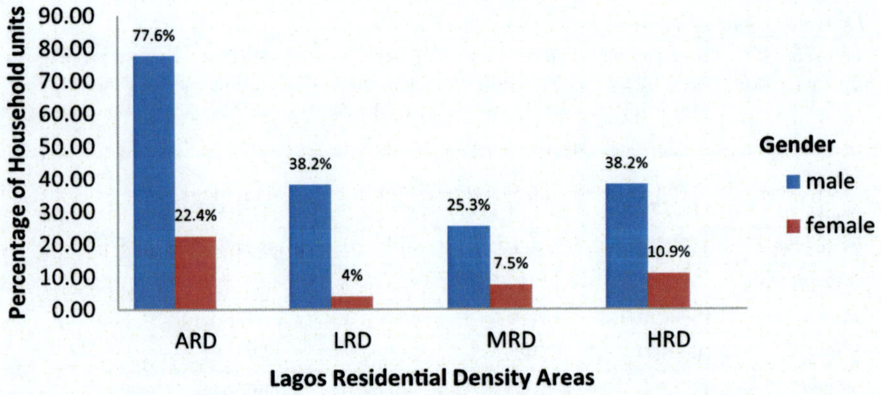

Fig. 6.1 Spatial pattern of households' gender distribution

be pre-empted from this emerging fact. The pattern of household size is the same in each of the residential density areas and a significant independence exists among the density areas ($\chi^2 = 114.804, p < 0.01$). Very crucial for housing choice analysis is the number of children or dependants within a household that are above 18 years of age. Knowing the distribution of the number of children over 18 years is important in order to see how the variable is factored in decision to take a type of residential unit. In this study, three categories of households based on the number of children above 18 years are observed and they are the households that have 1–3 children above 18 years, those that have 4–7 children above 18 years and those that do not have any child above 18 years. As indicated in Table 6.1 households with 1–3 children above 18 years constitute 38.9%, while those with 4–7 constitute 1.8% and 59.3% of the households have no child above 18 years. Finally, the ethnic compositions of the three density areas are analyzed. The study reveals that the Yoruba constitute 55.8%, other tribes in Nigeria 41.1% and others from outside of Nigeria constitute 3.1%. Although racial discrimination has not been found in any previous studies to be critical in housing choices in Nigeria, the variable is used to control for the existence of ethnic affiliation in residential choices in Lagos. In all the residential density areas Yoruba are obviously in the majority.

The spatial variations in the distribution of demographic variables in Lagos are quite interesting. Looking once more at Table 6.1 one would easily notice that males are in the majority in all the residential density areas, especially the LRD and the HRD with 38.5% each. The females are found more in the HRD than in other residential areas. Perhaps this pattern of gender distribution is totally at odd with the census figure which gives nearly equal proportions of males and females in the city (see NPC 2006). One reason why the males always dominate studies of this nature is not unconnected with the patriarchy family system in Nigeria where the household heads are always the males. The same variations noted for the gender distribution are also noted for the marital status, age, number of children, household size and ethnic affiliation. On all these demographic variables, the HRD has higher proportion followed by the MRD and the least being the LRD.

6.2 Socioeconomic Characteristics of Households

Just as the demographic variables are very important in housing quality and preference studies so the socioeconomic characteristics of households are crucial to the understanding and explanation of housing preference formation. Four variables are used in this study to describe the socioeconomic characteristics of the respondents. These variables include education, income, occupation and religious affiliation. The summary of the socioeconomic characteristics of respondents is presented in Table 6.2. According to Table 6.2, the educational attainment of respondents are split into three levels, namely no formal education or primary school certificate, secondary school certificate and first degree, M.Sc. or Ph.D. holders. Out of 1485 respondents, 39.3% are graduates, 56.6% are secondary and technical certificate holders while 4.4% are primary school holders and illiterates. The Chi-square χ^2 value of 21.97 at $p < 0.01$ shows that there is a significant intergroup independence in the educational attainment of respondents. Going by the general level of education in the study, it appears majority of the respondents could read and write and with graduates constituting nearly 40% and hence their residential choices and tastes may likely be similar. It is reasoned that the high representation of graduates in this study could be attributed to the fact that those who regarded themselves as graduates might possess some Diploma and National Certificate of Education (NCE). Occupation variable is split into four groups, namely unemployed, artisans and traders, private sector workers and civil servants. The unemployed constitute 1.8%, artisans and Traders 32.5%, private worker 50.6% and civil servants 15.1%. The least number of unemployed people is recorded in the LRD, and the highest in HRD. Conversely, the highest number of artisans and traders is recorded in HRD. Intergroup independence as shown by Chi-square χ^2 value of 83.667 is significant at $p < 0.01$.

The next socioeconomic variable considered in the study is income of household heads. The income status is categorized into four groups, namely the low-income earners N0-N74,999 who form 44.1% of the households interviewed, the average-income earners N75,000-N149,999 who form 48.1%, the middle-income earners N150,000-N224,999 who constitute 7.1% and the high-income earners N225,000 and above who constitute 0.7%. According to information in Table 6.2 over 90% of the high-income earners are from the LRD and close to three-quarter of the low-income earners are from HRD. The Chi-square χ^2 value of 158.154 at $p < 0.01$ indicates a significant intergroup independence in the spatial distribution of income among the respondents as illustrated in Fig. 6.2. The fourth socioeconomic variable of the households examined is the religious affiliation. The creed of respondents is split into three: Islam, Christianity and other faiths. Moslems constitute 34.9%, Christians 64.8% and others constitute 0.3%. From the findings in this study, the Christians households are in the majority. The implication of this distribution pattern

Table 6.2 Socioeconomic characteristics of households

Household characteristic	Total sample ARD (N = 1485) %	LRD subsample (N = 270) %	MRD subsample (N = 486) %	HRD subsample (N = 729) %	Test of intergroup independence χ^2
Education					
Ph.D./M.Sc./ graduate	584(39.3)	79(5.3)	172(11.6)	333(22.4)	21.97 $p <$ 0.000
Secondary/ technical	834(56.2)	183(12.3)	305(20.5)	340(23.5)	
No education/ primary	67(4.5)	9(0.6)	9(0.6)	48(3.2)	
Occupation					
Civil servant	224(15.1)	45(3.0)	58(3.9)	122(8.2)	83.667 $p <$ 0.000
Private worker	751(50.6)	159(10.7)	300(20.2)	292(19.7)	
Artisan/trader	483(32.5)	65(4.4)	120(8.1)	297(20.0)	
Unemployed	27(1.8)	1(0.1)	7(0.5)	18(1.2)	
Income					
N74,999 and less	655(44.1)	104(7.0)	134(9.0)	417(28.1)	158.154 $p <$ 0.000
N75,000–149,999	715(48.1)	120(8.1)	310(20.9)	284(19.1)	
N150,000–224,999	105(7.1)	37(2.5)	40(2.7)	28(1.9)	
N225,000 and above	10(0.7)	9(0.6)	1(0.1)	(1)0.1	
Religion					
Islam	518(34.9)	68(4.6)	145(9.8)	304(20.5)	48.604 $p <$ 0.000
Christianity	962(64.8)	197(13.3)	341(22.9)	425(28.6)	
Others	5(0.3)	5(0.3)	0(0.0)	0(0.0)	

of households on housing choices and quality would be shown in further analyses in the study, even though no literature has cited residential choice behaviors resulting from religious status of home seekers in Lagos.

6.3 Experiential and Familiarity Attributes of Households

Apart from demographic and socioeconomic characteristics, the households examined in this study were also studied from the points of their experience and familiarity with the Lagos environment. Two variables are used in the study to represent the households' awareness and their knowledge of Lagos environment and these are number of years worked and number of years spent in Lagos. While the first accounts

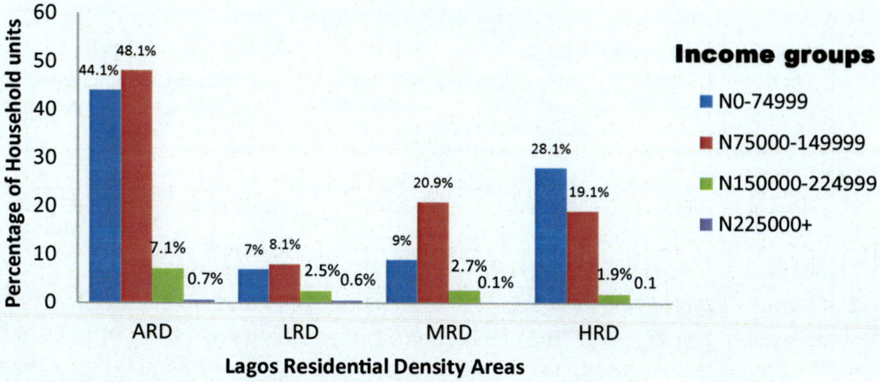

Fig. 6.2 Spatial pattern of households' income levels

for the life experience including residency, the second variable accounts for awareness of the situations in Lagos. Although these two variables are hardly employed in the past studies, they are considered in this study because of the potential impact they might have on the households' choices of home in future as envisaged by the stated model of housing preferences. Experience is categorized into three based on the number of years worked by households. As indicated in Table 6.3, households that have worked for 10 years and less constitute 26.3%, those that have worked for between 11 years and 20 years constitute 57.9%, those that have worked for between 21 years and 35 years are 14.0% and the rest 1.8% are those that have worked for 36 years and above. On the account of familiarity with Lagos environment, the study discovered that those who have lived in Lagos for 5 years and less constitute 3.8%, those who have lived between 6 years and 20 years make 37.6% while the majority 58.5% have lived for 21 years and more in Lagos. Intergroup independence is significant at $p < 0.01$ and Chi-square χ^2 value of 17.374. Figure 6.3 further graphically illustrates the spatial pattern of households' experience in Lagos.

This result implies that close to 60% of the households have spent over 20 years in Lagos and hence are very conversant with Lagos environment and lifestyles. Coupled with the fact that nearly four-fifths (73.7% have worked between 11 years and more) of them have spent more than 10 years on their respective jobs the households are very experienced and might have gotten a definite idea on the residential quality and choices of their desire.

Table 6.3 Experiential and environmental familiarity of households

Household characteristic	Total sample ARD (*N* = 1485) %	LRD subsample (*N* = 270) %	MRD subsample (*N* = 486) %	HRD subsample (*N* = 729) %	Test of intergroup independence χ^2
Experience					
10 years and less	390(26.3)	59(4.0)	92(6.2)	239(16.1)	38.685 $p <$ 0.000
11–20 years	860(57.9)	166(11.2)	310(20.9)	383(25.8)	
21–35 years	208(14.0)	37(2.5)	79(5.3)	92(6.2)	
36 years and more	27(1.8)	7(0.5)	4(0.3)	15(1.0)	
Familiarity					
5 years and less	57(3.8)	12(0.8)	16(1.1)	28(1.9)	17.374 $p <$ 0.002
6–20 years	558(37.6)	131(8.8)	171(11.5)	258(17.4)	
21 years and above	870(58.6)	128(8.6)	208(20.1)	443(29.8)	

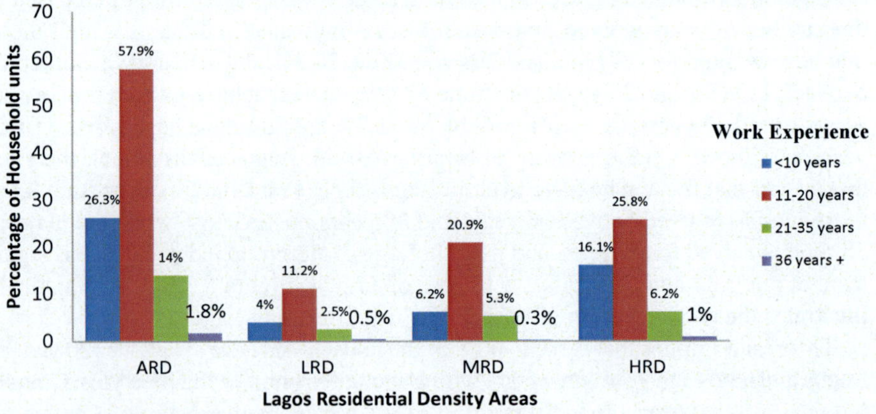

Fig. 6.3 Spatial pattern of households' experience

6.4 Residential Quality Variables that Shape Housing Choice Formation

A major aspect of the attributes of households covered in the study is the residential quality status as contained in the neighborhood and structural attributes of dwelling units of the respondents. It is believed that the quality of dwellings interact with the socioeconomic variables to influence home choices of households in each of the residential density areas. In this study, eleven variables are used to represent neighborhood quality of households in the study area. The neighborhood variables are metropolitan characteristics, distance to workplace, closeness to public school, closeness to hospital, closeness to friends and relations, distance to market, closeness to place of worship, security, accessibility, layout and environmental quality. The structural quality of households' dwelling units is summarized using nine variables, namely house type, number of rooms, room space, water, toilet, kitchen, structural quality of dwelling unit, type of tenure and price. Tables 6.4 and 6.5 contain the percentage distribution of the twenty residential quality variables across the residential density areas. Invariably, these neighborhood and structural quality indicators are taken as the residential quality choices of the individual residents as dictated by the prevalent conditions at the time they took their respective dwelling units. Therefore, these residential quality indicators have implications for the description of the revealed housing choices of the households. The first neighborhood residential quality of Lagos households to be observed in the study is the metropolitan characteristic which is divided into city core, outer city core and city suburbs. As indicated in Table 6.4, exactly 42.0% of the households decided to choose their dwellings in the city CBD, 34.3% in the outer CBD and 23.75% of them live in the CBD suburb.

From Table 6.4, it is noticeable that the core city area is not as more preferred for dwelling as the outer city and suburb areas of Lagos metropolis. Households that prefer the city core are barely 34.3% compared with 65.7% that do not wish to live in the city core. Intergroup independence of the pattern shows a significant variation with χ^2 value of 411.67 being significant at $p < 0.01$. Six variables are used to indicate spatial proximity to activity centers namely proximity to workplace, proximity to school, proximity to market, proximity to worship places, proximity to hospital and closeness to friends and relations all indicated by two categories 0–4 km and 5 km and more. Majority of the households making 54.5% chose to live in neighborhoods 0–4 km close to their places of work, 65% of them lived 0–4 km close to hospital, 68.1% lived in neighborhoods 0–4 km close to their children schools, 63.1% choose to live in localities 0–4 km close to their religious centers (churches and mosques) and 63.6% lived close to local markets or shopping centers. While the majority seem to live closer to the activity places, there are a significant number of the households that live 5 km and more faraway as represented by at least 32% of the households on each of the six location variables. These spatial behavioral patterns reflect the tendency among the residents in the study area to minimize the cost of transportation to the activity places.

Accessibility is viewed in this study as having unhindered opportunity to public transport as many of the households are not private car owners. There are two categories of the accessibility variable namely limited accessibility and reasonable accessibility. Findings as shown in Table 6.4 and illustrated in Fig. 6.4 indicate that majority of the households interviewed in Lagos, that is 82.9%, live in areas that are reasonably accessible to public transport, 78.3% live in places with mixed layout, 94.9% live in areas that are environmentally above average and 82.5% of the households live under public security. While the residents are willing to stay closer to the places of economic and social relevance to their livelihoods, they are however unable to have accommodation in places that have some organized layout and closer to relations and

Table 6.4 Neighborhood quality indicators of households' residential units

Residential attribute	Total sample ARD (*N* = 1485)	LRD subsample (*N* = 270)	MRD subsample (*N* = 486)	HRD subsample (*N* = 729)	Test of intergroup independence χ^2
Metropolitan characteristics					
City core	509(34.3)	203(13.7)	49(3.3)	257(17.3)	411.667 $p <$ 0.000
Outer city core	624(42.0)	64(4.3)	309(20.8)	251(16.9)	
Suburban	352(23.7)	1(0.1)	128(8.6)	221(14.9)	
Work					
0–4 km	809(54.5)	200(13.5)	251(16.9)	356(24.0)	55.649 $p <$ 0.000
5+ km	676(45.5)	68(4.6)	236(15.9)	371(25.0)	
School					
0–4 km	1011(68.1)	235(15.8)	361(24.3)	416(28.0)	106.537 p < 0.000
5+ km	474(31.9)	36(2.4)	125(8.4)	313(21.1)	
Hospital					
0–4 km	965(65.0)	221(14.9)	342(23.0)	402(27.1)	98.492 $p <$ 0.000
5+ km	511(35.0)	49(3.3)	144(9.7)	327(22.0)	
Friends					
5+ km	650(43.8)	146(9.8)	183(12.3)	322(21.7)	19.071 $p <$ 0.000
0–4 km	835(56.2)	125(8.4)	303(20.4)	407(27.4)	
Market					
0–4 km	944(63.6)	206(13.9)	340(22.9)	398(26.8)	130.190 $p <$ 0.000
5+ km	541(36.4)	62(4.2)	147(9.9)	331(22.3)	
Worship					
0–4 km	937(63.1)	206(13.9)	321(21.6)	408(27.5)	58.373 $p <$ 0.000
5+ km	548(36.9)	64(4.3)	165(11.1)	319(21.5)	
Accessibility					
Limited	254(17.1)	68(4.6)	137(9.2)	49(3.3)	133.296 $p <$ 0.000
Reasonable	1231(82.9)	202(13.6)	350(23.6)	680(45.8)	
Layout					
Well organized	322(21.7)	88(6.9)	200(13.5)	19(1.3)	418.336 $p <$ 0.000
Mixed land use	1163(78.3)	168(11.3)	285(19.2)	711(47.9)	
Ext. quality					
Poor	76(5.1)	51(3.4)	22(1.5)	3(0.2)	265.580 $p <$ 0.000
Good	1409(94.9)	220(14.8)	463(31.2)	728(49.0)	
Security					

(continued)

Table 6.4 (continued)

Residential attribute	Total sample ARD (*N* = 1485)	LRD subsample (*N* = 270)	MRD subsample (*N* = 486)	HRD subsample (*N* = 729)	Test of intergroup independence χ^2
Police	1225(82.5)	190(12.8)	413(27.8)	622(41.9)	39.878 $p <$ 0.001
Private	260(17.5)	80(5.4)	73(4.9)	107(7.20)	

friends. All these choices are spatially independent of one another and significantly so too. The second aspect of the residential quality attributes of Lagos households consists of the structural attributes of their dwelling units. The structural quality of the households is summarized under nine attributes as displayed in Table 6.5.

The first structural quality of Lagos residents' dwellings to be assessed in this study is the house type which is categorized into duplex, flat and multifamily units. From Table 6.5, it is obvious that majority of respondents in the study area have predilection for multifamily "face-me-I-face-you" unit housing as represented by 66.1% that choose to live in the type of house, followed by 31.2% that choose to live in flat units and the remaining 2.7% that choose duplex units as residential domicile. A high proportion of the households who choose duplex are actually from the LRD and majority of those who choose the multifamily units are from the HRD (see the spatial pattern in Fig. 6.5). Following the house type is the number of rooms occupied by each household. The number of rooms is categorized into two that is 1–2 rooms and 3 rooms and above. According to information in Table 6.5, majority of the respondents representing 55% of the households choose to live in 1–2 rooms, while 44.9% of them choose to live in dwelling units with 3 rooms and above. Again, the room space available to the households within their dwelling units is also examined and findings indicate that 56.9% choose to live in large 3×4 m^2 living rooms, while 43.1% live in small 3×3 m^2 size rooms (see Table 6.5).

The fourth structural quality variable examined is the type of water available to households within each dwelling unit and analysis shows that majority making 59.3% of the households live in dwellings that have pipe-borne/borehole water and 40.7% live in dwellings that have well/water vendor. The fifth attribute of the dwelling units available to the households studied is the number of toilets and baths provided within each household dwelling in the study area. Analysis indicates that 86.8% of the households reside in dwellings that have 1 bath and 1 toilet facility, and the rest 13.2% of them reside in dwellings that possess 2–3 toilet and bath facilities. The sixth structural quality variable of the households' residential units examined is the possession of tiled kitchen and results show that 78.2% of the households' residential units actually have untiled kitchen, compared with 21.8% of the units that do have tiled kitchen. Other structural quality variables of interest in this study include the interior quality, water sources, tenure type and annual rents. With regard to interior quality, dwelling units are examined to see how many deficiencies they possess in terms of cracks in walls, leaking roofing, cracked flooring and decrepit plumbing. The interior quality of the dwelling unit available to individual households is categorized

Table 6.5 Dwelling quality indicators of households' residential units

Residential attribute	Total sample ARD (N = 1485)	LRD subsample ($N = 270$)	MRD subsample ($N = 486$)	HRD subsample ($N = 729$)	Test of intergroup independence χ^2
House type					
Duplex	40(2.7)	16(1.1)	15(1.0)	9(0.6)	131.771 $p < 0.000$
Flat	463(31.2)	111(7.5)	214(14.4)	138(9.3)	
Multifamily	982(66.1)	143(9.6)	257(17.3)	582(39.2)	
NROOM					
1–2 ROOMS	817(55.0)	117(7.9)	183(12.3)	518(34.9)	151.346 $p < 0.000$
3 and above	667(44.9)	153(10.3)	303(20.5)	211(14.2)	
Room space					
3 × 4 m^2	845(56.9)	195(13.1)	336(22.6)	315(21.2)	109.997 $p < 0.000$
3 × 3 m^2	640(43.1)	76(5.1)	150(10.1)	414(27.9)	
Water					
Pipe-borne	881(59.3)	238(16.0)	350(23.6)	293(19.7)	233.496 $p < 0.000$
Well	604(40.7)	32(2.2)	136(9.2)	436(29.4)	
Toilet/bath					
2 TAB	867(58.4)	180(12.1)	361(24.3)	326(21.9)	201.700 $p < 0.000$
1 TAB	618(41.6)	90(6.1)	125(8.4)	403(27.1)	
Kitchen					
Tiled	325(21.9)	137(9.2)	108(7.3)	79(5.3)	393.214 $p < 0.000$
Untiled	1161(78.2)	134(9.0)	378(25.4)	650(43.8)	
Int. quality					
Good (1–2 deficiencies)	62(4.2)	28(1.9)	24(1.6)	10(0.7)	62.022 $p < 0.000$
Poor (3–4 deficiencies)	142 3(95.8)	242(16.3)	462(31.1)	719(48.4)	
Tenure					
Owner occupied	601(40.5)	80(5.4)	187(12.6)	334(22.5)	318. 975 $p < 0.000$
Renter	884(59.5)	190(12.8)	298(20.1)	395(26.6)	
Arent					
N200,000 and less	644(43.4)	86(5.8)	91(6.1)	467(31.4)	348.890 $p < 0.000$
N201,000–400,000	658(44.3)	128(8.6)	279(18.8)	251(17.0)	
N401,000 and above	183(12.3)	56(3.8)	116(7.8)	11(0.7)	

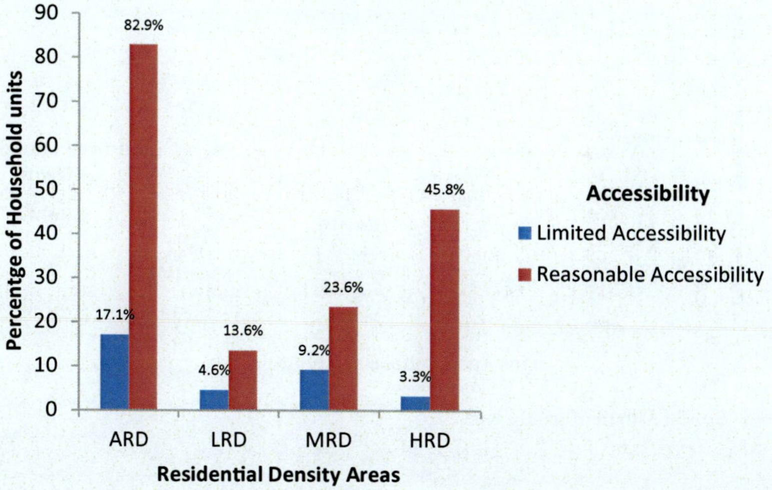

Fig. 6.4 Spatial pattern of residential neighborhoods' accessibility

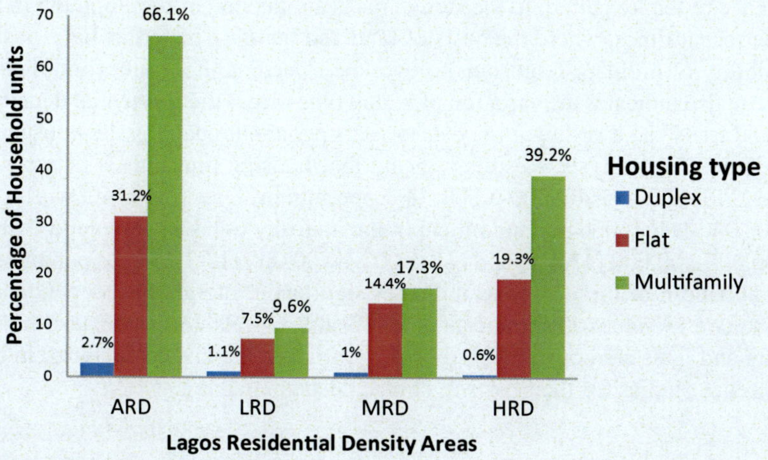

Fig. 6.5 Spatial pattern of house type

into two, namely good interior quality: residential units with 1–2 deficiencies and poor interior quality: residential units with 3–4 deficiencies. Results presented in Table 6.5 indicate that about 4% of the dwellings can be said to be of good quality given their interior conditions, while 96% of the dwelling units are poor. That is to say that majority of the dwellings of respondents have some defects ranging from poor plastering, leaking roofing, painting defects to cracks in the walls. The issue of tenure often reflects in the macroeconomic performance of the country and it is a measure of urban economic performance. The tenure type is split into two that is

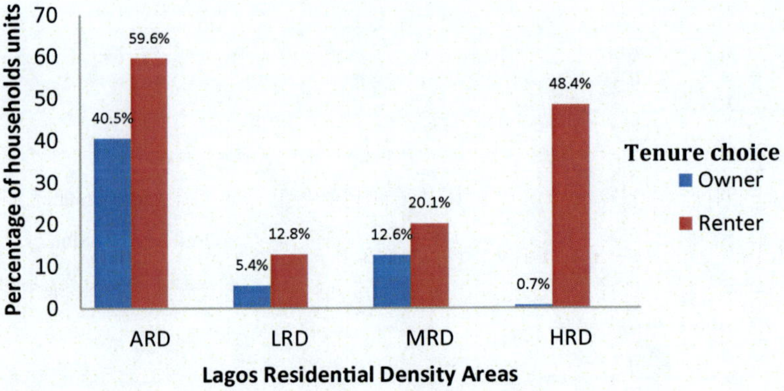

Fig. 6.6 Spatial pattern of tenure type

owner-occupier and renter. From the information in Table 6.5, the renters form the majority as 59.5% of the households interviewed choose renting compared 40.5% of the households that choose to live in a dwelling of their own. This emerging evidence of tenure pattern in the study area is a reflection of development in the city in the recent times, where the costs of land and building materials have pushed the possibility of ordinary Lagosians to own their personal homes beyond their reach. Fig. 6.6 also indicates the variation of tenure type across the residential density areas.

And lastly the dwelling unit costs or rents per annum paid by the households are considered for analysis. Results indicate that housing rent ranges between N100, 000-N200, 000 to N401000-N800, 000 per annum. Dwelling units with a rent of N201, 000-N401, 000 per annum are in the majority (44.3%) compared with others N100,000-200,000 (43.4%) and N401,000-N800,000 (12.3%) rents per annum. The spatial pattern of these choices indicates significant intergroup independence with Chi-square χ^2 values all significant at 99.9% alpha levels. In a more strict sense, both tenure and rents are not residential quality variables but always included in housing preference studies for their roles in choice decision making.

6.5 Analysis of Association Between Residential Choices and Households' Characteristics

A fundamental interest in this study is the examination and description of the association between households' characteristics and the attributes of their chosen present dwelling units. Two approaches in this study are employed in explaining the relationship between the two variable components. The first is the use of the univariate cross-tabulation method, and the second is the use of bivariate correlation techniques to display the pattern of association between the households' socioeconomic groupings and their residential attributes. Essentially, the cross-tabulations give more information on the distribution of housing quality variables across different urban dwellers in the study area. This is important in understanding how residential quality and socioeconomic attributes of residents interact in shaping their housing choices. The results of the cross-tabulation of households' and dwelling attributes can be gleaned in Tables 6.6, 6.7, 6.8, 6.9, 6.10 and 6.11.

Table 6.6 contains information on the distribution of residential quality variables across marital status. As can be seen from the table, the married households dominated all the house types. But 78.8% of the single households prefer multiunit housing, compared to 64.7% of the married and 71.4% of the widowed households. Among the married households, 29.5% prefer flat compared to 14% and 26% of the single and the widowed households, respectively. The single households have the highest preference for duplex making 7.1% of them, compared to 5.7% of the married and 2.0% of the widowed households. Although renters are in the majority in Lagos, it is the single households that lead the renter tenure with 86.9% of them, followed by the married 80.9% and the widowed 69.4%. More of the widowed households like to own their dwellings as depicted by 30.6% compared to single 13.1% and the married 19.1%.

The number of rooms available to the households also varies across marital status, and this is not unexpected as the stage in the lifecycle determines the type of dwellings needed (Krivo 1986). Results in Table 6.6 further show that the single households that live in 1–2 rooms are 75.8%, the widowed 71.4% and lastly the married 62.5%. Conversely, the married lead in the households that live in 3 rooms and above with 37.5% of them, followed by the widowed 28.6% and the single 24.2%. The distribution of room space among the three marital groups indicates that the majority of the single representing 59% occupies dwellings with small room space, and majority of the married 51.9% and the widowed 53.1% live in dwelling units with big rooms. The residents generally live in dwelling units with 1 toilet facility. Kitchens without tiles dominate the dwelling units across marital status. While the structural quality of homes by the single is generally poor, the married and the widowed are found in dwellings with high structural quality. Apart from the marital status, the residential quality variables of households' dwellings are also cross-tabulated against the occupational status of households and the results are presented in Table 6.7. The results show that majority of the unemployed (96.2%) are found in multiunit housing, so also the artisans (71.4%), civil servants (71.0%) and to a lesser proportion private sector workers (61.1%). Flat housing units are dominated by private sector workers (31.5%) and same for duplex units.

Regarding tenure, it is discovered that all the households irrespective of their occupation prefer renter to owning a dwelling although the artisan and the private workers lead with 82.8% and 81.3%, respectively. On account of number of rooms available to households, analysis shows that virtually all the unemployed (96.2%) are found in 1–2 rooms, private sector workers with 41.3% and civil servants with 29.9% live in dwellings that have 3 rooms and above. As regards room space, 73.0% of the unemployed are found in small rooms of $3 \times 3\text{m}^2$ while 27% of them live in large rooms of $3 \times 4\ \text{m}^2$. This is quite different from the workers—artisans/ traders, private and civil servants whom 49.5%, 56.2% and 38.4% respectively live in large

Table 6.6 Cross-tabulation of residential quality variables and marital status

Residential quality variable	Marital status		
House type	Single ($N = 99$)	Married ($N = 1337$)	Widowed/divorced ($N = 49$)
Multiunit	78(78.8)	865(64.7)	35(71.4)
Flat	14(14.1)	396(29.6)	13(26.5)
Duplex	7(7.1)	76(5.7)	1(2.0)
Total	99(100)	1337(100)	49(100)
Tenure			
Owner-occupier	13(13.1)	255(19.1)	15(30.6)
Renter	86(86.9)	1082(80.9)	34(69.4)
Total	99(100)	1337(100)	49(100)
Number of rooms			
1–2 rooms	75(75.8)	836(62.5)	35(71.4)
3+ rooms	24(24.2)	501(37.5)	14(28.6)
Total	99(100)	1337(100)	49(100)
Room space			
3×4 m^2	40(40.4)	694(51.9)	26(53.1)
3×3 m^2	59(59.6)	643(48.1)	13(46.9)
Total	99(100)	1337(100)	49(100)
Water			
Potable	45(45.5)	810(60.6)	24(49.0)
Well	54(54.5)	527(39.4)	25(51.0)
Total	99(100)	1337(100)	49(100)
Toilet/bath			
2 + toilets/2 + baths	29(29.3)	551(41.2)	16(32.7)
1 toilet/1 bath	70(70.7)	786(58.8)	33(67.3)
Total	99(100)	1337(100)	49(100)
Kitchen			
Tiled	16(16.2)	467(34.9)	12(24.5)
Untiled	83(83.8)	870(65.1)	37(75.5)
Total	99(100)	1337(65.1)	49(100)
IQT			
Good	39(39.4)	925(69.2)	34(69.4)
Poor	60(60.6)	412(30.8)	15(30.6)
Total	99(100)	1337(100)	49(100)

Table 6.7 Cross-tabulation of residential quality variables and occupation

Residential quality variable	Occupation			
House type	Unemployed (*N* = 26)	Artisan/trader (*N* = 483)	Private sector worker (*N* = 752)	Civil servant (*N* = 224)
Multiunit	25(96.2)	345(71.4)	459(61.1)	159(71.0)
Flat	0.0(0)	124(25.7)	237(31.5)	54(24.1)
Duplex	1(3.8)	14(2.9)	56(7.4)	11(4.9)
Total	26(100)	483(100)	752(100)	224(100)
Tenure				
Owner-occupier	6(23.1)	83(17.2)	141(18.7)	50(22.3)
Renter	20(76.9)	400(82.8)	611(81.3)	174(77.7)
Total	26(100)	483(100)	752(100)	224(100)
Number of rooms				
1–2 Rooms	25(96.2)	333(68.9)	441(58.7)	157(70.1)
3+ Rooms	1(3.8)	150(31.1)	311(41.3)	67(29.9)
Total	26(100)	483(100)	752(100)	224(100)
Room space				
3×4 m^2	7(26.9)	239(49.5)	423(56.2)	86(38.4)
3×3 m^2	19(73.1)	244(50.5)	329(43.8)	138(61.6)
Total	26(100)	483(100)	752(100)	224(100)
Water				
Potable	9(34.6)	255(52.8)	488(64.9)	122(54.5)
Well	17(65.4)	228(47.2)	264(35.1)	102(45.5)
Total	26(100)	483(100)	752(100)	224(100)
Toilet/bath				
2+ toilets/baths	1(3.8)	154(31.9)	361(48.0)	72(32.1)
1 toilet/bath	25(96.2)	329(68.1)	391(52.0)	152(67.9)
Total	26(100)	483(100)	752(100)	224(100)
Kitchen				
Tiled	2(7.7)	113(23.4)	312(41.5)	63(28.1)
Untiled	24(92.3)	370(76.6)	440(58.5)	161(71.9)
Total	26(100)	483(100)	752(100)	224(100)
IQT				
Good	15(57.7)	307(63.6)	550(73.2)	141(62.9)
Poor	11(42.3)	176(36.4)	202(26.8)	83(37.1)
Total	26(100)	483(100)	752(100)	224(100)

Table 6.8 Cross-tabulation of residential quality variables and income

Residential quality variable	Income groups			
House type	N0-74, 999 (*N* = 653)	N75,000–149, 999 (*N* = 710)	N150, 000–224,999 (*N* = 111)	N225, 000 and above (*N* = 11)
Multiunit	539(82.5)	390(54.9)	48(43.2)	1(9.1)
Flat	97(14.9)	277(39.0)	42(37.8)	7(63.6)
Duplex	17(2.6)	43(6.1)	21(18.9)	3(27.3)
Total	653(100)	710(100)	1110(100)	11(100)
Tenure				
Owner-occupier	157(24.0)	100(14.10)	22(19.8)	5(45.5)
Renter	496(76.0)	610(85.9)	89(80.2)	6(54.5)
Total	653(100)	710(100)	111(100)	11(100)
Number of rooms				
1–2 rooms	517(79.2)	380(53.5)	48(43.2)	1(9.1)
3+ rooms	136(20.8)	330(46.5)	63(56.8)	10(90.9)
Total	653(100)	710(100)	111(100)	11(100)
Room space				
3×4 m^2	226(34.6)	450(63.4)	75(67.6)	9(81.8)
3×3 m^2	427(65.4)	260(36.6)	36(32.4)	2(18.2)
Total	653(100)	710(100)	111(100)	11(100)
Water				
Potable	278(42.6)	491(69.2)	97(87.4)	11(100)
Well	375(57.4)	219(30.8)	14(12.6)	0(0)
Total	653(100)	710(100)	111(100)	11(100)
Toilet/bath				
2+ toilets/baths	143(21.9)	364(51.3)	79(71.2)	10(90.9)
1 toilet/bath	510(78.1)	346(48.7)	32(28.8)	1(9.1)
Total	653(100)	710(100)	111(100)	11(100)
Kitchen				
Tiled	98(15.0)	304(42.8)	82(73.9)	11(100)
Untiled	555(85.0)	406(57.2)	29(26.1)	0(0)
Total	653(100)	710(100)	111(100)	11(100)
IQT				
Good	382(58.5)	536(75.5)	90(81.1)	11(100)
Poor	271(41.5)	174(24.5)	21(18.9)	0(0)
Total	653(100)	710(100)	111(100)	11(100)

Table 6.9 Cross-tabulation of residential quality variables and education

Residential quality variable	Educational groups		
House type	Primary/no education ($N = 66$)	Technical/secondary ($N = 584$)	Graduate/M.Sc./Ph.D. ($N = 835$)
Multiunit	55(83.3)	423(72.4)	500(59.9)
Flat	11(16.7)	144(24.7)	268(32.1)
Duplex	0.0(0)	17(2.9)	67(8.0)
Total	66(100)	584(100)	835(100)
Tenure			
Owner-occupier	15(22.7)	90(15.4)	179(21.4)
Renter	51(77.3)	494(84.6)	656(78.6)
Total	66(100)	584(100)	835(100)
Number of rooms			
1–2 rooms	54(81.8)	405(69.3)	487(58.3)
3+ rooms	12(18.2)	179(30.7)	348(41.7)
Total	66(100)	584(100)	835(100)
Room space			
3 × 4 m^2	25(37.9)	296(50.7)	439(52.6)
3 × 3 m^2	41(62.1)	288(49.3)	386(47.4)
Total	66(100)	584(100)	835(100)
Water			
Potable	25(37.9)	320(54.8)	534(64.0)
Well	41(62.1)	264(45.2)	301(36.0)
Total	66(100)	584(100)	835(100)
Toilet/bath			
2+ toilets/baths	15(22.7)	181(31.0)	400(47.9)
1 toilet/bath	51(77.3)	403(69.0)	435(52.1)
Total	66(100)	584(100)	835(100)
Kitchen			
Tiled	7(10.6)	138(23.6)	350(41.9)
Untiled	59(89.4)	446(76.4)	485(58.1)
Total	66(100)	584(100)	835(100)
IQT			
Good	41(62.1)	383(65.6)	595(71.3)
Poor	25(37.9)	201(34.4)	240(28.7)
Total	66(100)	584(100)	835(100)

Table 6.10 Cross-tabulation of residential quality variables and household size

Residential quality variable	Household size groups		
House type	1–2 members ($N =$ 117)	3–6 members ($N =$ 1143)	7 and above members ($N = 225$)
Multiunit	90(76.9)	792(69.3)	96(42.7)
Flat	20(17.1)	295(25.8)	108(48.0)
Duplex	7(6.0)	56(4.9)	21(9.3)
Total	117(100)	1143(100)	225(100)
Tenure			
Owner-occupier	22(18.8)	233(20.4)	29(12.9)
Renter	95(81.2)	910(79.6)	196(87.1)
Total	117(100)	1143(100)	225(100)
Number of rooms			
1–2 rooms	89(76.1)	764(66.8)	93(41.3)
3+ rooms	28(23.9)	379(33.2)	132(58.7)
Total	117(100)	1143(100)	225(100)
Room space			
3×4 m^2	44(37.6)	536(46.9)	180(80.0)
3×3 m^2	73(62.4)	607(53.1)	45(20.0)
Total	117(100)	1143(100)	225(100)
Water			
Potable	57(48.7)	648(56.7)	174(77.3)
Well	60(51.3)	495(43.3)	51(22.7)
Total	117(100)	1143(100)	225(100)
Toilet/bath			
2+ toilets/baths	31(26.5)	435(38.1)	130(57.8)
1 toilet/bath	86(73.5)	708(61.9)	95(42.2)
Total	117(100)	1143(100)	225(100)
Kitchen			
Tiled	22(18.8)	376(32.9)	119(52.9)
Untiled	95(81.2)	767(67.1)	106(47.1)
Total	117(100)	1143(100)	225(100)
IQT			
Good	66(56.4)	786(68.8)	167(74.2)
Poor	51(43.6)	357(31.2)	58(25.8)
Total	117(100)	1143(100)	225(100)

Table 6.11 Cross-tabulation of residential quality variables and age

Residential quality variable	Age groups		
House type	21–40 yrs ($N = 624$)	41–60 yrs ($N = 801$)	61 yrs and above ($N = 60$)
Multiunit	463(74.2)	488(60.9)	27(45.0)
Flat	129(20.7)	264(33.0)	30(50.0)
Duplex	32(5.1)	49(6.1)	3(5.0)
Total	624(100)	801(100)	60(100)
Tenure			
Owner-occupier	121(19.4)	147(18.4)	16(26.7)
Renter	503(80.6)	654(81.6)	44(73.3)
Total	624(100)	801(100)	60(100)
Number of rooms			
1–2 rooms	442(70.8)	477(59.6)	27(45.0)
3+ rooms	182(29.2)	324(40.4)	33(55.0)
Total	624(100)	801(100)	60(100)
Room space			
3×4 m^2	273(43.7)	442(55.2)	47(78.3)
3×3 m^2	351(56.3)	359(44.8)	13(21.7)
Total	624(100)	801(100)	60(100)
Water			
Potable	284(45.5)	553(69.0)	42(70.0)
Well	340(54.5)	248(31.0)	18(30.0)
Total	624(100)	801(100)	60(100)
Toilet/bath			
2+ toilets/baths	204(32.7)	359(44.8)	33(55.0)
1 toilet/bath	420(67.3)	442(55.2)	27(45.0)
Total	624(100)	801(100)	60(100)
Kitchen			
Tiled	139(22.3)	332(41.4)	1.6(40.0)
Untiled	485(77.7)	469(58.6)	2.4(60.0)
Total	624(100)	801(100)	4.0(100)
IQT			
Good	397(63.6)	579(72.3)	2.9(71.7)
Poor	227(36.4)	222(27.7)	1.1(28.3)
Total	624(100)	801(100)	4.0(100)

rooms. While 34.6% of the unemployed live in dwelling units with potable water, 52.8%, 64.9% and 54.5% of the artisans/traders, private workers and civil servants respectively live in homes that have potable water. There is generally high proportion of the respondents based on occupation that live in dwellings with 1 toilet and bath facilities compared to 2 toilets and baths. Dwellings without tiled kitchen dominate the choices of respondents across occupational groups as 92.6% of the unemployed, 76.2% of the artisans/traders, 58.6% of the private workers and 71.9% of the civil servants live in dwelling units without tiled kitchen (see information in Table 6.7). Another aspect of the cross-tabulation is the examination of residential quality across income groups. As presented in Table 6.8, the house type varies across the four income-earning groups. Incidentally the type of house follows income distribution. For instance, 82.5% of the low-income earners live in multiunit housing, 63.6% of the highly rich (Table 6.8, last column) live in flat housing, majority of the high-income earners (56.7%) live in either flat or duplex dwelling units (see Table 6.8).

On account of tenure, analysis shows that all income groups prefer renting but a substantial proportion of the very rich group (45.5%) prefer owner-occupied housing. Concerning the distribution of households across number of rooms, results in Table 6.8 also show that the low-income earners (79.2%) live majorly in 1–2 rooms while the very rich households (90.9%) live mainly in dwellings with 3 rooms and above followed by the high-income group (56.8%), and 46.5% of the middle-income earners live in 3 rooms and above. Based on the number of rooms occupied by the households, analysis revealed that 79.2% of the low-income earners are contained in 1–2 room apartments, while only 9.1% of the rich are found in 1–2 room dwellings. Conversely, 90.9% of the rich live in dwellings with 3 rooms and more while 20.8% of the low-income earners live in 3 room apartments. There is a steady gradation among the respondents on the account of room space. For instance, while a paltry 34.6% of the low-income earners live in large rooms 81.8% of the rich live in large room ($3 \times 4\ m^2$) dwellings. Among the rich respondents surveyed none live in dwellings with well water that means all of them have potable water unlike the 42.7% of the low-income earners who live in dwellings with potable water. The low-income earners (78.1%) live generally in houses with only 1 toilet and 1 bath as shown in Table 6.8, while 90.9% of the rich live in dwelling with 2 toilets and more. All the respondents in the higher-income group live in dwellings with tiled kitchen while 85% of the low-income earners have no access to tiled kitchen. The next household attribute examined across the residential quality of Lagos residents is education. Table 6.9 shows the distribution of house type, tenure and number of rooms across three educationally differentiated households. Results show that 83.3% of the primary school holders live in multiunit housing, 72.4% of technical/secondary holders live in multiunit and 59.9% of the graduate households live in multiunit housing. The results further indicate that graduates dominate the flat and the duplex housing with 32.1% and 8.0%, respectively. No primary school certificate holder household is found in duplex and barely 2.9% of the technical certificate households are found in the duplex units.

On the basis of education, the tenure distribution across the study area is quite similar. For instance, 84.5% of the respondents with secondary and technical certificates are renters as against 77% of the primary and 78.2% of the graduates. Educational influence on number of rooms is not so significantly different as 81.8% of the primary school holders live in 1–2 rooms, followed by 61.3% of the secondary and 58.3% of the graduates. Also, 62.1% of the primary certificate holders are found in small rooms while 47.4% of the graduates are found in small rooms. More graduates 64.0% actually have access to potable water than the less educated groups. The primary schools holders live in dwellings within 1 toilet and bath while 47.0% of the graduates live in dwellings with 2 toilets and baths or more. A high percentage of 89.0% of the less educated residents live in housing units that have no tiled kitchen compared to 58% of the graduates with kitchens without tiles (Table 6.9). After residential quality distribution by occupational groups, residential quality distribution is examined across household size. Along the three household size groups results from analysis presented in Table 6.10 show that choice of house type follows household size as households with 1–2 members dominate the multiunit (76.9%), households with 7 and above members dominate both the flat and the duplex housing units (48.0% and 9.3%, respectively). Regarding tenure, analysis indicates that all the household size types prefer renting to owning dwelling. On account of number of rooms occupied, results from analysis show that the smaller household that is 1–2 members prefer 1–2 rooms (76.1%), while majority of the large member households (7 and above) prefer 3 rooms and above. These distribution patterns tally with expected results as the larger the household the higher the number of rooms required for the members (Krivo 1986; Rosenbaum 1995).

Table 6.10 further shows that household sizes also influence the room size desired by households. For instance, 80% of households with 7 members and more live in large rooms while 62% of households with 1–2 members live in small rooms. As regards with access to potable water, 77.3% of the households with 7 and more members have actually live in dwellings with potable water compared with 48.7% of the households with 1–2 members. Also, the 77.5% of the households with fewer members live in dwelling units with 1 toilet and bath facilities while 57.8% of the larger households have 2 toilets and baths' facilities. With regard to tiled kitchen, 81.2% of the households with 1–2 members are found in dwellings without tile kitchen while 52.9% of the households with 7 and more live in houses with tiled kitchens. Also considered for analysis is the residential quality variables across age groups. Results as presented in Table 6.11 indicate critical variations in the choices of households. From the point of house type, analysis shows that the young households, that is, 21–40 years prefer multiunit housing as indicated by 74.2% of them, and the old households 61 years and above prefer flat units as indicated by 50.0% of them and the middle-aged households 41–60 years prefer more than any other groups duplex units even though majority also dwell in multiunit housing as indicated by 60.9% of them. On account of tenure, it is discovered that there is no serious variation in the preference of households based on age as all of them prefer renter to owner-occupier. Conversely, as regards the number of rooms occupied by the households, analysis indicates that the young households (70.8%) prefer 1–2 rooms and the old households (55%) prefer 3 rooms and above. The preference for number of rooms by the middle-aged households is closely divided between 1–2 rooms (59.6%) and 3 rooms and above (40.4%).

On account of room space, the majority of the old people 78.3% choose to live in dwellings with large room space unlike the young residents whose majority 56.3% choose to live in smaller rooms. The old household headers actually choose to live in dwelling with potable water as 70.0% of them demonstrated, and majority (54.5%) of the households between 21 and 40 years of age choose dwellings with well water. The distribution of kitchen facilities among the age groups shows that the old people prefer homes with 2 toilets and baths or more while the middle age and young people prefer homes with 1 toilet and bath. Although many of these choices are questionable, the residents were constrained by the quality (structurally, locationally and environmentally) and affordability of available homes against their socioeconomic strength.

6.6 Correlation Between Housing Attributes and Households Characteristics

Having described the results of the cross-tabulation of socioeconomic and residential quality indicators of the respondents interviewed in this study, it is important that the bivariate associations between these variables be given in detail. A means of doing this is to use correlation techniques. The bivariate correlation analysis explicitly reveals the level and nature of associations that exist among the different variable components. In this study, the results from the bivariate analysis are essential for two reasons: they reveal the existence of potential collinearity between the dependent variables, and secondly, they furnish us with the nature of association either negative or positive (Saroj 1981; Robinson 1998; Hardy and Bryan 2006). Definitely high correlation coefficients would indicate a potential multicollinearity and vice versa. In this study, the twenty residential variables and thirteen socioeconomic and demographic variables are correlated. The results presented in Table 6.12 indicate correlation coefficients of the neighborhood and households' attributes, while Table 6.13 contains correlation coefficients of the structural and households' attributes observed in the study area.

According to the bivariate correlation results in Tables 6.12 and 6.13, many of the residential quality variables correlate significantly with the household characteristics although they do so in low values. For instance, metropolitan characteristics (MPC) correlate significantly with gender, occupation, education and ethnicity, children above 18 years, household size and income (see Table 6.12 column 2). On the other hand, housing type (TYP) also correlates significantly with age, household size, occupation, education, income and gender. The number of rooms also correlates significantly with gender, age, income, occupation and all other households' characteristics except marital status. The most uncorrelated variables are proximity

Table 6.12 Zero-order correlation coefficients of neighborhood and households' characteristics

VAR	MPC 1	WRK 2	MKT 3	SCH 4	HOS 5	WOR 6	SOC 7	ACC 8	SEC 9	LAY 10	EQT 11
1	1										
2	– 0.323**	1									
3	– 0.214**	0.647**	1								
4	– 0.104**	0.552**	0.738**	1							
5	– 0.016	0.491**	0.665**	0.713**	1						
6	– 0.041	0.449**	0.582**	0.627**	0.696**	1					
7	– 0.174**	0.051*	0.015	0.021	0.039	0.073**	1				
8	– 0.078**	0.201**	0.219**	0.210**	0.201**	0.235**	0.077**	1			
9	0.046	0.017	0.085**	0.111**	0.089**	0.081**	– 0.146**	– 0.058*	1		
10	– 0.033	0.203**	0.269**	0.260**	0.244**	0.282**	0.018	0.482**	– 0.020	1	
11	0.056*	0.141**	0.173**	0.211**	0.207**	0.224**	0.001	0.375**	0.003	0.752**	1
12	0.060*	– 0.255**	– 0.279**	– 0.249**	0.255**	– 0.290**	– 0.003	– 0.136**	– 0.108**	– 0.097**	– 0.056*
13	– 0.016	0.002	0.008	0.004	0.019	– 0.008	0.047	– 0.016	– 0.050	0.008	0.010
14	– 0.011	0.055*	0.123**	0.100**	0.130**	0.145**	0.032	0.031	– 0.031	0.115**	0.045
15	0.099**	– 0.005	0.018	0.027	0.060*	0.045	0.008	– 0.005	– 0.033	0.048	0.013
16	0.105**	0.087**	0.192**	0.176**	0.218**	0.198**	– 0.052*	0.162**	0.042	0.206**	0.149**
17	0.046	0.005	0.061*	0.041	0.072**	0.046	0.005	0.078**	– 0.034	0.126**	0.086**
18	0.135**	– 0.010	0.006	0.060*	0.041	0.014	– 0.017	0.031	– 0.069**	0.093**	0.112**
19	0.075**	– 0.153**	– 0.188**	– 0.151**	– 0.173**	– 0.190**	– 0.001	– 0.057*	– 0.092**	– 0.175**	– 0.105**
20	– 0.094**	– 0.011	– 0.004	– 0.048	– 0.019	– 0.044	– 0.024	0.052*	– 0.073**	0.126**	0.087**
21	– 0.064*	0.013	– 0.011	– 0.006	– 0.042	– 0.068**	– 0.013	0.036	– 0.072**	0.064*	0.044

(continued)

Table 6.12 (continued)

VAR	MPC 1	WRK 2	MKT 3	SCH 4	HOS 5	WOR 6	SOC 7	ACC 8	SEC 9	LAY 10	EQT 11
22	– 0.032	0.012	0.001	– 0.016	– 0.003	– 0.069**	– 0.010	– 0.019	– 0.043	0.027	0.030
23	– 0.074**	0.121**	0.198**	0.193**	0.199**	0.167**	0.040	0.214**	– 0.133**	0.274**	0.201**

VAR	GEN 12	MAR 13	AGE 14	CHD 15	HHS 16	REG 17	ETH 18	CHD18 19	EDU 20	OCC 21	EXP 22	INC 23
1												
2												
3												
4												
5												
6												
7												
8												
9												
10												
11												
12	1											
13	– 0.135**	1										
14	– 0.059*	0.347**	1									
15	– 0.003	0.478**	0.593**	1								
16	– 0.105**	0.274**	0.396**	0.588**	1							
17	– 0.012	– 0.082**	– 0.123**	– 0.171**	– 0.090**	1						

(continued)

Table 6.12 (continued)

VAR	GEN 12	MAR 13	AGE 14	CHD 15	HHS 16	REG 17	ETH 18	CHD18 19	EDU 20	OCC 21	EXP 22	INC 23
18	0.028	– 0.094**	– 0.075**	– 0.069**	0.005	0.288**						
19	0.169**	– 0.258**	– 0.587**	– 0.503**	– 0.411**	0.142**	0.162**	1				
20	0.098**	– 0.082**	– 0.086**	– 0.148**	– 0.149**	0.165**	– 0.089**	0.088**	1			
21	0.126**	0.069**	– 0.018	0.003	– 0.082**	0.052*	– 0.123**	0.002	0.526**	1		
22	0.079**	0.328**	0.449**	0.532**	0.299**	– 0.078**	– 0.024	– 0.386**	– 0.003	0.044	1	
23	– 0.021	0.121**	0.257**	0.221**	0.240**	0.068**	0.054*	– 0.207**	0.211**	0.138**	0.294**	1

**Correlation is significant at the 0.01 level (2-tailed)

*Correlation is significant at the 0.05 level (2-tailed)

Note MPC = % of households that live in outer city metropolitan area; WRK = % that live 0–4 km to work; MKT = % that live 0–4 km to market; SCH = % that live 0–4 km to school; HOS = % that live 0–4 km to hospital; WOR = % that live 0–4 km to place of worship; REL = % that live 0–4 km to relations; ACC = % that have reasonable accessibility to transport; SEC = % that have formal security; LAY = % that live in mixed layout neighborhoods; EQT = % that live in neighbourhood with good exterior quality

Table 6.13 Zero-order correlation coefficients of dwelling and households' characteristics

VAR	HTP 1	NRM 2	SPC 3	WAT 4	TAB 5	KIT 6	IQT 7	TEN 8	PRC 9	GEN 10
1	1									
2	0.864**	1								
3	0.366**	0.365**	1							
4	0.296**	0.308**	0.288**	1						
5	0.791**	0.822**	0.349**	0.364**	1					
6	0.544**	0.521**	0.285**	0.392**	0.587**	1				
7	0.392**	0.420**	0.263**	0.407**	0.450**	0.401**	1			
8	– 0.026	– 0.042	0.005	– 0.055*	– 0.038	– 0.070**	– 0.030	1		
9	0.720**	0.712**	0.381**	0.391**	0.707**	0.545**	0.390**	– 0.141**	1	
10	– 0.107**	– 0.094**	– 0.254**	– 0.013	– 0.097**	– 0.014	– 0.068**	– 0.093**	– 0.013	1
11	0.025	0.036	0.050	0.038	0.031	0.058*	0.038	– 0.063*	0.073**	– 0.135**
12	0.136**	0.139**	0.155**	0.224**	0.135**	0.185**	0.085**	– 0.009	0.183**	– 0.059*
13	0.066*	0.070**	0.088**	0.103**	0.060*	0.076**	0.026	– 0.011	0.141**	– 0.003
14	0.175**	0.191**	0.229**	0.153**	0.161**	0.145**	0.082**	0.049	0.213****	– 0.105**
15	0.106**	0.090**	0.052*	0.159**	0.105**	0.115**	0.073**	– 0.005	0.133**	– 0.012
16	0.055*	0.062*	– 0.024	0.081**	0.069**	0.107**	0.087**	0.004	0.107*	0.028
17	– 0.169**	– 0.167**	– 0.241**	– 0.155**	– 0.162**	– 0.129**	– 0.065*	0.019	– 0.147**	0.169**
18	0.166**	0.137**	0.047	0.127**	0.180**	0.213**	0.066*	– 0.050	0.173**	0.098**
19	0.097**	0.081**	0.002	0.077**	0.100**	0.113**	0.052*	– 0.049	0.096**	0.126**
20	0.084**	0.081**	– 0.023	0.142**	0.095**	0.150**	0.063*	– 0.041	0.118**	0.079**
21	0.325**	0.293**	0.276**	0.314**	0.349**	0.395**	0.194**	0.067**	0.375**	– 0.021

(continued)

Table 6.13 (continued)

VAR	MAR 11	AGE 12	CHD 13	HHS 14	REL 15	ETH 16	CHD18 17	EDU 18	OCC 19	EXP 20	INC 21
1											
2											
3											
4											
5											
6											
7											
8											
9											
10											
11	1										
12	0.347**	1									
13	0.478**	0.593**	1								
14	0.274**	0.396**	0.588**	1							
15	− 0.082**	− 0.123**	− 0.171**	− 0.090**	1						
16	− 0.094**	− 0.075**	− 0.069**	0.005	0.288**	1					
17	− 0.258**	− 0.587**	− 0.503**	− 0.411**	0.142**	0.162**	1				
18	− 0.082**	− 0.086**	− 0.148**	− 0.149**	0.165**	− 0.089**	0.088**	1			
19	0.069**	− 0.018	0.003	− 0.082**	0.052*	− 0.123**	0.002	0.526**	1		

(continued)

Table 6.13 (continued)

VAR	MAR 11	AGE 12	CHD 13	HHS 14	REL 15	ETH 16	CHD18 17	EDU 18	OCC 19	EXP 20	INC 21
20	0.328**	0.449**	0.532**	0.299**	– 0.078**	– 0.024	– 0.386**	– 0.003	0.044	1	
21	0.121**	0.257**	0.221**	0.240**	0.068**	0.054*	– 0.207**	0.211**	0.138**	0.294**	1

**Correlation is significant at the 0.01 level (2-tailed)

*Correlation is significant at the 0.05 level (2-tailed)

Note HTP = % of households that live in multiunit house type; NRM = % that live in 1–2 number of rooms; SPC = % that live in 3 × 4 m^2 room space; WAT = % that live in dwellings with potable water; TAB = % that live in dwellings with 1 toilet and 1 bath; KIT = % that live in dwellings without tiled kitchen; IQT = % that live in dwellings with poor interior quality; TEN = % that are renters; PRC = % that pay less N400,000 rent per annum.

to friends, marital status and tenure. These three variables have many lowly and insignificant correlations with all other variables. For instance, marital status has no significant correlation with any of the residential quality variables except kitchen and rent, while tenure has very few instances of high correlations with residential quality variables. Also, gender and children above 18 years, and income are observed to possess negative correlations with residential quality variables. The most correlated variables are gender, age and household size, children above 18 years, income and experience. The preliminary inference one can make from the correlations of the residential variables and household characteristics is simply that the two sets of variables are not only lowly associated but significantly too.

6.7 Testing of Hypotheses

The first hypothesis raised and tested in this study is:

Research Hypothesis I:

Ho1: *There is no significant association between residential quality and residents' characteristics.*

Ha1: *There is a significant association between residential quality and residents' characteristics.*

The results of the correlation analysis in Section 6.6 provided overwhelming evidence to validate the veracity of the first hypothesis set in this study. A fundamental aspect of the analysis is the test of hypothesis that there is a significant association between residential quality and residents' attributes. The correlation coefficients in Tables 6.12 and 6.13 indicate that there are indeed significant associations between the residential quality variables and residents' characteristics. However, the correlations are quite low but significant at both 5 and 1% levels of confidence. Hence, the null hypothesis is false and is therefore rejected for the research hypothesis which says that there are significant correlations between residential quality variables and households' attributes in the study area.

6.8 Summary

The results from the analysis of the socioeconomic and demographic variables of households sampled in the study have shown that the respondents have more males than females, middle-aged households, more married household heads with household sizes between 3 and 6, medium-income earners and spent over 16 years in Lagos. Their residential qualities display visible variations. The households prefer neighborhoods that are within the city core, 0–4 km from places of work, market, hospital, far from friends, formal security, mixed layout and good exterior quality.

They are also found more in dwellings that possess 1–2 rooms, large rooms, potable water, 1 toilet and bath, and poor structural quality. The majority of the households prefer multiunit dwellings, rental units and rents between N201,000 and N400,000. These background characteristics of the households actually were correlated with their housing attributes of choice. It was found that lower correlations exist between the attributes and residential attributes of households dwelling units. However, there are strongly significant but low correlations among the residential quality and households' variables. Having presented and discussed the background information of Lagos households in this part of the book, the next chapter will dwell on the pattern of residential quality and the revealed preferences exhibited in the study area.

References

Hardy M, Bryan A (eds) (2006) Handbook on data analysis. SAGE, London
Krivo JL (1986) Home ownership differences between hispanics and anglos in the united states. J Soc Soc Probl, 33(4), 319–333
Neumann WL (1997) Social research methods. Routledge, London
National Population Commission (2006). Nigerian population census. Abuja: NPC
Robinson MG (1998) Methods and techniques in human geography. Wiley, New York
Rosenbaum J (1995) Changing the geography of opportunity by expanding residential choice: lessons from the Gatreaux Program. Hous Policy Debate 6(1):231–269
Rosenbaum J (1996) The influence of race on Hispanic housing choices in New York City 1978–1987. Urban Aff Rev 32(2):217–243
Saroj KP (1981) Statistical techniques: a basic approach to geography. McGraw Hill, New Delhi

Chapter 7
Residential Quality and Revealed Housing Preferences in Lagos

Abstract This part of the book focuses on the results of the principal component analysis (PCA) and multinomial logit (MNL) regression analysis performed on the residential quality of existing housing choices already made by the respondents. The results of analyses presented give information on the nature of associations that exist among the residential quality variables, the important components that account for variations in the data, and the housing choice formation of home seekers based on the contextual residential quality variables and individual characteristics. Although there seems to be in reality a slight difference between preference and choice, in housing studies the two terms are conceptually the same. Empirical studies on renters' housing behavior have generally regarded housing preferences and housing choices as synonymous, and it is only in terms of variable operationalization that scholars make any serious demarcations. This study, however, uses both preferences and choices interchangeably. Discussion in this section is therefore pursued along four levels: patterns of residential quality variables that influence housing choices, spatial pattern of PCA scores on locations, housing choice modeling results and summary.

Keywords Residential quality · Revealed housing preference · Principal component analysis · Multinomial logit regression · Housing choice formation

This chapter focuses on the results of the principal component analysis (PCA) and multinomial logit (MNL) regression analysis performed on the residential quality of existing housing choices already made by the respondents. The results of analyses presented give information on the nature of associations that exist among the residential quality variables, the important components that account for variations in the data, and the housing choice formation of home seekers based on the contextual residential quality variables and individual characteristics. Although there seems to be in reality a slight difference between preference and choice, in housing studies the two terms are conceptually the same. Empirical studies on renters' housing behavior have generally regarded housing preferences and housing choices as synonymous, and it is only in terms of variable operationalization that scholars make any serious demarcations (see Wang and Li 2004; Cirman 2006; Earnhart 2001; Tayyaran and

© The Author(s), under exclusive license to Springer Nature Switzerland AG 2024

I. R. Aliu, *Urban Private Housing in Nigeria*, The Urban Book Series,
https://doi.org/10.1007/978-3-031-47432-3_7

Khan 2007). This study, however, uses both preferences and choices interchangeably. Discussion in this chapter is therefore pursued along four levels: patterns of residential quality variables that influence housing choices, spatial pattern of PCA scores on locations, housing choice modeling results and summary.

7.1 Principal Residential Quality Components that Shape Revealed Housing Choices

7.1.1 Zero-Order Bivariate Analysis of Residential Quality Variables

Although dwellings often display varying number of quality indicators only few of these indicators actually influence housing choices. In order to determine these few residential quality variables, we use PCA. However, the normal practice when using PCA is to begin with the correlation of the variables of interest as this provides the initial insights into the nature and extent of associations among the variables (Robinson 1998; Hardy and Bryan 2006). In this study, there are twenty residential variables of interest. Bivariate zero-order correlation analysis shows that these variables correlate lowly with one another. According to information in Table 7.1, the highest correlations exist between multiunit house type and 1–2 room units ($r = 0.864$) as also between 1 toilet/bath and 1–2 room dwellings ($r = 0.822$). The lowest correlations exist between dwellings with formal security and neighborhoods with poor exterior quality ($r = 0.003$) and between 0 and 4 km proximity to relations and neighborhoods with poor exterior quality ($r = 0.001$). Both 0–4 km proximity to relations and renter tenure type variables have low correlations with majority of the variables. As depicted in the tables, each has low and insignificant correlations with eleven variables (see Table 7.1, rows 7 and 19).

The implication is that variables with strong correlations with one another are expected to load similarly on the same PCA latent components. Hence, from the results of the correlations in Table 7.1, one might begin to see that variables such as price/rent, number of rooms, TAB and KIT would load on the same component, just as variables that have extremely low coefficients load separately on different components. Among the neighborhood residential quality variables location proximity ones such as proximity market, work and hospital display the highest correlation with other variables. For instance, workplace 0–4 km is correlated highly and significantly with market ($r = 0.647$) and school ($r = 0.552$), while market is correlated highly and significantly with school ($r = 0.738$), hospital ($r = 0.665$) and worship ($r = 0.582$) and school 0–4 km also correlates highly and significantly with hospital ($r = 0.713$) and worship ($r = 0.627$) while hospital 0–4 km correlates highly and significantly with worship ($r = 0.696$). There is also a high correlation between environmental quality and layout ($r = 0.752$). Among the structural quality variables house type,

Table 7.1 Zero-order correlation coefficients of residential quality variables

VAR	MPC 1	WRK 2	MKT 3	SCH 4	HOS 5	WOR 6	SOC 7	ACC 8	SEC 9	LAY 10
1	1									
2	– 0.323**	1								
3	– 0.214**	0.647**	1							
4	– 0.104**	0.552**	0.738**	1						
5	– 0.016	0.491**	0.665**	0.713**	1					
6	– 0.041	0.449**	0.582**	0.627**	0.696**	1				
7	– 0.174**	0.051*	0.015	0.021	0.039	0.073**	1			
8	– 0.078**	0.201**	0.219**	0.210**	0.201**	0.235**	0.077**	1		
9	0.046	0.017	0.085**	0.111**	0.089**	0.081**	– 0.146**	– 0.058*	1	
10	– 0.033	0.203**	0.269**	0.260**	0.244**	0.282**	0.018	0.482**	– 0.020	1
11	0.056*	0.141**	0.173**	0.211**	0.207**	0.224**	0.001	0.375**	0.003	0.752**
12	– 0.183**	0.199**	0.249**	0.251**	0.221****	0.219**	0.018	0.260**	– 0.036	0.381**
13	– 0.153**	0.191**	0.261**	0.266**	0.254**	0.246**	– 0.006	0.213**	– 0.005	0.322**
14	– 0.097**	0.314**	0.385**	0.362**	0.404**	0.420**	– 0.019	0.182**	0.032	0.377**
15	– 0.182**	0.124**	0.217**	0.168**	0.158**	0.160**	0.016	0.213**	– 0.098**	0.249**
16	– 0.252**	0.214**	0.269**	0.248**	0.248**	0.237**	0.052*	0.263**	– 0.087**	0.340**
17	– 0.113**	0.140**	0.166**	0.176**	0.183**	0.161**	0.081**	0.280**	– 0.132**	0.508**
18	– 0.153**	0.152**	0.179**	0.154**	0.148**	0.115**	0.059*	0.135**	– 0.062*	0.180**
19	0.043	0.097**	0.121**	0.131**	0.096**	0.111**	0.012	0.017	– 0.013	0.046
20	– 0.097**	0.107**	0.173**	0.180**	0.188**	0.160**	0.027	0.246**	– 0.073**	0.414**

(continued)

Table 7.1 (continued)

VAR	EQT 11	HTP 12	NRM 13	SPC 14	WAT 15	TAB 16	KIT 17	IQT 18	TEN 19	PRC 20
1										
2										
3										
4										
5										
6										
7										
8										
9										
10										
11	1									
12	0.285**	1								
13	0.248**	0.864**	1							
14	0.238**	0.366**	0.365**	1						
15	0.113**	0.296**	0.308**	0.288**	1					
16	0.257**	0.791**	0.822**	0.349**	0.364**	1				
17	0.465**	0.544**	0.521**	0.285**	0.392**	0.587**	1			
18	0.115**	0.392**	0.420**	0.263**	0.407**	0.450**	0.401**	1		
19	– 0.010	– 0.026	– 0.042	0.005	– 0.055*	– 0.038	– 0.070**	– 0.030	1	
20	0.331**	0.720**	0.712**	0.381**	0.391**	0.707**	0.545**	0.390**	– 0.141**	1

** Significant at $p < 0.01$ and * Significant at $p < 0.05$

Note MPC = % of households that live in outer city metropolitan area; WRK = % that live 0–4 km to work; MKT = % that live 0–4 km to market; SCH = % that live 0–4 km to school; HOS = % that live 0–4 km to hospital; WOR = % that live 0–4 km to place of worship; SOC = % that live 0–4 km to relations; ACC = % that have reasonable accessibility to transport; SEC = % that have formal security; LAY = % that live in mixed layout neighborhoods; EQT = % that live in neighborhood with good exterior quality; HTP = % that live in multiunit house type; NRM = % that live in 1–2 number of rooms; SPC = % that live in 3 × 4 m^2 room space; WAT = % that live in dwellings with potable water; TAB = % that live in dwellings with 1 toilet and 1 bath; KIT = % that live in dwellings without tiled kitchen; IQT = % that live in dwellings with poor interior quality; TEN = % that are renters; PRC = % that pay less N400,000 rent per annum.

number of rooms, toilet and bath, kitchen and price have high and significant correlations with a number of other variables. For instance, HTP is highly and significantly correlated with number of rooms ($r = 0.864$), toilet and bath ($r = 0.791$), kitchen ($r = 0.544$) and price ($r = 0.720$). This means that housing types are associated with rooms, number of toilets and baths, nature of kitchen and home rentals level. The number of rooms is also significantly correlated with toilet and bath ($r = 0.822$), kitchen ($r = 0.521$) and price ($r = 0.712$). The association between price and number of rooms is understandable as room number is a function of cost per room. Toilet and bath correlates with kitchen ($r = 0.587$) and price ($r = 0.707$) and kitchen correlates highly with price ($r = 0.545$). The high correlations of structural quality variables with price are highly indicative of the place of affordability in housing quality of households in the study area. However, two variables stand out very distinctively among the neighborhood variables in their unique low and negative correlations with other variables and these are social relations and security (see Table 7.1, Columns 1 and 7).

7.1.2 *Extraction of Important Residential Quality Components*

After the correlation matrix, the important residential quality components were extracted. As indicated in Tables 7.2, 7.3, 7.4 and 7.5, four PCA results are generated for explaining the essential components that summarily describe residential quality structure in Lagos. During analysis, eight latent variables were extracted from the rotated principal component analysis of twenty original variables used to represent the neighborhood and structural quality of dwelling units of Lagos residents. The PCA components of variables with a minimum loading of 0.40 and at least two distinct variables were used in order to facilitate easy explanation. The eight latent component variables extracted in this study accounted for 77.66% of the variance in the data set in ARD, 71.36% in LRD, 80.04% in MRD and 77.79% in HRD, respectively. The KMO tests of data adequacy are respectively 0.874, 0.791, 0.848 and 0.862 and are all significantly high. However, based upon theoretical assumption of the Kaiser criterion only five of these eight components are important to the explanation of the total variance of 64.14% of residential attributes that shape housing choice decision making. The remaining components have less than 1.0 Eigenvalue and just one significantly high loading variable on each of them.

A cursory look at Table 7.2 indicates that five dwelling unit quality variables, namely number of rooms, house type, number of toilets and baths, kitchen and price/rent strongly load on Component I with Eigenvalue of 6.14 and variance of 30.69%. This component is therefore named "Dwelling Facility-Quality" since it contains dwelling variables that are of immense usefulness within the residential unit structure. The second component contains six variables, namely proximity to hospital, school, market, worship, work and space with loadings well over 0.40 each. This component

Table 7.2 PCA rotated component loadings for all residential density areas (ARD, $N = 1485$)

Residential quality variable	Component								Communality
	I	II	III	IV	V	VI	VII	VIII	
%HOUSEHOLDS NROOM = 1–2	0.915	0.173	0.081	0.107	0.041	– 0.027	0.009	0.034	0.854
% HOUSEHOLDS HOUSE TYPE = FLAT	0.902	0.141	0.160	0.079	0.084	– 0.013	0.026	0.006	0.712
% HOUSEHOLDS TOILETs/BATHs = 1	0.864	0.152	0.131	0.184	0.143	0.030	0.010	– 0.054	0.779
% HOUSEHOLDS RENT = N201000-40,000	0.786	0.078	0.230	0.225	– 0.047	– 0.001	– 0.144	– 0.037	0.758
% HOUSEHOLDS KITCHEN = UNTILED	0.534	0.048	0.461	0.331	– 0.006	0.080	– 0.052	– 0.109	0.792
% HOUSEHOLDS TO HOSPITAL = 0–4 km	0.114	0.868	0.079	0.051	– 0.111	0.054	0.003	0.023	0.714
% HOUSEHOLDS TO SCHOOL = 0–4 km	0.117	0.850	0.100	0.034	0.061	– 0.006	0.068	0.055	0.971
% HOUSEHOLDS TO MARKET = 0–4 km	0.096	0.827	0.098	0.087	0.245	– 0.059	0.064	0.022	0.503
% HOUSEHOLDS TO WORSHIP = 0–4 km	0.097	0.812	0.136	0.042	– 0.110	0.110	0.023	0.032	0.985
%HOUSEHOLDS TO WORK = 0–4 km	0.054	0.671	0.108	– 0.005	0.488	– 0.060	0.052	– 0.061	0.836
% HOUSEHOLDS IN RSPACE = 3 × 4 m^2	0.277	0.478	0.187	0.313	– 0.066	– 0.088	– 0.084	0.043	0.791

(continued)

Table 7.2 (continued)

Residential quality variable	Component								Communality
	I	II	III	IV	V	VI	VII	VIII	
%HOUSEHOLDS LAYOUT = MIXED	0.230	0.176	0.859	0.106	– 0.027	– 0.028	0.032	0.019	0.872
% HOUSEHOLDS EXT. QUALITY = GOOD	0.179	0.117	0.853	– 0.032	– 0.119	– 0.017	– 0.034	0.044	0.888
% HOUSEHOLDS ACCESSIBILITY = REASONABLE	0.089	0.149	0.656	0.086	0.160	0.060	0.030	– 0.069	0.459
% HOUSEHOLDS WATER = POTABLE	0.166	0.112	0.138	0.826	0.094	– 0.048	– 0.061	– 0.086	0.763
% HOUSEHOLDS INT.QUALITY = POOR	0.368	0.076	0.005	0.700	0.053	0.084	0.057	0.031	0.845
% HOUSEHOLDS DISTRICT = OUTERCORE	– 0.127	– 0.042	0.013	– 0.113	– 0.899	– 0.115	0.041	– 0.003	0.631
% HOUSEHOLDS TO RELATIONS = 0–4 km	0.004	0.028	0.031	0.013	0.096	0.977	0.002	– 0.076	0.645
% HOUSEHOLDS TENURE = RENTER	– 0.060	0.104	0.017	– 0.022	– 0.028	0.002	0.982	– 0.014	0.980
% HOUSEHOLDS SECURITY = FORMAL	– 0.047	0.088	– 0.026	– 0.053	– 0.009	– 0.076	– 0.014	0.983	0.752
Eigenvalue **Variance %** **Total variance %**	**6.14** **30.69** **30.69**	**2.75** **13.76** **44.44**	**1.62** **8.12** **52.56**	**1.31** **6.53** **59.09**	**1.01** **5.06** **64.14**	**0.97** **4.85** **68.99**	**0.92** **4.58** **73.57**	**0.82** **4.09** **77.66**	**KMO = 0.874**

Table 7.3 PCA rotated component loadings for low residential density area (LRD, $N = 270$)

Residential attribute	LRD component								Communality
	I	II	III	IV	V	VI	VII	VIII	
%HOUSEHOLDS NROOM = 1–2	0.852	0.039	0.007	– 0.105	– 0.005	0.041	0.035	0.086	0.686
%HOUSEHOLDS HOUSE TYPE = FLAT	0.841	0.118	– 0.023	– 0.169	– 0.111	– 0.113	– 0.003	0.037	0.802
%HOUSEHOLDS TOILET/TAB = 1	0.758	0.079	0.065	0.073	– 0.159	0.142	– 0.046	– 0.129	0.788
%HOUSEHOLDS RENT = N200000-400,000	0.751	0.390	0.026	0.002	– 0.070	0.030	0.130	0.005	0.486
%HOUSEHOLDS KITCHEN = UNTILED	0.604	0.429	– 0.072	0.197	0.134	0.180	0.145	– 0.194	0.689
%HOUSEHOLDS INT. EQUALITY = POOR	0.432	0.197	– 0.109	– 0.066	0.407	0.276	0.072	– 0.251	0.747
%HOUSEHOLDS LAYOUT = MIXED	0.287	0.834	– 0.068	0.016	– 0.103	0.059	0.044	– 0.026	0.710
%HOUSEHOLDS EXT. QUALITY = GOOD	0.245	0.804	– 0.034	– 0.012	0.183	0.130	0.077	– 0.078	0.645
%HOUSEHOLDS ACCESSIBILITY = REASONABLE	0.043	0.599	– 0.026	0.145	– 0.469	0.119	– 0.043	– 0.164	0.833
%HOUSEHOLDS RSPACE = 3 × 4 m^2	0.371	0.412	– 0.037	0.232	0.128	– 0.401	0.079	0.269	0.799
%HOUSEHOLDS TO WORK = 0–4 km	0.039	0.109	0.878	– 0.041	0.013	0.099	– 0.038	0.059	0.769

(continued)

Table 7.3 (continued)

Residential attribute	LRD component								Communality
	I	II	III	IV	V	VI	VII	VIII	
%HOUSEHOLDS TO MARKET = 0–4 km	– 0.044	– 0.129	0.857	0.186	0.007	0.008	– 0.006	0.009	0.776
%HOUSEHOLDS TO SCHOOL = 0–4 km	0.050	– 0.096	0.577	0.228	0.001	– 0.261	0.031	– 0.145	0.748
%HOUSEHOLDS TO WORSHIP = 0-4 km	– 0.082	0.115	0.114	0.834	– 0.038	0.087	0.041	0.086	0.619
%HOUSEHOLDS TO HOSPITAL = 0-4 km	– 0.056	– 0.037	0.442	0.641	0.193	– 0.096	0.030	– 0.174	0.771
%HOUSEHOLDS DISTRICT = OUTER CITY	– 0.208	– 0.016	0.057	0.112	0.778	– 0.064	– 0.122	0.045	0.654
%HOUSEHOLDS WATER = POTABLE	0.160	0.198	– 0.050	0.079	– 0.043	0.828	0.055	0.083	0.702
%HOUSEHOLDS TENURE = RENTER	– 0.215	0.110	0.184	– 0.165	0.202	– 0.101	– 0.765	0.008	0.551
%HOUSEHOLDS TO RELATIONS = 0–4 km	– 0.110	0.410	0.223	– 0.107	0.096	– 0.060	0.675	– 0.008	0.755
% HOUSEHOLDS SECURITY = FORMAL	– 0.045	– 0.123	– 0.051	– 0.007	0.039	0.057	– 0.010	0.899	0.739
Eigenvalue **Variance %** **Total variance %**	**4.78** **23.91** **23.91**	**2.53** **12.66** **36.57**	**1.68** **8.40** **44.97**	**1.22** **6.08** **51.05**	**1.11** **5.56** **56.61**	**1.04** **5.19** **61.80**	**0.99** **4.95** **66.75**	**0.92** **4.61** **71.36**	**KMO = 0.791**

Table 7.4 PCA rotated component loadings for medium residential density area (MRD, $N = 486$)

Residential attribute	Component								Communality
	I	II	III	IV	V	VI	VII	VIII	
%HOUSEHOLDS NROOM = 1–2	0.906	0.208	0.071	0.062	– 0.035	0.044	0.131	– 0.017	0.850
%HOUSEHOLDS HOUSE TYPE = FLAT	0.888	0.149	0.159	0.081	0.040	0.047	0.135	– 0.006	0.610
%HOUSEHOLDS TOILET/TAB = 1	0.878	0.072	0.093	0.088	0.056	0.137	0.185	0.038	0.790
%HOUSEHOLDS RENT = N200000-400,000	0.840	0.017	0.149	– 0.109	– 0.022	0.114	– 0.042	– 0.064	0.815
%HOUSEHOLDS TO SCHOOL = 0–4 km	0.086	0.878	0.132	0.014	– 0.100	0.022	0.075	0.052	0.823
%HOUSEHOLDS TO HOSPITAL = 0–4 km	0.156	0.858	0.154	– 0.182	– 0.019	0.073	– 0.027	0.012	0.702
%HOUSEHOLDS TO MARKET = 0–4 km	0.078	0.855	0.175	0.095	– 0.108	– 0.006	0.003	0.040	0.827
%HOUSEHOLDS TO WORSHIP = 0–4 km	0.177	0.728	0.284	– 0.081	– 0.025	0.105	– 0.200	0.037	0.765
%HOUSEHOLDS TO WORK = 0–4 km	– 0.029	0.567	0.172	0.465	0.033	– 0.164	0.108	– 0.047	0.564
%HOUSEHOLDS LAYOUT = MIXED	0.141	0.282	0.894	0.001	– 0.052	0.003	– 0.006	0.028	0.902
%HOUSEHOLDS EXT. QUALITY = GOOD	0.148	0.316	0.876	– 0.003	– 0.074	– 0.026	0.024	0.013	0.896

(continued)

Table 7.4 (continued)

Residential attribute	Component								Communality
	I	II	III	IV	V	VI	VII	VIII	
%HOUSEHOLDS ACCESSIBILITY = REASONABLE	0.081	0.225	0.539	0.332	0.235	0.480	0.126	− 0.077	0.864
%HOUSEHOLDS RSPACE = 3 × 4 m^2	0.437	0.157	0.506	− 0.003	− 0.191	0.107	− 0.415	0.041	0.893
%HOUSEHOLDS DISTRICT = OUTER CITY	− 0.082	0.190	0.050	− 0.894	0.034	0.037	0.036	− 0.022	0.694
%HOUSEHOLDS SECURITY = FORMAL	0.009	0.319	0.036	0.497	− 0.452	− 0.025	0.033	− 0.092	0.896
%HOUSEHOLDS TO RELATIONS = 0–4 km	0.023	− 0.088	− 0.066	− 0.036	0.898	− 0.055	0.000	0.053	0.851
%HOUSEHOLDS WATER = POTABLE	0.251	0.015	0.009	− 0.130	− 0.096	0.896	0.048	− 0.021	0.793
%HOUSEHOLDS INT. QUALITY = POOR	0.441	− 0.052	− 0.021	0.069	− 0.051	0.095	0.715	− 0.013	0.726
%HOUSEHOLDS KITCHEN = UNTILED	0.433	0.090	0.512	− 0.203	0.017	0.070	0.533	0.067	0.989
%HOUSEHOLDS TENURE = RENTER	− 0.034	0.080	0.032	− 0.023	0.077	− 0.032	0.001	0.986	0.760
Eigenvalue **Variance %** **Total variance %**	**6.10** **30.51** **30.51**	**3.04** **15.21** **45.72**	**1.63** **8.15** **53.87**	**1.37** **6.86** **60.73**	**1.19** **5.93** **66.66**	**0.96** **4.78** **71.44**	**0.86** **4.32** **75.75**	**0.86** **4.29** **80.04**	**KMO = 0.848**

Table 7.5 PCA rotated component loadings for high residential density area (HRD, $N = 729$)

Residential attribute	Component								Communality
	I	II	III	IV	V	VI	VII	VIII	
%HOUSEHOLDS TO SCHOOL = 0–4 km	0.876	0.088	0.008	0.041	0.009	0.080	0.062	0.048	0.783
%HOUSEHOLDS TO HOSPITAL = 0–4 km	0.865	0.096	0.028	0.004	0.105	0.109	0.056	− 0.016	0.711
%HOUSEHOLDS TO MARKET = 0–4 km	0.840	0.088	0.096	− 0.062	− 0.182	− 0.027	0.017	0.063	0.764
%HOUSEHOLDS TO WORSHIP = 0–4 km	0.837	0.112	0.025	0.056	0.075	0.041	0.116	0.063	0.789
%HOUSEHOLDS TO WORK = 0–4 km	0.781	0.050	0.027	0.005	− 0.236	− 0.174	− 0.058	0.087	0.784
%HOUSEHOLDS RSPACE = 0–4 km	0.619	0.252	0.385	− 0.006	− 0.005	− 0.042	− 0.102	− 0.038	0.741
%HOUSEHOLDS NROOM = 1–2	0.178	0.937	0.076	− 0.001	− 0.027	− 0.011	− 0.003	0.037	0.886
%HOUSEHOLDS TOILET/TAB = 1	0.155	0.933	0.092	0.027	− 0.089	− 0.028	0.042	0.019	0.761
%HOUSEHOLDS HOUSE TYPE = FLAT	0.206	0.922	0.064	0.037	− 0.088	− 0.022	0.008	0.052	0.778
%HOUSEHOLDS RENT = N200000-400,000	0.037	0.781	0.239	0.011	0.083	0.005	− 0.066	− 0.249	0.723
%HOUSEHOLDS KITCHEN = UNTILED	− 0.073	0.522	0.314	0.336	− 0.211	− 0.060	0.038	− 0.161	0.760

(continued)

Table 7.5 (continued)

Residential attribute	Component								Communality
	I	II	III	IV	V	VI	VII	VIII	
%HOUSEHOLDS WATER = POTABLE	0.089	0.102	0.828	– 0.066	– 0.208	– 0.050	– 0.036	– 0.089	0.910
%HOUSEHOLDS INT. QUALITY = POOR	0.134	0.308	0.759	0.019	0.095	0.010	0.093	0.064	0.917
%HOUSEHOLDS EXT. QUALITY = GOOD	– 0.058	0.003	– 0.208	0.803	0.217	0.071	0.019	– 0.130	0.608
%HOUSEHOLDS LAYOUT = MIXED	0.104	0.096	0.126	0.799	– 0.149	– 0.110	– 0.002	0.120	0.763
%HOUSEHOLDS DISTRICT = OUTER CITY	– 0.173	– 0.156	– 0.113	0.037	0.802	0.112	– 0.239	– 0.032	0.915
%HOUSEHOLDS SECURITY = FORMAL	0.133	– 0.040	– 0.055	– 0.069	0.204	0.840	0.068	0.012	0.565
%HOUSEHOLDS ACCESSIBILITY = REASONABLE	0.216	0.027	– 0.024	– 0.048	0.430	– 0.617	0.377	0.056	0.712
%HOUSEHOLDS TO RELATIONS = 0–4 km	0.055	– 0.011	0.030	0.023	– 0.174	– 0.024	0.922	0.005	0.945
%HOUSEHOLDS TENURE = RENTER	0.130	– 0.098	– 0.037	– 0.010	– 0.018	– 0.011	0.010	0.957	0.741
Eigenvalue	**5.52**	**3.08**	**1.53**	**1.43**	**1.18**	**1.02**	**0.96**	**0.83**	**KMO = 0.862**
Variance %	**27.61**	**15.41**	**7.63**	**7.13**	**5.92**	**5.11**	**4.80**	**4.18**	
Total variance %	**27.61**	**43.02**	**50.65**	**57.79**	**63.70**	**68.81**	**73.61**	**77.79**	

is appropriately named "Location Proximity-Quality." The third component has high loadings on three variables layout, exterior quality and accessibility. This component is therefore named "Neighborhood Exterior-Quality." The fourth component contains high loadings on two structural quality variables of water and interior quality, and it is therefore called "Dwelling Interior Water-Quality." Metropolitan characteristic variable loads singly and negatively on the fifth component which is also called "Neighborhood-Integrity."

The fifth component contains variables with many negative loadings indicating lack of association between the district of residence and such variables as proximity to work, place of worship, market, school and layout. The sixth, seventh and eighth components also contain quite a number of variables with low and negative loadings except relations which loads very strongly on the sixth (Social Bond), tenure on the seventh (Barrier to entry) and security on the eighth component (Security/Safety Quality).

However, spatial variations exist in the structure of the components across residential density areas. As indicated in Table 7.3, for instance in the LRD, the first component "Dwelling Facility-Quality" accounts for nearly 24% of the total variance in the set, the second "Dwelling Exterior-Quality" account for 12.7%, followed by "Location Proximity-Quality" (Components III and IV) 14.5%, "Neighborhood-Integrity" 5.6%, "Dwelling Interior-Quality" 5.2%, "Barrier-to-entry" 5%, "Security/Safety-Quality" 4.6%. Six components based on the Kaiser Criterion are important in this LRD, and they account for 61.80% of the total variance. Incidentally, a component "Social-Bond" has no distinct presence in this region as it merges with Component VII. As there is slight rearrangement in the components so in the variables that account for them. Component I contains in addition to the previous variables interior quality, while hospital and worship load on Component IV.

The situation in the MRD presents a different revelation as the arrangement of the components is different from those discovered in LRD. Extracting the same eight components as in LRD, results of PCA components, in MRD are more interesting. The first component to be extracted in the MRD is "Dwelling Facility-Quality," followed by "Location Proximity-Quality," "Dwelling Exterior-Quality," "Integrity-Safety," "Social-Bond," "Dwelling Interior-Quality" and "Barrier-to-entry." Respectively the components account for 30.5%, 15.2%, 8.5%, 6.7%, 5.9%, 4.8%, 4.3% and 4.29% of the total variance in the data set (see Table 7.4). Although the same numbers of components were extracted in the LRD and MRD, the arrangement and loading values differ significantly. The MRD loadings perhaps display the most inconsistent orientation, as many variables load in multiples on different components—for instance, work, accessibility, space, security, interior quality and kitchen. Like the ARD components, the pattern displayed in MRD is a bit antithetical to the normal trend. The explanation for this unusual variation from expectation may be that the MRD, in terms of socioeconomic attributes, falls between the low economic status of residents in HRD and high economic status of residents in LRD. Only five components that account for 66.66% of the variance are important in explaining the residential quality variables for explaining housing choice decision making in the MRD of the study area. The PCA results in HRD as shown in Table 7.5

present a different pattern from the two previously discussed areas. Eight components account for 77.79% of the total variation in residential quality data used in the study. The first component "Location Proximity-Quality" accounts for 27.6%, "Dwelling Facility-Quality" 15.4%, "Dwelling Interior-Quality" 7.6%, "Dwelling Exterior-Quality" 7.1%, "Neighborhood-Integrity" 5.9%, "Security/Safety-Quality" 5.1%, "Social-Bond" 4.8% and "Barrier-to-entry" 4.2% of the variance observed in the set. Six variables loaded heavily and positively on the first component.

According to Table 7.5, out of the four variables that loaded on the second component number of rooms, number of toilets and baths, and house type are the most substantial residential quality variables. All the variables except accessibility consistently load on the expected components. The accessibility variable loads on two components (V and VI), and this confirms its inconsistency in housing quality choices. Incidentally, only six components that account for 68.81% of the variance are important in explaining the residential quality variables for explaining housing choice decision making in the HRD part of the study area. The implication is that the extracted eight components from the PCA can be appropriately used in summarizing the residential quality of the households in the HRD far better than in the LRD and MRD. There are some other revelations one can notice in the PCA analysis done so far. In all four rotated matrices, price/rent is consistently high and positively loaded on Dwelling Facility-Quality component. And beside HRD the Dwelling Facility-Quality component remains the most important residential quality component favored by the Lagos residents. These findings have diverse implications. It shows that the most important price determining quality variables are the dwelling facility variables and that residents would probably consider the price first in considering housing choices. Resulting from the rotated components are the spatial patterns of the components along the twelve LGAs. A transformation of the PCA components gives scores of the components on the LGAs as presented in Sect. 7.2.

7.2 Spatial Pattern of Residential Quality Component Scores on LGAs

After factoring the twenty residential variables giving an orthogonal matrix of loadings and eight components, the extracted components are factored to load on the geographic locations and the results are presented in Table 7.6. The performance of each LGA on the components is reflected in four groups, namely (i) = + 0.51 and above (ii) = + 0.50 to 0 (iii) = 0 to − 0.50 and (iv) = − 0.51 and less.

Grouping of Component Scores for Mapping

(i) Very High = + 0.50 and above
(ii) Moderate = + 0.50 to 0
(iii) Low = 0 to − 0.50
(iv) Very Low = − 0.51 and less.

Table 7.6 Spatial pattern of residential quality component scores on LGAs

LGA	Component							
	Dwelling facility I	Location proximity II	Exterior quality III	Interior water IV	Neighborhood V	Social bond VI	Barrier to entry VII	Security VIII
Etiosa	– 0.005	0.552	– 0.280	– 0.384	– 0.722	– 0.473	2.343	– 0.881
Lagos Island	– 0.216	0.094	– 0.092	1.347	0.140	– 0.821	0.982	– 0.875
Ajeromi-Ifelodun	0.074	– 0.203	– 0.668	1.343	0.052	0.536	– 0.215	0.283
Apapa	– 0.089	0.137	0.143	– 0.188	– 0.396	0.496	– 0.593	2.600
Mainland	– 0.166	– 0.157	1.440	– 0.491	0.302	0.230	– 0.009	1.316
Mushin	– 0.025	– 0.089	1.067	– 0.020	– 0.144	0.227	– 0.497	– 1.243
Oshodi-isolo	0.153	– 0.243	0.068	0.152	0.526	0.509	– 0.324	0.174
Somolu	0.159	– 0.031	– 0.198	– 0.305	– 0.419	2.428	– 0.963	0.670
Agege	0.590	0.087	– 0.159	– 0.634	– 0.892	– 1.759	0.844	– 1.577
Ikeja	– 0.029	0.662	– 0.312	– 0.645	– 0.492	– 0.060	– 1.921	– 0.502
Surulere	– 0.125	– 0.054	– 0.022	0.068	2.433	– 0.230	– 0.574	– 0.428
Amuwo-odofin	0.504	0.091	– 0.907	– 0.158	– 0.503	– 1.311	1.184	0.066

7.2.1 Variations in Dwelling Facility Quality Component Across LGAs

As indicated in Table 7.6, Component I, Dwelling Facility Quality, displays three patterns that divide Lagos metropolis diametrically into three based on the relevance of the residential quality variables. As can be seen in Fig. 7.1, Ajeromi, Oshodi and Shomolu three communities in the HRD belong to the same group with positive scores on Component I and Etiosa, Apapa, Ikeja (LRD), Island, Mainland, Surulere (MRD) belong to another group with negative scores on Component I. The negative scoring LGAs contribute less to the variation in the component in the study area. However, Agege and Amuwo LGAs in HRD and MRD respectively belong to the same high positive scoring locations on the Dwelling Facility Quality component. The implication of this spatial distribution pattern is the importance of the facility variables in each of the residential density areas HRD, MRD and LRD as depicted earlier in Tables 7.3, 7.4 and 7.5. The variables that account for this component in each of the RDAs such as number of rooms, house type, kitchen, toilets and baths and price shape housing choices more in the HRD than in the MRD and LRD. This further indicates the severity of poor dwelling facilities in the HRD compared to those in the two other RDAs.

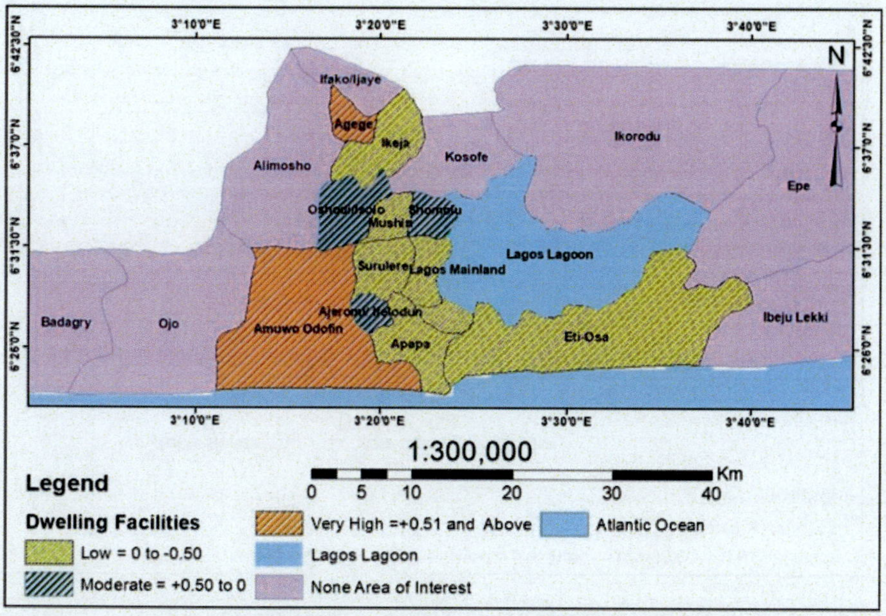

Fig. 7.1 Spatial pattern of Component I (dwelling facility) scores on LGAs

7.2.2 Variations in Location Proximity Quality Component Across LGAs

According to Table 7.6, Component II, Location proximity Quality, also divides Lagos metropolis into three namely the industrial conurbations of Etiosa and Ikeja (LRD) on the one hand, then Apapa (LRD), Island and Amuwo (MRD) on the other, while the third is composed of areas made of workers who live in faraway in Ajeromi, Mainland, Mushin, Oshodi (HRD), Surulere and Somolu LGAs (MRD). The locations that have negative scores contribute less to the variation in the location quality of dwelling conditions in Lagos. The implication of this spatial distribution pattern of location proximity quality of dwellings finds support in the loadings of the variables that account for the component in each of the RDAs depicted in Tables 7.3, 7.4 and 7.5. The variables that account for this component in each of the RDAs including proximity to work, market, school, worship centers, and friends and relations all have more representation in the LRD than in MRD and HRD. This indicates the fact that location proximity shapes housing choices more in the LRD compared to those in the two other RDAs. The spatial pattern of Component II is graphically presented in Fig. 7.2.

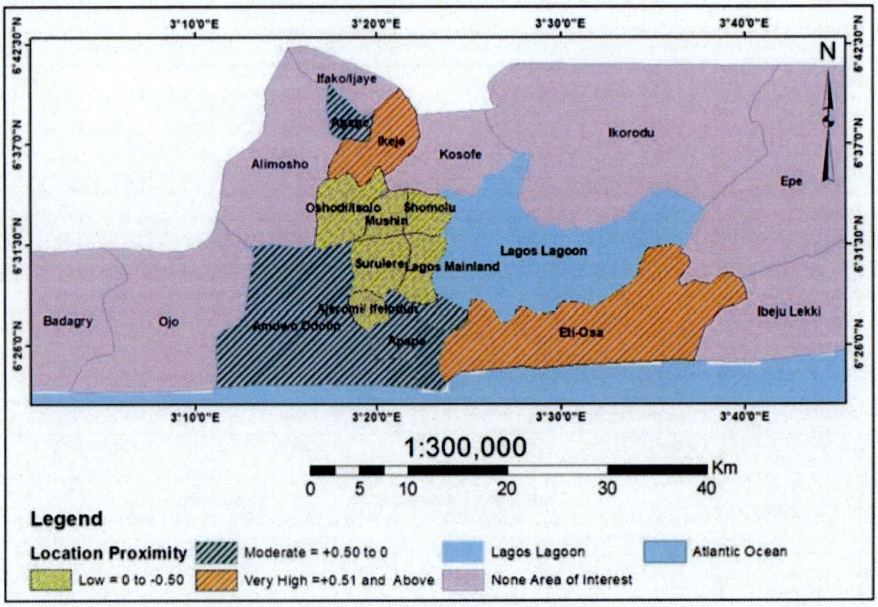

Fig. 7.2 Spatial pattern of Component II (location proximity) scores on LGAs

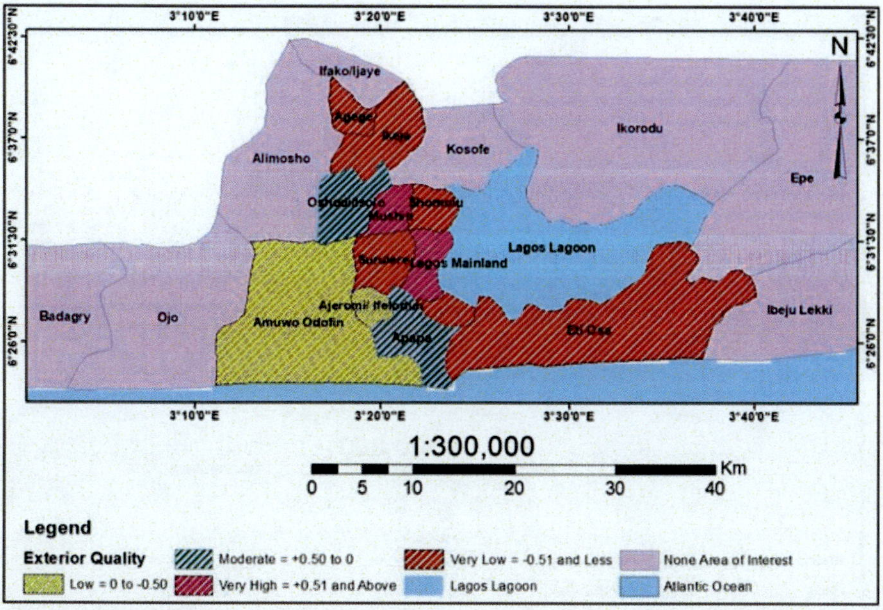

Fig. 7.3 Spatial pattern of Component III (Exterior Quality) scores on LGAs

7.2.3 Variations in Exterior Quality Component Across LGAs

According to Table 7.6 and Fig. 7.3, Component III, Exterior Quality, divides the study area into four distinct regions; the first being composed of high-density areas of Mushin and Mainland (HRD), followed by the second region consisting of Apapa (LRD), and Oshodi (HRD), the third region consists of Etiosa, Ikeja (LRD), Island, Agege (HRD), Somolu and Surulere (MRD). The last region comprises Ajeromi (HRD) and Amuwo (MRD) two LGAs that have high negative scores – 0.668 and – 0.907, respectively. The implication of this spatial distribution pattern is the importance of exterior neighborhood conditions in each of the residential density areas HRD, MRD and LRD as depicted in Tables 7.3, 7.4 and 7.5. The variables that account for this component in each of the RDAs are layout, exterior quality and accessibility. These variables shape more greatly residential choice decision making in the HRD compared to MRD and LRD.

7.2.4 Variations in Interior Quality Across LGAs

Component IV, Interior Quality, as shown in Table 7.6, has the highest scores on two LGAs, namely Island (1.347) and Ajeromi (1.343) both in the HRD area. These two settlements share attributes of high-density and low-residential quality areas. The

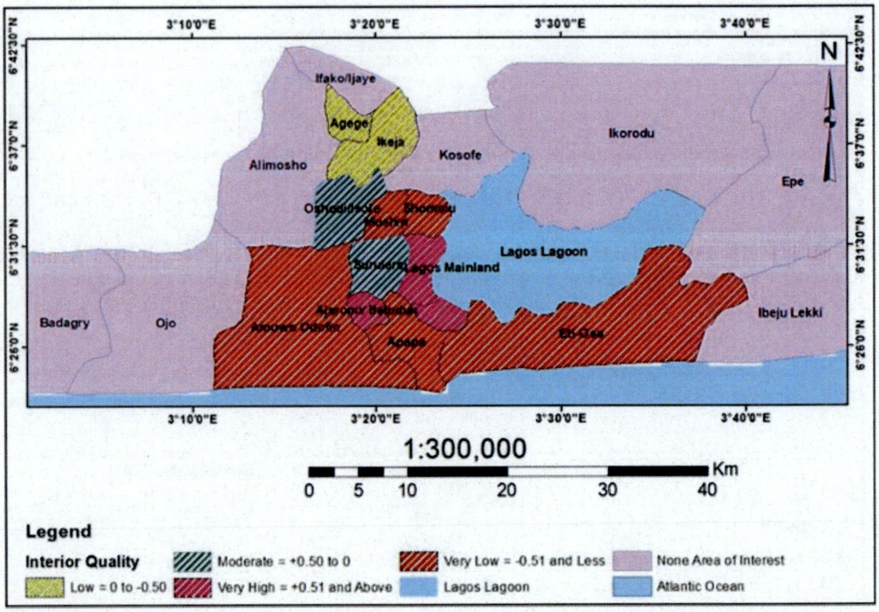

Fig. 7.4 Spatial pattern of Component IV (Interior Water Quality) scores on LGAs

second group based on the Interior quality contains two LGAs, namely Oshodi and Surulere. The third group is made of Etiosa, Apapa (LRD), Mainland and Mushin (HRD) while the last group consists of Agege and Ikeja (Fig. 7.4 shows the spatial pattern of the component graphically). The implication of this spatial distribution pattern is the importance of water facility variables in each of the residential density areas HRD, MRD and LRD as depicted in Tables 7.3, 7.4 and 7.5. The variable that accounts for this component—water facility—is very important in residential choice decision in each of the RDAs. Water sources and quality play a great role in home choices in all the residential density areas.

7.2.5 *Variations in Neighborhood Integrity Across LGAs*

A cursory look at Table 7.6 again shows that Component V—Neighborhood Integrity—divides the study area into four. The first region is made of Oshodi (HRD) and Surulere (MRD), the second region comprises Island, Ajeromi (HRD) and Mainland, while the third region consists of Apapa, Mushin, Somolu and Ikeja. The last region along neighborhood integrity is made of Etiosa, Agege and Amuwo (see Fig. 7.5 for the spatial pattern of Component V on the LGAs). The implication of this spatial distribution pattern is the importance of the metropolitan characteristics

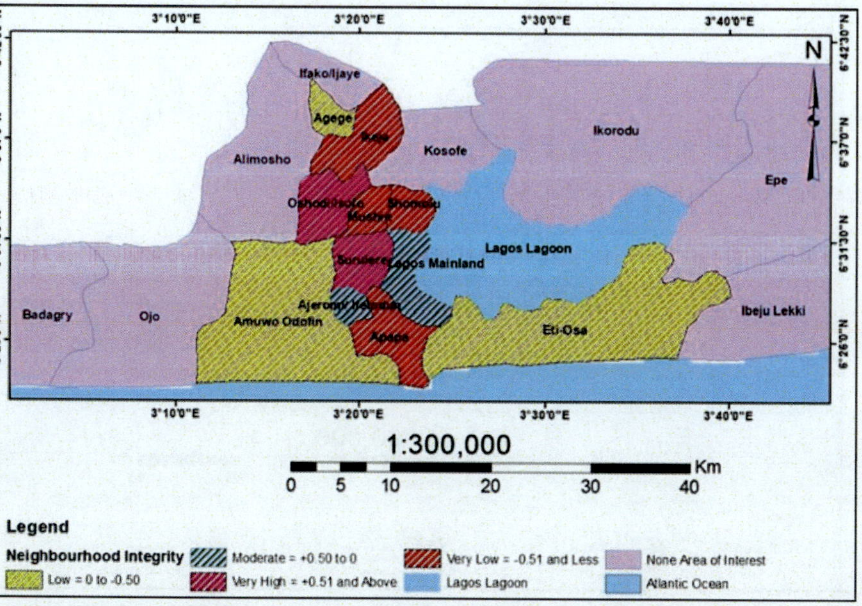

Fig. 7.5 Spatial pattern of Component V (Neighborhood Integrity) scores on LGAs

variable in each of the residential density areas HRD, MRD and LRD as earlier depicted in Tables 7.3, 7.4 and 7.5.

7.2.6 Variations in Social, Barrier and Security Components Across LGAs

Component VI, that is Social Bond, also divides Lagos into four distinct areas. The first area is composed of Ajeromi, Oshodi and Somolu. The second group contains Apapa, Mainland and Mushin, while the third area is made of Etiosa, Ikeja and Surulere. The last area comprises Island and Amuwo. Component VII, that is Barrier to entry, divides Lagos into three. The first group is made of Island, Agege and Amuwo. The second group is made of Ajeromi, Mailand, Mushin and Oshodi while the third group contains Apapa, Somolu, Ikeja and Surulere LGAs. Lastly, Component VIII, which is security, splits the study area into four. The first group consists of Somolu, Apapa and Mainland, while the second is made of Ajeromi, Oshodi and Amuwo. The third group consists of Surulere alone and the last group comprises Etiosa, Island, Mushin, Agege and Ikeja (Figs. 7.6, 7.7 and 7.8 show the spatial pattern of the components on LGAs).

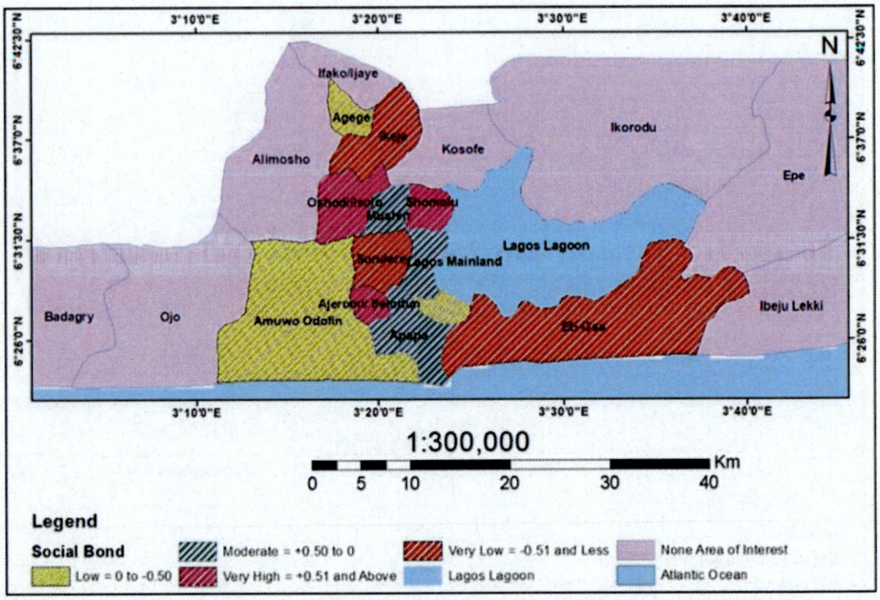

Fig. 7.6 Spatial pattern of Component VI (Social Bond) scores on LGA

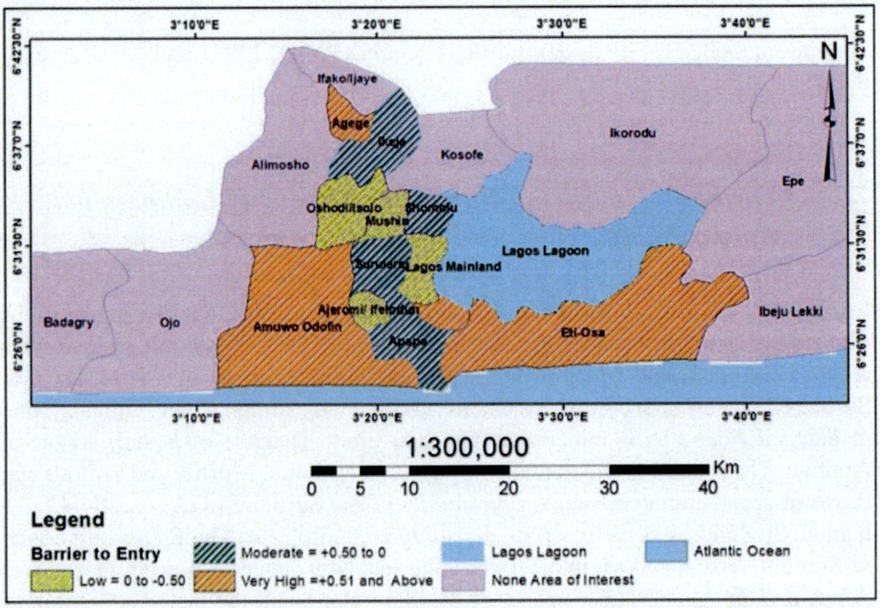

Fig. 7.7 Spatial pattern of Component VII (Barrier to Entry) scores on LGAs

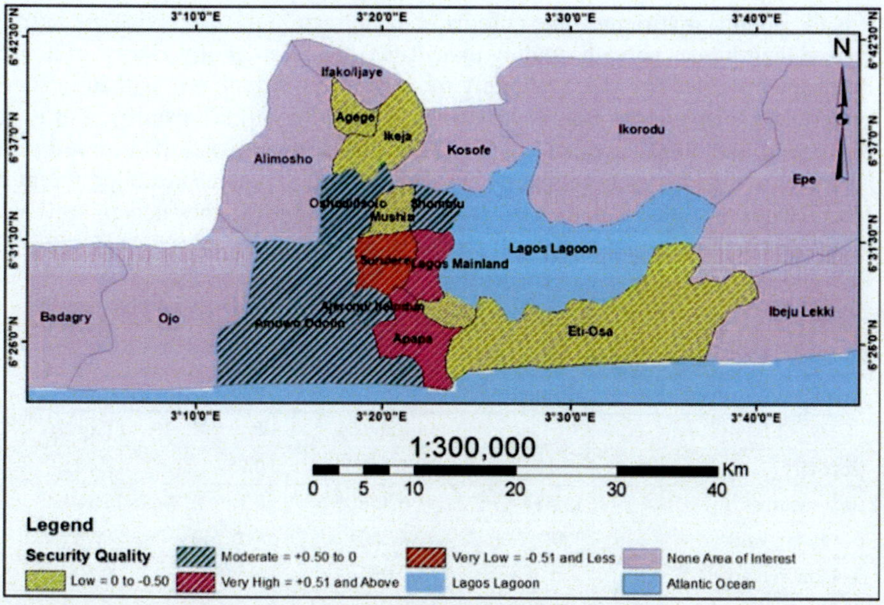

Fig. 7.8 Spatial pattern of Component VIII (Security) scores on LGAs

7.3 Revealed Housing Choice Modeling Results

An important objective of this study is to examine the spatial manifestations of housing choices within the study area. To achieve this objective attempt was made to analyze the choices of residents for housing type and the corresponding residential quality variables that shape home choices within the residential density areas. As indicated in the earlier part of this chapter, three housing types were chosen by the residents, namely the multiunit, flat and duplex housing types. Four multinomial logit models were set with housing type as the dependent and the residential quality variables as independent variables. Results from the analyses are presented in Tables 7.7, 7.8, 7.9 and 7.10. Five other choice models were fitted to estimate the probabilities of residents choosing their dwelling units based on the features of homes and their characteristics. The first model was fitted to estimate the socioeconomic attributes that determine housing choices. The second model was fitted to estimate the variations in choices based upon marital groups. The third model was fitted to estimate the variations in choices based on age while the fourth model estimated the choices based on income level. The fifth model was fitted to estimate choices based on location within the city. These models were fitted using the multinomial logit regression (MNL) model which is appropriate for categorical discrete choice data used in this study. The argument for the use of this approach is premised upon the fact that renters in practice weigh the attributes of houses including the environmental and structural attributes to make decision on the choice of residence. Sometimes, it is the dominant attributes that command the attraction of renters that are used to choose their homes notwithstanding many times the affordability aspects of houses determine revealed choices. Definitely more in revealed preferences than in stated preferences, consumers often make decisions based upon affordability. But if the issue of affordability is relaxed the choices of renters are controlled more by the attributes of the houses. In this study, we decided to interpret the behavior of renters from the positions taken on the attributes of residences which they occupy (revealed preferences). The results of these models are presented in Tables 7.11, 7.12, 7.13, 7.14 and 7.15.

Table 7.7 MNL parameter estimates of housing choices in LRD

Residential attribute	Multiunit		Flat	
	B	Exp (*B*)	*B*	Exp (*B*)
Core city	12.171***	1.93E05	0.752	2.121
City suburbs	13.437***	6.85E05	0.169	1.184
0–4 km to work	3.481**	32.504	– 0.242	0.785
0–4 km to market	– 3.388	0.034	– 0.693	0.500
0–4 km to school	– 0.288	0.750	1.628*	5.092
0–4 km to hospital	– 3.801**	0.022	– 0.134	0.874
0–4 km to worship	0.538	1.713	– 1.585**	0.205
0–4 km to relations	– 0.088	0.915	0.072	1.075
Reasonable accessibility	– 3.633**	0.026	0.969*	2.635
Formal security	– 1.120	0.326	– 0.840*	0.432
Mixed layout	1.867	6.471	– 0.533	0.587
Good exterior quality	– 3.667***	0.026	– 0.428	0.652
3+ number of rooms	6.020***	411.403	0.447	1.564
Small room space	1.029	2.798	– 0.040	0.961
Potable	– 2.643**	0.071	– 0.951	0.386
1 toilet and 1 bath	14.954***	3.12E06	11.708***	1.22E05
Untiled kitchen	4.151***	63.529	1.049	2.854
Poor interior quality	– 0.211	0.809	0.935	2.547
Owner	– 0.136	0.873	0.768	2.155
N200000 and less	7.954***	2848.138	0.247	1.280
N201-N400000	6.593***	729.762	1.805**	6.081
Intercept	– 17.299***		– 0.456	
Model parameters	**Number of observations = 486; -2likelihood = 170.637 Chi-square $\chi^2 = 334.095; p = 0.000$; McFadden $\rho^2 = 0.630$**			

The reference category is: DUPLEX
***Significant at 1%; ** at 5% and * at 10%

Table 7.8 MNL parameter estimates of housing choices in MRD

Residential attribute	Multiunit		Flat	
	B	Exp (*B*)	*B*	Exp (*B*)
0–4 km to work	− 1.822	0.162	1.614***	5.025
0–4 km to market	− 2.444	0.087	− 0.982	0.374
0–4 km to school	0.272	1.312	− 1.663	0.190
0–4 km to hospital	1.649	5.200	1.209	3.351
0–4 km to worship	0.399	1.491	− 0.955	0.385
0–4 km to relations	− 0.734	0.480	0.779*	2.178
Reasonable access	− 0.682	0.506	0.709	2.031
Private security	0.091	1.096	0.847	2.333
Mixed layout	− 2.530	0.080	− 0.962	0.382
Good exterior quality	8.624***	5564.197	1.765*	5.842
3+ number of rooms	8.443***	4642.602	− 2.956**	0.052
Small room space	2.153	8.614	0.462	1.588
Potable water	− 2.159	0.115	− 0.571	0.565
1 Toilet and 1 bath	3.543**	34.587	− 0.848	0.428
Untiled kitchen	− 0.840	0.432	− 0.601	0.549
Poor interior quality	2.322	10.192	− 0.540	0.583
Owner	− 0.124	0.883	0.541	1.718
N200000 and less	3.243*	25.603	1.679	5.360
N201-N400000	− 1.659	0.190	2.251***	9.501
Intercept	− 6.935***		− 1.183**	
Model Parameters	**Number of observation = 486; -2Loglikelihood = 165.708 Chi-square χ^2 = 703.228; p = 0.000; McFadden ρ^2 = 0.770**			

The reference category is: DUPLEX
***Significant at 1%; **at 5% and *at 10%

7.3.1 *Spatial Polarization of Residential Quality and Revealed Housing Choices*

The first logit model was set to estimate the effects of residential quality variables on home choices in the low residential density area. In Table 7.7, the results of the effects of neighborhood and structural variables on housing type choices in the low residential density (LRD) area are presented.

Out of the nineteen residential quality variables employed metropolitan characteristics, proximity to work, hospital, accessibility, exterior quality, number of rooms, potable water, toilet and kitchen, and of course, rent are of immense importance in the type of housing chosen in the LRD area. While the intercept of the model is

Table 7.9 MNL parameter estimates of housing choices in HRD

Residential attribute	Multiunit		Flat	
	B	Exp (*B*)	*B*	Exp (*B*)
City core	– 0.785	0.456	– 0.665	0.514
City suburbs	– 0.141	0.869	0.013	1.013
0–4 km to work	0.772	2.165	0.870	2.387
0–4 km to market	0.384	1.469	0.161	1.175
0–4 km to school	0.046	1.047	0.005	1.005
0–4 km to hospital	– 0.329	0.719	– 0.318	0.728
0–4 km to worship	0.699	2.012	0.638	1.894
0–4 km to relations	– 0.116	0.891	– 0.022	0.978
Reasonable access	– 0.901	0.406	– 1.043	0.352
Private security	0.760	2.138	1.016	2.762
Mixed layout	3.024**	20.564	2.694**	14.786
Good exterior quality	0.916	2.499	0.981	2.668
3+ number of rooms	2.703**	14.918	– 0.546	0.579
Small room space	– 1.147	0.318	– 1.336*	0.263
Potable water	0.514	1.672	0.606	1.834
1 toilet and 1 bath	2.367*	10.670	– 0.156	0.856
Untiled kitchen	0.946	2.576	1.172	3.230
Poor interior quality	– 0.359	0.698	– 0.318	0.728
Owner	– 0.426	0.653	– 0.693	0.500
N200000 and less	7.983***	2929.267	– 27.223***	1.50E–012
N201-400,000	7.978***	2917.538	– 26.865***	2.15E–012
Intercept	– 11.515***		26.721***	
Model parameters	**Number of observations = 729; -2likelihood = 302.023 Chi-square χ^2 = 490.712; p = 0.000; McFadden ρ^2 = 0.612**			

The reference category is: DUPLEX
***Significant at 1%; **at 5% and *at 10%

very significant in multiunit housing its value of – 0.456 is rather insignificant in flat choice. The reference category is duplex unit. However, the model predicted the choice behavior very adequately given the McFadden ρ^2 value of 0.630.

The second logit model is set to estimate the effects of residential quality in the choice of homes in the medium residential density (MRD) area. The results for the MRD are presented in Table 7.8. However, the metropolitan characteristics variable was removed due to its inconsistent effects on the outcome of the model. Hence, eighteen variables were used to observe the influence of residential quality on housing choices.

Table 7.10 MNL parameter estimates of housing choices in ARD

Residential attribute	Multiunit		Flat	
	B	Exp (*B*)	*B*	Exp (*B*)
City core	– 14.438***	5.36E–007	– 17.766***	1.92E–008
City suburbs	– 14.691***	4.16E–007	– 18.013***	1.50E–008
0–4 km to work	0.117	1.124	1.006**	2.734
0–4 km to market	1.445	4.244	– 0.692	0.500
0–4 km to school	0.919	2.508	0.775	2.170
0–4 km to hospital	– 1.574*	0.207	– 0.024	0.977
0–4 km to worship	– 0.015	0.985	– 1.389***	0.249
0–4 km to relations	– 0.495	0.609	0.018	1.019
Reasonable access	– 0.336	0.715	0.721**	2.057
Private security	0.278	1.321	– 0.485	0.615
Mixed layout	2.785***	16.200	– 0.275	0.759
Good exterior quality	– 2.781***	0.062	0.123	1.131
3+ number of rooms	6.121***	455.258	0.115	1.122
Small room space	1.260**	3.525	– 0.269	0.764
Potable water	– 1.586**	0.205	– 0.325	0.723
1 Toilet and 1 bath	19.223***	2.23E08	14.586***	2.16E06
Untiled kitchen	1.782***	5.939	0.768*	2.156
Poor interior quality	0.422	1.524	– 0.057	0.945
Owner	– 0.102	0.903	0.348	1.416
N200000 and less	5.318****	204.059	1.369	3.932
N201-N400000	3.784****	43.972	2.067***	7.900
Intercept	8.692*		17.786****	
Model parameters	**Number of observation = 1485; -2likelihood = 451.324 Chi-square χ^2 = 1832.020; p = 0.000; McFadden ρ^2 = 0.777**			

The reference category is: DUPLEX
***Significant at $p < 1\%$; **at $p < 5\%$ and *at $p < 10\%$

Based on the type of house occupied by residents, analysis shows that proximity to work, exterior quality, 1–2 number of rooms, toilet and rents shape the housing behavior of the residents in this residential area. The model also predicted the outcome very soundly. While the McFadden ρ^2 value of 0.770 is very significant at $p < 0.01$, the intercepts for the multiunit (– 6.935) and flat units (– 1.183) are very significant at both 1% and 5% confidence levels, respectively. Next is the situation in the high residential density area. The results presented in Table 7.9 are the outcomes of the analysis in the high residential density (HRD) area. In choosing multiunit and flat housing types the residents in this area lay emphasis on layout, number of rooms,

Table 7.11 MNL odd ratios for estimating determinants of house type choices

Household attribute	Flat		Duplex	
	B	Exp (*B*)	*B*	Exp (*B*)
Number of children	0.013	1.013	0.323*	1.382
Female	– 0.283	0.753	– 0.465	0.628
Single versus divorced	0.454	1.574	– 1.194	0.303
Married versus divorced	0.448	1.565	– 0.884	0.413
21–40 years old versus 61+	0.822	2.276	1.745*	5.727
41–60 years old versus 61+	0.755	2.127	1.932**	6.901
1–2 members versus 7+	– 0.978	0.376	1.563*	4.775
3–6 members versus 7+	– 0.553	0.575	0.595	1.813
1–3 above 18 years versus none	0.552	1.737	0.639	1.895
4–7 above 18 years versus none	0.845	2.329	2.101**	8.172
Pry/No education versus graduate	– 0.113	0.893	0.335	1.398
Tech/secondary versus graduate	– 0.241	0.786	– 0.505	0.604
< 10 years of work versus 36 years+	0.325	1.384	0.514	1.672
11–20 years of work versus 36 years+	0.397	1.488	0.594	1.812
21–35 years of work versus 36 years+	0.156	1.169	– 0.227	0.797
0–74,999 versus 225,000+	– 14.777***	3.82E−007	– 18.048***	1.45E−008
75–149,999 versus 225,000+	– 14.924***	3.30E−007	– 16.949***	4.36E−008
150–224,999 versus 225,000+	– 15.468***	1.92E−007	– 15.333***	2.19E−007
<5 years of stay versus 21 years	0.668	1.951	– 0.753	0.471
6–20 years of stay versus 21 years	0.281	1.325	0.283	1.327
Intercept	16.289***	–	14.234***	–
Model parameters	**Number of observation = 1485; -2Loglikelihood = 1573.552 Chi-square χ^2 = 255.743; p = 0.000; McFadden ρ^2 = 0.090**			

*Significant at $p < 10\%$, **Significant at $p < 5\%$, ***Significant at $p < 1\%$ (multiunit is the reference category)

room space, toilet and rent. The single most important residential quality variable that shapes housing choice decision is rent which is very significant at 1%.

Specifically, among the residents that choose multiunit as against duplex, the 1–2 rooms, 1 toilet and bath and rent below N400000 are more influential in their choice decision making. Conversely, the residents in the flat units have less concern for rent at the two lower levels. The model predicted the outcomes very highly given the McFadden ρ^2 value of 0.612 being significant at 1%. The intercepts of the multiunit and flat units are correspondingly negative and positive indicating that the residential

Table 7.12 MNL odd ratios for estimating revealed residential choices by marital status

Housing quality variable	Single versus divorced		Married versus divorced	
	B	Exp (*B*)	*B*	Exp (*B*)
City core	– 16.117***	1.00E–007	– 15.198***	2.51E–007
Outer city	– 14.765***	3.87E–007	– 13.829***	9.86E–007
0–4 km to work	0.216	1.241	0.187	1.206
0–4 km to market	0.016	1.017	0.051	1.053
0–4 km to school	– 0.506	0.603	– 0.815	0.442
0–4 km to hospital	0.517	1.677	0.233	1.263
0–4 km to worship	– 0.507	0.602	– 0.321	0.726
0–4 km to relations	0.663*	1.940	0.303	1.353
Reasonable	– 0.417	0.659	0.038	1.039
Private security	– 0.667	0.513	0.090	1.094
Mixed layout	– 1.081	0.339	– 1.394*	0.248
Good exterior quality	0.108	1.114	0.328	1.388
Duplex	– 0.624	0.536	0.454	1.574
Flat	– 2.304*	0.100	– 0.582	0.559
3+ rooms	– 1.066	0.344	– 0.708	0.493
Large rooms (3 × 4 m^2)	1.116**	3.052	1.129***	3.091
Well	– 0.041	0.960	– 0.310	0.734
1 toilet and 1 bath	– 1.083	0.338	– 0.184	0.832
Untiled kitchen	0.489	1.631	– 0.279	0.756
Poor interior quality	0.283	1.327	0.394	1.484
Owner	– 0.651	0.521	– 0.329	0.719
N200,000 and less	1.176	3.243	– 1.578	0.206
N201000-400,000	0.280	1.323	– 1.285	0.277
Intercept	18.128***		20.610***	
Model parameter	**Number of observation = 1485** **-2Loglikelihood = 870.004** **Chi-square χ^2 = 97.198; p = 0.000 McFadden ρ^2 = 0.084**			

*Significant at $p < 10\%$, **Significant at $p < 5\%$, ***Significant at $p < 1\%$ (divorced is the reference category)

quality variables have respectively inverse and direct effects on choice decisions in the area.

Finally, information in Table 7.10 gives a general picture of the effects of residential quality variables on the choice of homes in the metropolitan area of Lagos. Accordingly, it would be noticed that those who choose multiunit housing are influenced significantly by metropolitan characteristics good layout, exterior quality, 1–2

Table 7.13 MNL odd ratios for estimating revealed residential choices by age

Housing quality variable	Middle age group 41–60 years		Old age group 61 years and above	
	B	Exp (*B*)	*B*	Exp (*B*)
0–4 km to work	0.005	1.005	0.626*	1.871
0–4 km to market	0.024	1.024	– 1.315**	0.268
0–4 km to school	0.166	1.180	0.559	1.748
0–4 km to hospital	– 0.334*	0.716	0.308	1.361
0–4 km to worship	– 0.375**	0.687	– 0.563	0.569
0–4 km to friends	– 0.083	0.920	– 0.224	0.799
Reasonable	0.455**	1.576	0.123	1.131
Private security	0.237	1.268	– 0.603	0.547
Mixed layout	– 0.204	0.815	– 0.292	0.747
Good ext. quality	0.464**	1.590	0.317	1.374
Duplex	– 0.341	0.711	– 0.378	0.685
Flat	0.453	1.573	1.051	2.862
3+ rooms	0.488	1.629	0.510	1.665
Large rooms (3 × 4 m^2)	0.049	1.051	– 0.982**	0.374
Well water	– 0.801***	0.449	– 0.414	0.661
1 bath and 1 toilet	0.558**	1.748	0.913	2.493
Untiled kitchen	– 0.843***	0.430	– 0.152	0.859
Poor interior	0.231	1.260	0.571	1.769
Owner	– 0.152	0.859	0.351	1.420
N200,000 and less	– 0.636**	0.530	– 1.732***	0.177
N201000-N400,000	– 0.369	0.692	– 0.947**	0.388
Intercept	0.696**	–	– 1.578**	–
Model parameter	**Number of observation = 1485;-2Loglikelihood = 1662.789 Chi-square χ^2 = 200.188; p = 0.000 McFadden ρ^2 = 0.087**			

*Significant at $p < 10\%$, **Significant at $p < 5\%$, ***Significant at $p < 1\%$ (21–40 years is the reference category)

rooms, small rooms, water, toilet, kitchen and lower rents. Compared to duplex units, the choice of flat is metropolitan characteristics, proximity to workplace, place of worship, accessibility, toilets and rents. The intercepts of the model are positive and significant at 1%, and the McFadden ρ^2 value of 0.777 is quite high and implicative of high predicting model (Table 7.10).

Table 7.14 MNL odd ratios for estimating revealed residential choices by income

Residential quality variable	Low-income earners N0-N74,999		Middle-income earners N75,000-N149,999		High-income earners N150,000-N224,999	
	B	Exp (*B*)	*B*	Exp (*B*)	*B*	Exp (*B*)
City core	– 15.085***	2.81E–007	– 16.088***	1.03E–007	– 15.210***	2.48E–007
Outer city	– 14.718***	4.06E–007	– 15.035***	2.95E–007	– 14.693***	4.16E–007
0–4 km to work	2.400*	11.019	2.947**	19.055	3.159**	23.540
0–4 km to market	– 1.671	0.188	– 2.436	0.087	– 1.772	0.170
0–4 km to school	– 2.819**	0.060	– 3.336***	0.036	– 3.075**	0.046
0–4 km to hospital	– 0.098	0.907	– 0.244	0.783	– 0.920	0.398
0–4 km to worship	0.863	2.371	1.170	3.221	1.071	2.918
0–4 km to friends	– 2.022*	0.132	– 2.031*	0.131	– 1.994*	0.136
Reasonable	1.669	5.309	1.458	4.299	1.021	2.776
Private security	– 0.005	0.995	0.508	1.662	0.930	2.533
Mixed layout	– 0.436	0.646	– 0.378	0.685	– 0.158	0.854
Good ext. quality	– 0.285	0.752	– 0.353	0.703	0.011	1.011
Duplex	– 0.219	0.804	– 0.349	0.705	– 0.938	0.392
Flat	– 0.430	0.651	– 0.096	0.908	– 0.833	0.435
3+ rooms	0.024	1.024	0.513	1.670	1.312	3.715
Large rooms (3 × 4 m^2)	0.182	1.199	– 0.121	0.886	– 0.235	0.790
Well water	12.116***	1.83E005	11.635***	1.13E005	10.971***	5.82E004
1 bath and 1 toilet	0.285	1.330	0.157	1.170	– 0.580	0.560

(continued)

Table 7.14 (continued)

Residential quality variable	Low-income earners N0-N74,999		Middle-income earners N75,000-N149,999		High-income earners N150,000-N224,999	
	B	Exp (*B*)	*B*	Exp (*B*)	*B*	Exp (*B*)
Untiled kitchen	15.164***	3.85E006	14.292***	1.61E006	13.061***	4.70E005
Poor interior	11.687***	1.19E005	11.916***	1.45E006	12.728***	3.37E005
Owner	− 0.684	0.505	− 1.453	0.234	− 1.464	0.231
N200,000 and less	16.834***	2.05E007	16.124***	1.01E007	15.096***	3.60E006
N201000-N400,000	3.390**	29.658	3.250**	25.799	2.444*	11.515
Intercept	17.199***		19.522***		18.446***	
Model parameters	**Number of observation = 1485; -2Loglikelihood = 1915.378 Chi-square $\chi^2 = 581.617$; $p = 0.000$ McFadden $\rho^2 = 0.207$**					

*Significant at $p < 10\%$, **Significant at $p < 5\%$, ***Significant at $p < 1\%$ (N225,000 and above is the reference category)

Table 7.15 MNL odd ratios for estimating revealed residential choices by metropolitan locations

Residential quality variable	City core versus suburb		Outer city core versus suburb	
	B	Exp (*B*)	*B*	Exp (*B*)
0–4 km to work	1.859***	6.417	2.494***	12.115
0–4 km to market	0.892**	2.441	0.614	1.847
0–4 km to school	0.667*	1.949	0.217	1.243
0–4 km to hospital	0.237	1.268	– 0.107	0.898
0–4 km to worship	– 0.540*	0.583	0.000	1.000
0–4 km to friends	0.268	1.307	0.705***	2.023
Limited access	– 0.368	0.692	– 0.975***	0.377
Private security	– 0.871***	0.419	– 0.849***	0.428
Mixed layout	1.950***	7.030	– 1.451***	0.234
Good env. quality	0.841**	2.319	0.947***	2.577
Duplex	– 1.713**	0.180	– 1.331**	0.264
Flat	0.716	2.045	0.423	1.526
3+ rooms	– 0.350	0.705	– 0.422	0.656
Large rooms (3 × 4 m^2)	– 1.167***	0.311	– 0.372*	0.689
Well	2.005***	7.426	1.013***	2.753
1 bath and 1 toilet	3.213***	24.844	2.432***	11.379
Untiled kitchen	0.179	1.197	0.465*	1.593
Poor interior quality	– 0.277	0.758	– 0.446*	0.640
Owner	0.190	1.209	– 0.881***	0.415
<N200,000	2.403***	11.052	0.739*	2.093
N201-N400,000	1.870***	6.491	0.934***	2.545
Intercept	– 4.592***	–	– 0.286	–
Model parameters	**Number of observation = 1485; -2Loglikelihood = 1723.922 Chi-square χ^2 = 1003.110; p = 0.000 McFadden ρ^2 = 0.330**			

*Significant at $p < 10\%$, **Significant at $p < 5\%$, ***Significant at $p < 1\%$

7.3.2 *Determinants of Housing Preferences in Lagos*

A major objective of the study is the determination of factors that influence housing choices in the study area. In order to determine the predictors of the choices exhibited in the study area, a MNL model is fitted using the housing type choice as a dependent variable and the household characteristics as independent variables. Results as displayed in Table 7.11 show information on the results of the attributes of households that determine their choice of house selected. The children in the household, marital status, age, number of children above 18, income, length of stay in Lagos are very important in determining the housing choices of the households as they have odd ratios greater than 1.0 on each attribute. According to Table 7.11, households based on the number of children, with odd ratio 1.38, prefer duplex to other forms of housing unit, while the married, with odd ratio 1.94, prefer multiunit to other type of unit, the older households, with odd ratio 5.73 and 6.90, prefer duplex more; households with more children above 18 years with odd ratio 8.17, prefer duplex more; households that spent below 10 years with odd ratio 2.13, prefer multiunit dwellings; the model is significant in all the three housing choices and though the McFadden ρ^2 of 0.090 is rather quite low signifying the fact that there are other variables that account for variance in the data.

A number of households' variables that determine housing choices are significant. Out of these significant variables, income is the most significant statistically. Looking at the variables again one will only conclude that income level (affordability) is the decisive determinant of residential choices in Lagos. This is the variable that is statistically significant at 1% confidence levels across the housing types. The beta coefficients of the values in Table 7.11 show the impact of households' variables on the probability of choosing residential type—flat, multiunit or duplex. With regard to flat dwelling units, variables such number of children, single and married status, 21–40 and 41–60 years old, households with 1–3 and 4–7 children above 18 years, work experience, 5 years and less and 6–10 years of stay in Lagos have more influence on the probability of choosing flat unit. On the other hand, variables such as female households' heads, 1–2 and 3–6 households' members, primary education, secondary education and income contribute less to the probability of households choosing flat compared to multiunit dwellings. With regard to duplex dwelling units, variables like number of children, age 21–40 and 41–60 years, households with 1–3 and 4–7 children above 18 years, work experience, and 6–20 years of stay in Lagos impact positively on the probability of choosing duplex compared to multiunit dwelling. But households' variables such as female, single, married, secondary school and income contribute less to the prediction of the probability of choosing duplex units in comparison with multiunit dwelling units.

7.3.3 Estimating Residential Quality Choices Based on the Marital Status of Households

An attempt was made to estimate the variations in housing choices based on socioeconomic status of households in Lagos. The first MNL model to be estimated in this respect is for the prediction of the housing quality and home choices of households based on their marital status. We used three categories of marital status: the single, the married and the widowed/divorced. However, the divorced/widowed was taken as the reference category (see Table 7.12). The results of multinomial model across marital status as shown in Table 7.12 indicate that both the single and married households compared to the divorced households share similar sentiments on certain important housing quality variables except in accessibility, security, house type, number of rooms, kitchen and rent. Actually, the single households have more preference for closer neighborhood 5 km and above to place of work, market, hospital and relations going by their positive beta values and their corresponding odd ratios that are greater than 1.0. The single and the married households conversely prefer less, areas with limited accessibility, security problem, duplex housing, one-room apartment, homes without potable water, 1 toilet and bath, and owner homes compared with the divorced. Besides metropolitan characteristics, space, relations, flat house type and land use, none of the remaining variables are significant in the two marital groups. Interestingly, the model is significant at 1% confidence levels as shown by the intercept values of 18.13 and 20.61, respectively. The preference for house rent among the households differs as the married have 0.21 times less preference for lower house rents while the single households have 3.24 times more preference for lower house rents. These preference behaviors are understandable especially when viewed from the fact that most of the single households occupy multiunit one-room apartments which cost less. The most essential residential quality variables that contribute to the households' residential preference prediction are perhaps the metropolitan area and space of residences. A cursory look at the odd ratios of residential quality variables in Table 7.12 again shows that the married households in comparison with the divorced households have more preference for neighborhood 3 km and above to work, market, hospital, and far from friends, limited accessibility, formal security, poor exterior quality, multiunit housing, small rooms and poor interior quality units.

7.3.4 Estimating Residential Quality Choices Based on Households' Age

The second MNL model fitted on the household attributes was to predict the residential choices of households based upon their age differentials. In the study the age groups are three: the young that are 21–40 years, the active adults that are 41–60 years and the old groups that are 61 years and above. The old-aged group is the reference group. Results from the estimations are presented in Table 7.13. Information in Table 7.13 contains parameters on another multinomial model of residential quality across age groups using nineteen variables. The metropolitan variable provided inconsistent and awkward coefficients on the model and was promptly removed. The remaining variables give significant results at 5% level of statistical confidence. Along age groups, Lagos households display marked variations in the choice of quality variables and these differences in many instances are significant. For instance, compared to the young households the middle-aged households prefer 1.005 times more, 1.024 times more, 1.180 times more, places that are 5 km and more to work, market and school, respectively. The middle-aged households also have 0.17 and 0.687 times less preference for places that are 5 km and more distance to hospitals and places of worship, respectively. They also exhibit higher preference for places with limited accessibility (odd ratio 1.576 times more), formal security (odd ratio 1.268 times more), poor exterior quality environment (odd ratio 1.590 times more), flat units (odd ratio 1.573 times more), 1–2 living rooms (1.629 times more), small room (1.051 times more), 1 bath and toilet homes (1.748) and poor interior units (1.260 times more).

On the other hand, compared to the young age group the older households prefer neighborhood 1.871 times more, 1.738 times more, 1.361 times more places that are 3 km and more to work, school and hospital, respectively. They also have more predilections for neighborhoods with limited accessibility, poor environmental quality, flat, 1–2 rooms, 1 bath and toilet, poor interior quality and owner tenure. Only few of these variables are, however, significant, and this implies that not all of them are actually important to housing choice decision making by the age groups.

7.3.5 Estimating Residential Quality Choices Based on Income Groups

The third MNL model was fitted to examine variations in residential quality choice probabilities across households based on their incomes. We have four income groups, and the reference group is the rich-very-high-income-earning group. Since from the theoretical and empirical points of view, house seekers make real choices by actual effective demand, it is crucial that the influence of income on residential choice making be examined. Results from the analysis are presented in Table 7.14. The third multinomial model was fitted to see the influence of income status of households on their residential quality choices. Results in Table 7.14 show that there are consistent variations in the residential quality of households among the different income groups in the city of Lagos. Compared with the very rich group (the reference category), the low-income, middle-income and high-income households show less odd probabilities of staying in the three locations of Lagos that is, core city, outer city and suburbs.

There are more consistent odd probabilities among the three groups compared to the very rich households to prefer neighborhoods that are far from work, have limited accessibility, houses with 1–2 rooms, possess well water, untiled kitchen, interior equality and low rents. The low and the medium-income earners have high preference for both N100,000–N200,000 and N201,000–N400,000 rents compared with the very rich households. There is general less likelihood that the lower-, middle- and high-income households would prefer neighborhoods far from market, school and hospital, close relations, mixed layout, multiunit and flat and owner tenure. The significance of these variables, especially metropolitan, place of work, market, school and rent, makes the results more interesting. It is however quite interesting to note that the huge odd ratios of housing structural quality variables such as water, kitchen and interior quality are statistically significant at all three confidence levels. On the whole, the model is very significant at 1% considering their intercept values of 17.199, 19.522 and 18.446 (see Table 7.14 last two rows). The MNL model adequately predicted the residential choices of respondents given the McFadden ρ^2 value of 0.207.

7.3.6 Estimating Residential Choices by Metropolitan Location

A logit model was fitted to examine the influence of location within the city on households' dwelling choices. The metropolitan characteristic variable was regressed against the residential quality variables, and the results are presented in Table 7.15. Out of the three locations, the city suburb is taken as reference location. The pattern of the revealed residential quality preferences is made apparent by examining the odd ratios of residential quality variables within the study area, and this is done by comparing their odd ratios with one another. As displayed in Table 7.15, the odd ratios of residential variable values in the city core compared with those of outer city core reveal striking variation in magnitudes. The intercept value (− 0.286) for the outer city, is however not significant at 1%, 5% or 10% levels of confidence. Compared with the city core, households are more interested in neighborhoods that are close to places of work, market and school.

This spatial behavior is consistent with the earlier findings from the analysis of the marital, age and income groups. Lagos households in the core city and outer core city areas are more likely to dwell in housing units with 1 toilet, untiled kitchen, 1–2 rooms, well water and low rents per annum compared to households in the suburb. The explanation for this emerging pattern of housing behavior among the households in core city and outer core city areas compared to those in the suburb is anchored on the high socioeconomic status of the households. The McFadden ρ^2 value of 0.33 shows that the MNL model predicted the outcomes of the choices quite adequately. Generally, the McFadden ρ^2 that accompanies MNL model estimations though tries in theory to mimic the R^2 in the linear regression models is considerably lower than the R^2 in the OLS. There is no evidence that a higher value of ρ^2 can generate more significant model results as the value does not actually determine the significance of the model. A relatively small value of ρ^2 may be very meaningful (Huang and Clark 2002).

7.4 Testing of Hypotheses

Two hypotheses were tested for veracity in this chapter, and they are:

Research Hypothesis II: Ho2: The residential quality variables that shape housing choices could not be explained by few variables. **Ha2:** The residential quality variables that shape housing choices could be explained by few variables. The second hypothesis in this study concerns about the essential residential quality variables that actually shape housing preference formation of home renters and buyers. The essence of this hypothesis is to re-emphasize the impossibility of using the whole residential quality variables when searching for residential dwellings given affordability. From the PCA analysis done in this section, it is evident that residential quality variables that influence housing choices can be summarized in few components and these are majorly dwelling facility, location proximity, exterior, interior and neighborhood integrity. Hence, the null hypothesis is rejected. **Research Hypothesis III: Ho3:** Socioeconomic and lifecycles variables are not significant predictors of housing preferences. **Ha3:** Socioeconomic and lifecycles variables are significant predictors of housing preferences.

The third hypothesis examines the role of households' characteristics in home choice formation. Evidence from the study as shown in Sect. 5.11 has however confirmed the fact that not all socioeconomic and demographic variables are important in predicting housing choices. The most important variable is household's income which is directly linked to affordability. Three other variables, namely age, number of children and children above 18 years, are partially significant predictors of dwelling preferences in the study area. Hence, the hypothesis is not wholly true and therefore is rejected.

7.5 Summary

Analyses so far performed in this section of the book present the revealed residential quality and preferences of households in Lagos as observed in real-life situations. The quality of housing units of the respondents displayed both intra-group and spatial variations. There are differences between one group of households based upon their demographic and economic status as there are variations between households according to their location in the city. In the earlier part of the chapter, the twenty residential quality variables in the three distinct residential density areas are subjected to Factor Analysis (PCA). In understanding the patterns of choices in the study areas, analysis using the PCA was made to discover the underlying few components that could summarize the variables without a serious loss of information. This was successfully achieved as eight components were extracted to represent the twenty variables. These variables are the use value, location value, exterior value, interior value, neighborhood integrity, social bond, barrier to entry and safety. There are however striking similarities and little differences in the arrangement of components within the three residential density areas. The variations have been ascribed to the socioeconomic and cognitive status of the households. The spatial variations are indeed not unexpected as there are clear differences in the housing markets within the Lagos city. These are graphically represented by the maps generated from the component scores of the PCA.

The multinomial analysis of the revealed preference that was predicated upon the residential quality observed in the study areas shows some interesting results. Four multinomial logit models were estimated to predict the effects of housing quality on home choices. The results show the influence of location, and structural quality as well as prices of dwellings on residential types. Also, another five models were estimated to estimate the influence of households' characteristics on home choices and to determine the variation in residential choices across marital, age and income groups. The models are relatively significant and adequate to explain the variation in odd ratios of the households' residential quality choices across varying groups of residents in the study area. The results specifically reveal that Lagos households choose dwelling units based on location, neighborhood and structural quality of housing units. The place of work plays tremendous influence on the choice decision making, as in all the models estimated constant preferences are given more to neighborhoods that are close than to those that are far from the metropolis. The issue of affordability which underscores the crucial role of income in housing choices was adequately revealed in the study as the majority of the households prefer less costly units to N401,000–N800,000 per annum units. The spatial pattern of the choices also reveals the proclivity of the households in the HRD and MRD towards lower rent regimes compared with those in the LRD. There are apparent preferences for rooming homes, with well water, untiled kitchen, and 1 toilet by the residents in HRD and MRD compared with those in LRD. While this trend contrasts their demographic structure (more married and larger household sizes), the economic limitation might have guided their actions. Summarily, this chapter has clearly presented the results from the revealed choices and in the next chapter the discourse shifts to the results of analysis from the stated preference perspectives.

References

Cirman A (2006) Housing tenure Preferences in the Post-privatization period: the case of Slovenia. Hous Stud 21(1):113–134

Earnhart D (2001) Combining revealed and stated preference methods to value environmental amenities at residential locations. Land Econ 77(1):12–29

Hardy M, Bryan A (eds) (2006) Handbook on data analysis. SAGE, London

Huang Y, Clark WAV (2002) Housing tenure in transitional Urban China: a multilevel analysis. Urban Stud 39(1):3–7

Robinson MG (1998) Methods and techniques in human geography. John Wiley, New York

Tayyaran MR, Khan MA (2007) Telecommuting and residential location decisions: combined stated and revealed preferences model. Can J Civ Eng 34:1324–1333

Wang D, Li S-M (2004) Housing preferences in a transitional housing system: the case of Beijing China. Environ Plan A 36:69–87

Chapter 8
Residential Quality and Conjoint Housing Preferences in Lagos

Abstract The revealed preferences have shown that the available dwelling units and their quality attributes have to do with some prevailing condition within housing markets and of course, the households' socioeconomic and demographic circumstances. In this way, the revealed preference actually depicts the real behavior of consumers when looking for dwelling units to accommodate. The quality of the housing unit available is what is obtainable at that given period of time. Quite different from this scenario is the stated preference which bases residential quality and choices on normative assumption of equality of conditions. In essence, stated preference deals with ideal needs and aspirations of consumers barring any constraints. Discussion in this chapter therefore takes five levels: analysis of residential quality variables that drive stated housing preferences, modeling of stated housing preferences, spatial polarization of residential quality and stated housing preferences and testing of hypothesis. Aside from the stated preference analysis, the results from the SMART analysis are also presented in this chapter.

Keywords Residential quality · Stated choice models · Hypotheses testing · SMART analysis · Determinants of home choices

This chapter considers the desired residential quality from the perspective of stated preferences. The only difference between revealed and stated preferences is that in the case of the former decisions had been made on the residential quality attributes of dwelling units, but in the latter case decisions are yet to be made on desired residential quality and choice of dwelling units. The revealed preferences have shown that the available dwelling units and their quality attributes have to do with some prevailing condition within the housing markets and of course, the households' socioeconomic and demographic circumstances. In this way, the revealed preference actually depicts the real behavior of consumers when looking for dwelling units to accommodate. The quality of the housing unit available is what is obtainable at that given period of time. Quite different from this scenario is the stated preference which bases residential quality and choices on normative assumption of equality of conditions. In essence, stated preference deals with ideal needs and aspirations of consumers barring any

© The Author(s), under exclusive license to Springer Nature Switzerland AG 2024

I. R. Aliu, *Urban Private Housing in Nigeria*, The Urban Book Series,
https://doi.org/10.1007/978-3-031-47432-3_8

constraints. Discussion in this chapter therefore takes five levels: analysis of residential quality variables that drive stated housing preferences, modeling of stated housing preferences, spatial polarization of residential quality and stated housing preferences and testing of hypothesis. Aside from the stated preference analysis, the results from the SMART analysis are also presented in this chapter.

8.1 Analysis of Residential Quality Variables that Drive Stated Housing Preferences

8.1.1 Variation in Residential Quality Preferences in the Housing Density Areas

In order to establish future residential quality and choice desires, aspirations and expectations of Lagos households, we decided to probe into their normative preferences. Out of the twenty-five residential quality variables that home seekers usually wish to maximize when searching for accommodation in urban areas eleven are categorized as neighborhood while fourteen belong to the dwelling structural variables. Individuals were asked to rate these variables in accordance with their preferences knowing fully that the rankings are without constraints. This free rating method offered unfettered amplitude for the respondents to make choices of their ideal residential quality characteristics; the opportunity denied in the revealed choice condition. Using the results of the PCA components generated in Chap. 7 and partly based on the research theory in Chap. 3, the stated residential quality variables are summarized along two levels: neighborhood and structural attribute importance (see Tables 8.1 and 8.2).

As depicted in Table 8.1, the mean values of the attribute ratings reflect expected variations across residential density areas. Both relations and recreation quality variables have lower means less than 4.0 on a scale of 0–6, and security has the highest means with values higher than 5.0 in all localities. As for the structural quality preferences information in Table 8.2 shows that Lagos households pay little attention to patio, lot size, room space and aesthetics in future housing. Two most important facilities are light and water. Number of rooms and toilets and baths are of moderate importance with mean values slightly lower than 4.0. Most of the low ratings comes from the HRD area mostly number of rooms, CBD, toilet, kitchen, New house, worship and Tenure (Table 8.2 column 3).

ANOVA results in Tables 8.3 and 8.4 further advance the evidence supporting spatial variations in the perception of residential quality variables as drivers of housing choices and the significance of the intergroup variations. Twenty-two of the residential quality variables display significant spatial variations as their F values are greater than the table value of 2.30 at 5% confidence levels. However, proximity to school ($F = 1.085$; $p > 0.05$) and hospital ($F = 0.452$; $p > 0.05$) neighborhood

Table 8.1 Mean parameters of stated neighborhood residential quality

Residential quality variable	Mean total (N = 1485)	Mean HRD ($N = 729$)	Mean MRD ($N = 486$)	Mean LRD ($N = 270$)
Neighborhood quality (total mean)	**47.200**	**47.2374**	**49.5596**	**48.5112**
CBD	4.1603	3.9781	4.3539	4.3037
Market	4.1293	4.0878	4.0658	4.3556
School	4.8296	4.8642	4.8148	4.7630
Hospital	4.8310	4.8560	4.8066	4.8074
Worship	4.0135	3.9204	4.0617	4.1778
Workplace	4.2815	4.1207	4.4156	4.4741
Relations	3.5313	3.3937	3.6996	3.6000
Layout	4.7852	4.5103	5.2387	4.7111
Recreation	3.3751	3.1001	3.7819	3.3852
Accessibility	4.6923	4.7682	4.6214	4.6148
Security	5.6000	5.6379	5.6996	5.3185

Note Values are means of residential quality variables on a scale of 0–6

Table 8.2 Mean parameters of stated residential structural quality

Residential quality variable	Mean total ($N = 1485$)	Mean HRD ($N = 729$)	Mean MRD ($N = 486$)	Mean LRD ($N = 270$)
Structural quality (total mean)	**45.300**	**47.3965**	**51.5679**	**49.926**
NROOM	3.9933	3.9396	4.0206	4.0889
Toilet/bath	3.8492	3.6379	4.0741	4.0148
Kitchen	4.0269	3.7888	4.2757	4.2222
Water	5.5232	5.5528	5.6049	5.2963
Light	5.7670	5.7915	5.8477	5.5556
RSpace	3.8007	3.6324	3.9424	4.0000
HouseType	4.1549	4.0576	4.2634	4.2222
Newhouse	4.0485	3.9040	4.2510	4.0741
Aesthetics	3.4088	3.0672	3.8230	3.5852
Patio	3.3266	3.0261	3.7037	3.4593
LotSize	3.3630	3.0590	3.7202	3.5407
Tenure	3.9596	3.9396	4.0412	3.8667
Cost (mean)	**8.670**	**8.7024**	**8.7078**	**8.8889**
Caution	4.6734	4.6612	4.6708	4.7111
Price/rent	4.0646	4.0412	4.0370	4.1778

Note Values are means of residential quality variables on a scale of 0–6

variables are not significant to the residents in their consideration for housing choices and caution ($F = 0.238; p > 0.05$) remain insignificant as a structural quality variable.

8.1.2 Analysis of Stated Housing Preferences by the SMART Method

The descriptive univariate analysis of the stated housing preference data in Sect. 8.1.1 does not provide sufficient evidence on the most important utilities among neighborhood, structural and cost quality that influence housing choices in Lagos. What was revealed in that section is simply the spatial pattern of the residential attribute mean rankings in the LRD, MRD and HRD areas of Lagos. It is bounden task in this study to determine the variations in utilities across the housing submarkets. This is appropriately done with the SMART analytical framework. Eight steps are taken in realizing this objective: the identification of the decision makers, identification of decision issue, outline of choices to be made, stating of value dimensions, ranking of dimensions, allocation of weights "W_i," calculation of scores "S_j" and estimation of utilities ($\Sigma\, w_i * s_j$).

Tables 8.5, 8.6, 8.7 and 8.8 present the results of the SMART analysis as found in the stated preference data. On the aggregate sample as presented in Table 8.5, it is discovered that Lagos households, all things being equal, would prefer flat housing units ($U_j = 38.3$) to either multiunit ($U_j = 23.4$) or duplex ($U_j = 37.5$). They make their residential choice decisions based upon their perception of neighborhood quality variables ($U_j = 47.2$) compared to the structural ($U_j = 44.3$) and cost quality ($U_j = 7.7$) variables. Table 8.6 presents another dimension of the SMART results in HRD which show that respondents prefer the flat dwelling units ($U_j = 38.3$) compared with duplex ($U_j = 37.4$) and multiunit ($U_j = 23.3$). The neighborhood aspect of the house rather than the structural quality and cost takes precedence in their housing choice decision making.

While the residential choices of households in the HRD are very similar to the overall choice pattern, the choice behavior of households in the MRD and the HRD presents a different pattern completely. The households in MRD and HRD areas express a greater preference for the duplex housing units than the multiunit and flat dwelling units. In the MRD, the duplex unit with $U_j = 42.2$ and neighborhood attribute with $U_j = 47.9$ are mostly preferred by the respondents. In a similar fashion, households in the LRD also preferred more the duplex unit with $U_j = 42.8$ than flat $U_j = 38.4$ and multiunit $U_j = 23.1$. The pattern of residential choice behaviors in the study areas can be seen in the utility values displayed in Tables 8.7 and 8.8.

The spatial pattern of the SMART utilities indicating the first most preferred and second most preferred housing units is also reinforced by the maps presented in Figs. 8.1 and 8.2, respectively. The first map was generated from the first most preferred housing units in the LRD, MRD and HRD areas, while the second map was generated from the second most preferred housing units in the areas. According

Table 8.3 ANOVA of stated neighborhood quality preferences

Residential quality variable	Source of variance	Sum of squares	DF	Mean square	*F*	Sig
CBD	Between group variation	47.983	2	23.992	42.435	0.000
	Within group variation	837.873	1482	0.565		
	Total	885.856	1484			
Workplace	Between Group Variation	37.604	2	18.802	35.874	0.000
	Within Group Variation	776.737	1482	0.524		
	Total	814.341	1484			
Relations	Between group variation	28.843	2	14.422	14.164	0.000
	Within group variation	1508.951	1482	1.018		
	Total	1537.794	1484			
Accessibility	Between group variation	8.261	2	4.131	4.114	0.017
	Within group variation	1488.100	1482	1.004		
	Total	1496.361	1484			
Landuse	Between group variation	156.522	2	78.261	87.077	0.000
	Within group variation	1331.952	1482	0.899		
	Total	1488.474	1484			
Security	Between group variation	27.258	2	13.629	21.879	0.000
	Within group variation	923.142	1482	0.623		
	Total	950.400	1484			
Market	Between group variation	17.035	2	8.517	26.849	0.000
	Within group variation	470.141	1482	0.317		
	Total	487.176	1484			
School	Between group variation	2.178	2	1.089	1.085†	0.338
	Within group variation	1487.719	1482	1.004		
	Total	1489.896	1484			

(continued)

Table 8.3 (continued)

Residential quality variable	Source of variance	Sum of squares	DF	Mean square	*F*	Sig
Hospital	Between group variation	0.894	2	0.447	0.452†	0.636
	Within group variation	1465.681	1482	0.989		
	Total	1466.575	1484			
Worship	Between group variation	14.730	2	7.365	14.048	0.000
	Within group variation	777.000	1482	0.524		
	Total	791.731	1484			
Recreation	Between group variation	135.567	2	67.783	66.592	0.000
	Within group variation	1508.511	1482	1.018		
	Total	1644.078	1484			

Note †Value of "*F*" not significant at either 1% or 5% confidence level

to Fig. 8.1, both LRD and MRD have highest preference for the duplex unit and the HRD have highest preference for flat units. Conversely, in Fig. 8.2, the second most preferred housing unit in the LRD and MRD is flat unit, while the second choice in the HRD is duplex. The last preference in all the residential density area is the same and it is multiunit housing (the map is not generated because it does not show any variation).

Having discovered the behavioral pattern of households with regard to their ideal housing choices, the central issue is to estimate what and how residential quality variables influence their behavior. This task is performed using the multinomial regression model which was employed preferably to estimate the part-worth utilities of choice alternatives. Section 8.2 deals with the modeling results of stated preferences observed in the study.

8.2 Stated Housing Preference Modeling Results

In Sect. 8.1.2 (stated preference variables), an elaborate explanation was given concerning the variables used in the stated preference experimentation. The 36 profiles were collapsed into 6 choice sets. Instead of using the whole profiles, we decided to limit the choices to six feasible options for which it is more certain that any respondent would have a predilection. The respondents were asked to simply choose one out of the six hypothetical dwellings given their affordability. The question was put: "Given your level of affordability and attribute combinations of the six houses which of them would you prefer?" These choice sets are aggregated and the

Table 8.4 ANOVA of stated dwelling quality preferences

Residential quality variable	Source of variance	Sum of squares	DF	Mean square	F-Ratio	Sig
NROOM	Between group variation	4.927	2	2.464	9.533	0.000
	Within group variation	383.005	1482	0.258		
	Total	387.933	1484			
Toilet/bath	Between group variation	64.542	2	32.271	33.641	0.000
	Within group variation	1421.669	1482	0.959		
	Total	1486.211	1484			
Kitchen	Between group variation	81.735	2	40.867	27.366	0.000
	Within group variation	2213.188	1482	1.493		
	Total	2294.923	1484			
Water	Between group variation	17.787	2	8.894	11.889	0.000
	Within group variation	1108.661	1482	0.748		
	Total	1126.448	1484			
Light	Between group variation	15.677	2	7.838	19.242	0.000
	Within group variation	603.706	1482	0.407		
	Total	619.383	1484			
Housetype	Between group variation	13.842	2	6.921	16.165	0.000
	Within group variation	634.535	1482	0.428		
	Total	648.377	1484			
Newhouse	Between group variation	35.338	2	17.669	13.920	0.000
	Within group variation	1881.171	1482	1.269		
	Total	1916.509	1484			
Rspace	Between group variation	41.137	2	20.568	35.450	0.000
	Within group variation	859.863	1482	0.580		
	Total	900.999	1484			

(continued)

Table 8.4 (continued)

Residential quality variable	Source of variance	Sum of squares	DF	Mean square	*F*-Ratio	Sig
Aesthetics	Between group variation	176.857	2	88.429	102.062	0.000
	Within group variation	1284.029	1482	0.866		
	Total	1460.886	1484			
Patio	Between group variation	139.709	2	69.855	77.321	0.000
	Within group variation	1338.890	1482	0.903		
	Total	1478.599	1484			
Lotsize	Between group variation	137.905	2	68.953	73.864	0.000
	Within group variation	1383.458	1482	0.934		
	Total	1521.363	1484			
Tenure	Between group variation	5.854	2	2.927	7.432	0.001
	Within group variation	583.721	1482	0.394		
	Total	589.576	1484			
Caution	Between group variation	0.496	2	0.248	0.238†	0.788
	Within group variation	1542.103	1482	1.041		
	Total	1542.599	1484			
Price/rent	Between group variation	4.229	2	2.114	8.571	0.000
	Within group variation	365.565	1482	0.247		
	Total	369.794	1484			

Note †Value of "*F*" not significant at either 1% or 5% confidence level

variables are coded in interactive method. The dependent variable is the choice of a home with different attributes, and the results are as depicted in Table 8.9.

Results of the experimental stated preference data analysis in Table 8.9 and graphically displayed in Fig. 8.3 indicate that out of the six choices put across to the households to select from, Lagos households mostly prefer CHOICE 3 (34.3%), closely followed by CHOICE 4 (33.6%), next CHOICE 2 (21.0%), then CHOICE 5 (5.0%), then CHOICE 1 (3.1%) and lastly CHOICE 6 (2.4%). However, there is an apparent spatial polarization of choices across the residential density areas in Lagos. For instance, the most preferred housing choice by the HRD residents is CHOICE 3 with 39.8% of them going for the choice, while in the MRD the most preferred housing choice is CHOICE 4 as 42.2% of them choose this choice, and likewise the most

Table 8.5 SMART utilities of residential quality variables (ARD)

Residential choice of households	Choice value dimensions				Utility of residential choices (U_j)	Rank based on utility
	Weight	Max. NQ	Max. SQ	Min. cost		
Multiunit	W	0.2	0.2	0.6	**23.4**	3rd
	S	47.2	44.3	8.5		
	w * s	**9.4**	**8.9**	**5.1**		
Flat	W	0.4	0.4	0.2	**38.3**	1st
	S	47.2	44.3	8.5		
	w * s	**18.9**	**17.7**	**1.7**		
Duplex	W	0.4	0.4	0.1	**37.5**	2nd
	S	47.2	44.3	8.5		
	w * s	**18.9**	**17.7**	**0.9**		
Total		47.2	44.3	7.7	99.15	

Note NQ neighborhood, *SQ* structural quality, *ARD* total sample

Table 8.6 SMART stated utilities of residential quality variables in the HRD

Residential choice of households	Choice value dimensions				Utility of residential choices (U_j)	Rank based on utility
	Weight	Max. NQ	Max. SQ	Min. Cost		
Multiunit	W	0.2	0.2	0.6	**23.3**	3rd
	S	45.7	45.8	8.4		
	w * s	**9.1**	**9.2**	**5.0**		
Flat	W	0.4	0.4	0.2	**38.3**	1st
	S	45.7	45.8	8.4		
	w * s	**18.3**	**18.3**	**1.7**		
Duplex	W	0.4	0.4	0.1	**37.4**	2nd
	S	45.7	45.8	8.4		
	w * s	**18.3**	**18.3**	**0.8**		
Total		45.7	44.3	7.7	99.15	

Note NQ neighborhood quality, *SQ* structural quality

preferred housing choice in LRD is CHOICE 4 as 52.2% of them indicated. As regards the type of housing choices made, information in Table 8.9 shows that majority of the households in Lagos prefer residing in the flat units (67.9%), followed by households that prefer multiunit with reasonable accessibility (38.0%), except households in MRD that prefer reasonable accessibility (14.1%), formal security (63.5%), 3-4 rooms (49.0%), small-parlor-large-room (89.2%), potable water (73.0%), N201,000–N400,000 rent (45.6%), and flat housing unit (67.9%). The spatial pattern of these distributions is regular except the accessibility in the MRD where respondents prefer

Table 8.7 SMART stated utilities of residential quality variables in the MRD

Residential choice of households	Choice value dimensions				Utility of residential choices (U_j)	Rank based on utility
	Weight	Max. NQ	Max. SQ	Min. Cost		
Multiunit	W	0.2	0.2	0.6	**23.1**	3rd
	S	45.1	47.0	7.9		
	w * s	**9.0**	**9.4**	**4.7**		
Flat	W	0.4	0.4	0.2	**38.4**	2nd
	S	45.1	47.0	7.9		
	w * s	**18.0**	**18.8**	**1.6**		
Duplex	W	0.5	0.4	0.1	**42.2**	1st
	S	45.1	47.0	7.9		
	w * s	**22.6**	**18.8**	**0.8**		
Total		47.9	44.3	7.7	99.15	

Note NQ Neighborhood quality, *SQ* structural quality

Table 8.8 SMART stated utilities of residential quality variables in the LRD

Residential choice of households	Choice value dimensions				Utility of residential choices (U_j)	Rank based on utility
	Weight	Max. NQ	Max. SQ	Min. Cost		
Multiunit	W	0.2	0.2	0.6	**23.1**	3rd
	S	51.6	40.6	7.8		
	w * s	**10.3**	**8.1**	**4.7**		
Flat	W	0.4	0.4	0.2	**38.4**	2nd
	S	51.6	40.6	7.8		
	w * s	**20.6**	**16.2**	**1.6**		
Duplex	W	0.5	0.4	0.1	**42.8**	1st
	S	51.6	40.6	7.8		
	w * s	**25.8**	**16.2**	**0.8**		
Total		56.7	40.5	7.1	99.1	

Note NQ neighborhood quality, *SQ* structural quality

location with reasonable accessibility to high accessibility. The Chi-square distribution statistics shows that for all the eight residential quality preferences there is significant interlocation independence with values highly significant at 1% level of confidence. Incidentally, the descriptive analysis of choices and residential quality variables done in Table 8.9 cannot enforce explanation of choice behavior of households as potential home consumers. The task of predicting the choice behavior of households can only be achieved through the use of probabilistic models. Therefore, we turn to multinomial logit (MNL) models for a more penetrating explanation of

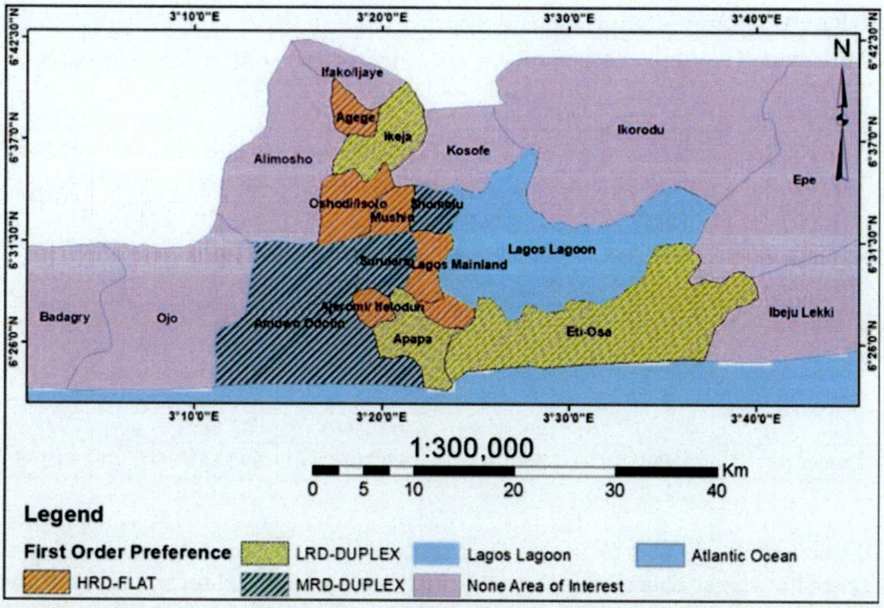

Fig. 8.1 Spatial pattern of housing preferences (first order) in Lagos Metropolis

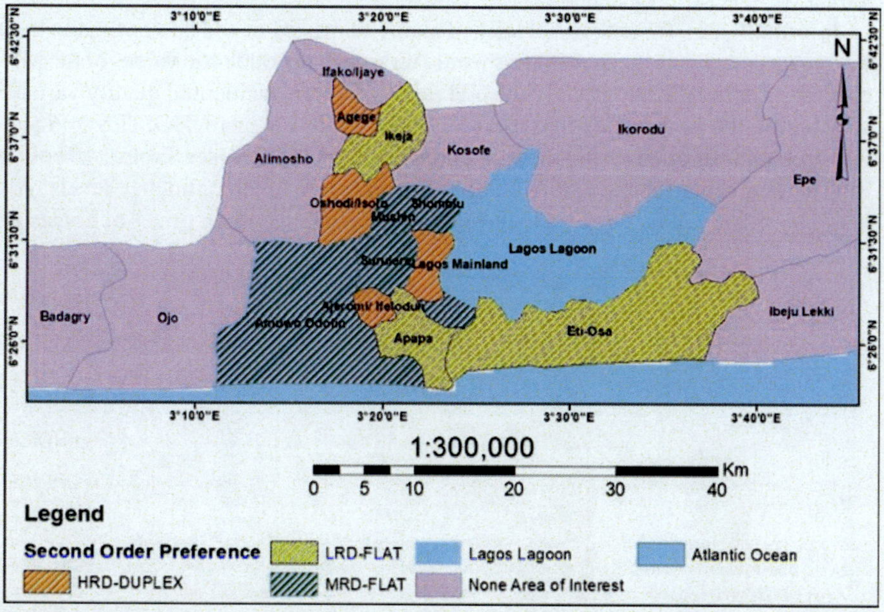

Fig. 8.2 Spatial pattern of housing preferences (second order) in Lagos Metropolis

Table 8.9 Summary of stated residential choices

Residential choice of households	Total = 1485 (%)	HRD = 729 (%)	MRD = 486 (%)	LRD = 270 (%)	Chi-square
CHOICE 1	46(3.1)	28(3.8)	18(3.7)	0(0.0)	$X^2 = 35.285$, $P = 0.000$
CHOICE 2	312(21.0)	213(29.2)	55(11.3)	44(16.3)	
CHOICE 3	**509(34.3)**	**290(39.8)**	171(35.2)	49(18.1)	
CHOICE 4	499(33.6)	153(21.0)	**205(42.2)**	**141(52.2)**	
CHOICE 5	83(5.6)	31(4.3)	24(4.9)	28(10.4)	
CHOICE 6	36(2.4)	14(1.9)	13(2.7)	8(3.0)	
House type—multiunit	358(24.1)	241(33.0)	73(15.0)	44(16.3)	$X^2 = 176.718$, $P = 0.000$
Flat	1008(67.9)	443(60.8)	376(77.4)	190(70.3)	
Duplex	119(8.0)	45(6.2)	37(7.6)	36(13.4)	

the households making choice decision. Four multinomial models were fitted on the stated preference data used in the study. First, the MNL model for whole sample was estimated, second is the MNL for HRD, third is the MNL for the MRD and fourth is the MNL for LRD. The results of the MNL model estimations are as presented in Tables 8.10, 8.11, 8.12 and 8.13.

Information in Table 8.10 actually contains estimates of the choices made in the aggregate data that is in the ARD. As would be seen in the odd ratio values of the MNL estimates for the ARD, virtually the odd ratios of all the residential quality variables selected by the households that prefer CHOICE 1 as against CHOICES 2–6 show less probabilities of choosing the residential quality variables (see Table 8.10 column 8). The intercepts for the Choices are all significant at 1% confidence levels. Also very importantly, it is observed that choices are predicated upon prices of homes and

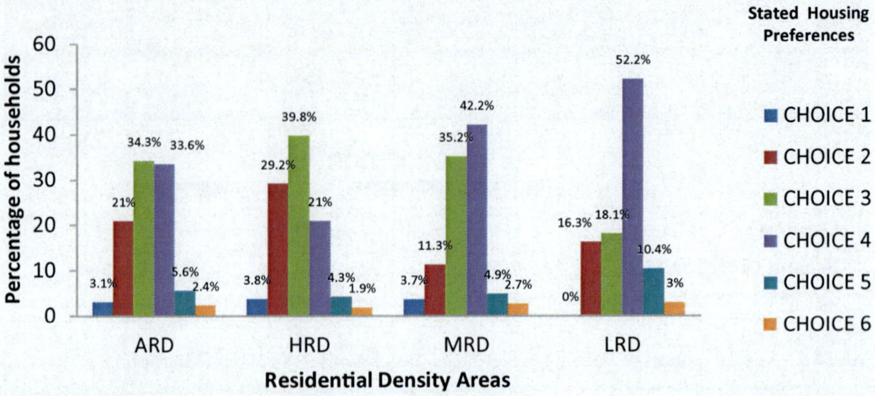

Fig. 8.3 Spatial pattern of stated housing choices/preferences

Table 8.10 MNL odd ratios for estimating stated residential choices

Residential quality variable	CHOICE 2		CHOICE 3		CHOICE 4		CHOICE 5		CHOICE 6	
	B	Exp (*B*)	*B*	Exp (*B*)	*B*	Exp (*B*)	*B*	Exp (*B*)	*B*	Exp (*B*)
Intercept	4.089***		4.086***		5.424***		4.258***		3.929***	
Metro location City core	– 0.593	0.553	– 0.681	0.506	– 0.906	0.404	– 0.431	0.650	– 1.452*	0.234
Outer city core	– 0.448	0.639	– 0.221	0.802	– 0.804	0.447	– 0.606	0.545	– 0.732	0.481
Accessibility Limited	– 0.131	0.877	– 0.077	0.926	– 0.259	0.772	– 0.706	0.494	– 0.495	0.610
Reasonable	– 0.808*	0.446	– 0.545	0.580	– 0.690	0.502	– 1.089**	0.337	– 0.595	0.551
Prox to market Market within 5 km+	– 0.705	0.494	– 0.568	0.567	– 0.442	0.643	– 0.383	0.682	– 1.136*	0.321
3–5 km	– 0.116	0.890	– 0.376	0.687	– 0.104	0.902	– 0.061	0.941	– 0.692	0.500
Number of rooms 1–2 rooms	– 0.759	0.468	– 0.775	0.461	– 0.645	0.525	– 0.963*	0.382	– 1.409**	0.244
3–4 rooms	– 0.328	0.720	– 0.234	0.792	– 0.160	0.852	– 0.104	0.901	– 0.960	0.383
Room space Small (3 × 3 m^2)	– 0.569	0.566	– 0.555	0.574	– 1.236	0.290	– 1.643**	0.193	– 1.121	0.326
Water Well	– 0.379	0.684	– 0.053	0.948	– 0.233	0.792	– 0.473	0.623	– 0.715	0.489
House rent < N200,000	0.052	1.053	0.272	1.312	– 0.388	0.678	– 0.452	0.636	0.033	1.034
N201-400,000	0.418	1.519	0.449	1.567	0.011	1.011	– 0.214	0.807	0.300	1.350

The reference category is CHOICE 1
*Significant at $p < 10\%$, **Significant at $p < 5\%$, ***Significant at $p < 1\%$

Table 8.11 MNL odd ratios for estimating stated residential choices in HRD

Residential quality variable	CHOICE 2		CHOICE 3		CHOICE 4		CHOICE 5		CHOICE 6	
	B	Exp (*B*)	*B*	Exp (*B*)	*B*	Exp (*B*)	*B*	Exp (*B*)	*B*	Exp (*B*)
Intercept	20.478***		21.210***		20.584***		19.993***		3.376	
Metro location City core	0.077	1.080	– 0.153	0.858	– 0.983	0.374	0.594	1.812	– 1.298	0.273
Outer city core	– 0.074	0.928	– 0.223	0.800	– 1.411	0.244	– 0.259	0.772	– 0.561	0.571
Accessibility Limited	– 0.007	0.993	0.113	1.120	0.085	1.089	– 0.577	0.562	– 0.564	0.569
Reasonable	– 1.534***	0.216	– 1.356*	0.258	– 1.858***	0.156	– 1.911***	0.148	– 1.111	0.329
Prox to market 5 km+	– 0.918	0.399	– 0.944	0.389	– 1.241*	0.289	– 1.361	0.256	– 1.474	0.229
3-5 km	0.577	1.781	0.120	1.127	0.418	1.518	0.626	1.871	– 1.383	0.251
Number of rooms 1–2 Rooms	– 1.452*	0.234	– 1.464*	0.231	– 0.683	0.505	– 1.342	0.261	– 1.202	0.301
3–4 Rooms	– 1.381*	0.251	– 1.336*	0.263	– 0.487	0.614	– 0.788	0.455	– 1.877	0.153
Room space Small (3×3 m^2)	– 15.737***	1.46E–007	– 16.533***	6.61E–008	– 15.479***	1.90E–007	– 16.592***	6.22E–008	0.451***	1.570
Water Well	– 0.733	0.480	– 0.326	0.722	– 0.719	0.487	– 1.397*	0.247	– 1.320	0.267
House rent < N200,000	– 0.660	0.517	– 0.118	0.889	– 0.972	0.378	– 0.653	0.521	– 0.886	0.412
N201000-400,000	0.386	1.471	0.469	1.598	0.113	1.120	– 0.535	0.586	0.579	1.784

The reference category is CHOICE 1
*Significant at $p < 10\%$, ***Significant at $p < 5\%$, ***Significant at $p < 1\%$

Table 8.12 MNL odd ratios for estimating stated residential choices in MRD

Residential quality variable	CHOICE 2		CHOICE 3		CHOICE 4		CHOICE 5		CHOICE 6	
	B	Exp (*B*)	*B*	Exp (*B*)	*B*	Exp (*B*)	*B*	Exp (*B*)	*B*	Exp (*B*)
Intercept	2.504		1.371		3.768***		– 0.579		– 13.503***	
Metro location City core	– 2.100*	0.122	– 1.625	0.197	– 1.796	0.166	– 2.119	0.120	– 1.186	0.306
Outer city core	– 1.871	0.154	– 0.596	0.551	– 0.975	0.377	– 0.969	0.379	– 0.740	0.477
Accessibility Limited	– 0.213	0.808	– 0.217	0.805	– 0.985	0.373	0.084	1.087	– 1.976	0.139
Reasonable	– 0.039	0.962	0.178	1.195	– 0.195	0.823	0.836	2.306	– 1.008	0.365
Prox to market Market within 5 km+	– 1.206	0.299	– 0.602	0.547	– 0.656	0.519	– 1.532	0.216	– 0.888	0.412
3–5 km	– 0.374	0.688	– 0.583	0.558	– 0.576	0.562	– 0.340	0.712	– 0.644	0.525
Number of rooms 1–2 rooms	– 0.601	0.548	– 0.665	0.514	– 0.507	0.602	– 0.710	0.492	– 1.779	0.169
3–4 rooms	0.987	2.684	0.941	2.563	0.679	1.972	1.129	3.094	0.484	1.622
Room space Small room	0.537	1.712	1.584	4.877	0.485	1.625	1.245	3.473	16.761***	1.90 E007
Water Well	0.109	1.116	0.668	1.951	0.406	1.500	1.764*	5.834	-0.317	0.729
House rent <N200,000	0.821	2.273	0.681	1.975	0.689	1.992	– 0.313	0.731	– 0.986	0.373
N201000–N400,000	0.175	1.192	0.354	1.424	– 0.064	0.938	– 0.359	0.698	– 0.648	0.523

The reference category is CHOICE 1
*Significant at $p < 10\%$, ***Significant at $p < 5\%$, ***Significant at $p < 1\%$

Table 8.13 MNL odd ratios for estimating stated residential choices in LRD

Residential quality variable	CHOICE 3		CHOICE 4		CHOICE 5		CHOICE 6	
	B	Exp (*B*)	*B*	Exp (*B*)	*B*	Exp (*B*)	*B*	Exp (*B*)
Intercept	– 0.098		1.289		0.214		– 18.149***	
Metro location City core	0.137	1.147	0.498	1.645	0.855	2.351	– 1.556	0.211
Outer city core	1.115	3.050	0.767	2.154	0.903	2.466	0.111	1.117
Accessibility Limited	– 0.536	0.585	– 0.667	0.513	– 1.591***	0.204	0.700	2.013
Reasonable	– 0.284	0.753	– 0.195	0.823	– 1.409*	0.244	0.225	1.253
Proximity to market Market within 5 km+	– 0.539	0.583	0.818	2.266	1.936***	6.929	1.080	2.946
3–5 km	0.068	1.070	0.422	1.525	0.736	2.088	1.275	3.580
Number of rooms 1–2 rooms	1.163	3.200	0.495	1.641	– 0.300	0.741	– 0.637	0.529
3–4 rooms	1.373*	3.945	0.509	1.664	0.349	1.418	– 0.805	0.447
Room space Small room	0.000	1.000	– 0.270	0.763	– 0.887	0.412	– 1.531	0.216
Water Well	– 0.068	0.934	0.375	1.455	0.075	1.077	– 0.245	0.782
House rent < N200,000	– 0.874	0.417	– 1.785***	0.168	– 1.769***	0.170	18.257***	8.5E007
N201000–N400,000	– 1.146*	0.318	– 1.395***	0.248	– 0.915	0.401	16.947***	2.3E007

The reference category is CHOICE 2 (nobody chose CHOICE 1 in the LRD)
*Significant at $p < 10\%$, ***Significant at $p < 5\%$, ***Significant at $p < 1\%$

the households that choose option CHOICE 1 (the reference category) lay greatest emphasis upon rent values more than the rest.

8.3 Spatial Polarization of Residential Quality and Stated Housing Preferences

Although we have presented the results of housing choices and residential quality based on the aggregate data in Sect. 8.2, there is need to explore the spatial pattern of the choices across residential density areas of Lagos. This was done by fitting three MNL models on the stated data split into residential density areas. The results are given in Tables 8.11, 8.12 and 8.13. The reference category for the choices is CHOICE 1 except in LRD where nobody chose CHOICE 1 making CHOICE 2 as the reference choice category. As given in Table 8.11, those households in the HRD that chose House 2 have a preference for city core and market at within 3–5 km. They also have less preference for outer city, high accessibility, reasonable accessibility, market within 0–2 km, 1–2 rooms, 3–4 rooms, large rooms, potable water and low rent housing units compared to those that choose CHOICE 1. Households that choose CHOICE 3 compared to CHOICE 1 have more preference for high accessibility and market within 3–5 km. Those that choose CHOICE 4 prefer dwellings that are located 3–5 km to market, highly accessible and rents within N200-4000, 000 per annum. Those that choose CHOICE 5 prefer to live in the core city and 3–5 km to market. And those who choose CHOICE 6 in preference for CHOICE 1 actually have less desire for virtually all the attributes save large rooms, and rents between N200,000 and N400,000.

Information in Table 8.12 represents the results of MNL estimation for the MRD. Those that choose CHOICE 2 have more preference for dwellings with 3–4 rooms, large rooms, potable water and lower rents to CHOICE 1 as can be gleaned from their odd ratios. Those households that choose CHOICE 3 as against CHOICE 1, given their odd ratios, prefer more locations that are reasonably accessible, dwellings with 3–4 rooms, large rooms and lower rents per annum. Similarly, from the odd ratio values in the same table it is apparent that households that choose CHOICE 4 over CHOICE 1 prefer 3–4 rooms, large rooms, potable water and the least rent per annum. Those that choose CHOICE 5 prefer neighborhood with high accessibility, 3–4 rooms, large rooms and potable water. The same for households that choose CHOICE 6 have more preference for only 3–4 rooms and large rooms.

For the LRD, Table 8.13 indicates that the households that choose CHOICE 3 as against CHOICE 2 prefer more city core, outer city, 3–5 km to market, 1–2 and 3–4 rooms and quite indifferent to room space. Those that choose CHOICE 4 prefer city core, outer city, 0–2 km, 3–5 km to market, 1–2 rooms and potable water. Those that choose CHOICE 5 also prefer city core and outer city, 0–2 km and 3–5 km to market, 3–4 rooms and potable water. Lastly those that choose CHOICE 6 prefer the outer city, highly and reasonably accessible neighborhood, 0–2 km and 3–5 km to market and lower rents per annum.

8.4 Testing of Hypotheses

The fourth hypothesis set and tested in this study states that

Research Hypothesis IV: **Ho4**: *There is no significant variation in the preferred residential quality variables within the study area.* **Ha4**: *There is a significant variation in the preferred residential quality variables within the study area.* According to the results of the Analysis of Variance ANOVA presented in Tables 8.3 and 8.4, there are significant variations in the residential quality variables in the study area. Virtually all neighborhood residential quality variables save two and all structural quality variables save one display significant variations in the twelve LGAs under study. Hence, on the strength of these variations evidence emanating from the study supports the hypothesis that actually there are significant variations in the residential quality variables across locations at both 0.01 and 0.05 levels of confidence. The null hypothesis is not true and therefore is rejected and the alternative hypothesis is accepted.

8.5 Summary

This chapter in contrast to Chap. 7 has dealt with the stated preferences exhibited by the households in Lagos. The analysis was made at three levels. One, the perceived preferences based upon ranking of residential quality variables were described and estimated using means of rankings and later ANOVA to determine variations among the groups and within the groups. The means of the residential quality variables indicate a higher perception of neighborhood variables over those of structural variables. Beside recreation and closeness to relations variables, no other neighborhood variable has less than 4.0 as mean. The ANOVA results also indicate that the intermarket variations are quite significant on all variables except school, hospital and caution (either at 5% or 1% alpha). Two, SMART analysis of SP data using the additive model of scores and weights was made. Results from the analysis indicate that how house renters combine residential quality variables to form residential decisions. The value placed on the neighborhood components of the dwelling units is more significant than that placed upon the structural variables and these value differentials expose the behavior pattern of home seekers. On the account of housing type the SMART analysis shows that Lagos households would generally prefer flat unit to either multifamily unit or duplex. Three, the multinomial logit model was employed to estimate the importance of dwelling attributes in the prediction of housing choices. The findings from the MNL analysis indicate that while the models are significant the dwelling variables that significantly influenced housing choice prediction are very quite few—accessibility to public transport, number of rooms and room space. The analyses performed so far in this section emphasize at regular interval the importance of differentiations in the submarkets. The final chapter discusses the summary of findings in this study, their implications and recommendations in light of the current results.

Chapter 9
Discussion and Implications of Empirical Findings on Residential Quality and Housing Preferences

Abstract This part of the book gives the key findings, explanation of findings and implications of findings as presented in early chapters of the book. Since the early chapters of results have produced a lot of outputs that were interpreted, it is vitally important to summarize the findings and explain the significance and relevance of the results. The discussion of findings gives more elaborate justification for the study in line with the goal and objectives.

Keywords Housing preference outcomes · Socioeconomic factors · Residential quality factors · Neighborhood quality factors · Policy implications · Theoretical implications · Practical implications

This part of the book presents the discussion and implications of findings as given in early chapters of the book. Since the early chapters of results (Chaps. 6–8) produced a lot of outputs that were interpreted, it is vitally important to summarize the findings and explain the significance and relevance of the results. The discussion of findings gives more elaborate justification for the study in line with the goal and objectives.

9.1 Discussion of Findings

9.1.1 Households' Sociodemographic and Residential Characteristics

Five specific objectives were set right from the outset to be achieved in this study. A basic objective of this study is to first and foremost *describe and analyze the characteristics of households interviewed in this study*. In light of the immense importance of households' characteristics to the prediction of housing quality and choice decision-making process, the results are of great value to this study. The demographic and socioeconomic attributes of Lagos households that participated in the study display

© The Author(s), under exclusive license to Springer Nature Switzerland AG 2024

I. R. Aliu, *Urban Private Housing in Nigeria*, The Urban Book Series,
https://doi.org/10.1007/978-3-031-47432-3_9

a remarkable variation within the residential density areas and the variation in households' attributes are perhaps the basis for different preferences and tastes. It is found in this study that the married are in the majority 77.6%, the males are dominant 90.0%, and the middle-aged respondents are in the largest proportion 53.9%. Majority of the households 77.0% have 3-6 members, households with children above 18 years are 38.9%, the low and middle income groups are in the majority 92.2%, and households are fairly educated as they are mostly secondary school leavers 56.2% but graduates are also substantial 39.3%. Majority of the respondents are private workers, artisans and traders 83.2%, while 64.8% of them are Christians. Most of the households 57.9% have worked for 11–20 years, and 58.6% of them have stayed in Lagos for 21 years and above. The findings are consistent with recent studies in Lagos (Aliu and Adebayo 2010; Towry-Coker 2012). The findings about the households' characteristics in Lagos imply that the households under study are the type that can only fairly compete in the urban housing market with varying qualities and prices (Towry-Coker 2012; Aluko 2000). This observation is more amplified in the analysis of the revealed preference data, although the veracity of this submission is highly masked in the stated preference data. Several other studies in developing economies have confirmed the fact that majority of households in the cities is of low socioeconomic status and their dwellings display widespread variations in neighborhood and structural quality terms (see Rosenbaum 1996; Li 2000; Wang and Li 2004; Opoku and Abdul-Muhmin 2010).

The delineation of the study area into three differentiated housing markets provides a unique opportunity to observe the spatial differentials in the households' socioeconomic characteristics. The majority for instance of the lower income earners, lower educational attainments, artisans and traders, are found in the HRD, while the majority of the high-income earners, graduates and private workers lived in the LRD. The MRD area is dominated by medium-income earners, married group and secondary school holders. Since the household attributes influence tremendously the behavioral tendencies of home seekers, it is expected that they rub-off on the quality of dwellings available to the individuals across the submarkets. Rosenbaum (1996) discovered that residential quality reflects racial differences in New York as the White Anglo are much better in socioeconomic characteristics and therefore have better residential quality than say the Black Americans or Hispanic whites. The second objective of the study is to *analyze the spatial variations in the neighborhood and structural attributes of houses in the study area.* Descriptive analysis of neighborhood quality of dwellings revealed that only 42.0% of the respondents chose the outer city core neighborhood, compared to 34.3% that chose city core and 23.7% that chose suburban areas of the city. This pattern of metropolitan characteristics of respondents replicates in all the residential areas sampled. Spatial behavior is exhibited in their choices of dwellings and this is more evident in the proximity of their dwelling neighborhoods to place of work, market, school, hospital and religious sanctuaries. Further, analysis indicated that 54.5% found dwellings in close neighborhood to work, 68.1% live close to children schools, 65% live close to hospital, 56.2% live close to friends, 63.6% live close to market, 82.9% live in neighborhood with reasonable accessibility to transport route, 78.3% live in mixed layout areas,

94.9% in areas described as good environmentally and 82.5% live in neighborhood covered by formal security system-police stations.

Analysis showed that majority 66.1% of the respondents chose to live in multiunit dwellings, compared with 31.2% that chose flat and 2.7% that chose duplex dwelling units. Majority of the residents that chose duplex are from the LRD; majority that chose multiunits are from the HRD. Further, analysis indicated that well over half of the respondents live in 1–2 room 55%, while 45% live 3 or more rooms. Large room apartment dominates the study area as 56.9% of the respondents indicated and 43.1% live in small room space apartments. This might due to old dwellings that were constructed with large room standard at the time when land was not so costly in the metropolis. In terms of water sources, analysis indicated a prevalence of dwellings 59.3% with pipe-borne potable water as against residences with well water 40.7%. As regards toilets and baths investigation revealed that 41.6% have 1 bath and 1 toilet, while majority 58.4% live in dwellings with 2 toilets and baths or more. On the nature of kitchen analysis indicated that majority of the dwellings and households 78.2% have untiled kitchen. Dwellings with poor interior quality or 3–4 structural defects constitute 95.8%. Majority of the households making 59.6% are renters, and they chose to live in dwellings with annual rent within the range of N201, 000-N400, 000. On a general note, in terms of residential quality, it is observed that the households are generally accommodated in modestly standard dwelling units. This contradicts the old studies that attempted to depict residential dwellings of Lagos residents as generally substandard (see Abiodun 1976; Onibokun 1985). A major improvement in property maintenance over the year must have led to the level observed in the study presently. Twenty residential quality variables were used to describe the residential quality of Lagos residents. Among these residential quality variables, the residents performed only averagely well on the neighborhood and the structural variables.

9.1.2 Association Between Residential Quality and Household's Characteristics

In recognition of the third objective of this study (that states: *analyze the association among residential quality and socioeconomic characteristics of households*), analysis of the association between the residential quality of households and their characteristics was performed. Results indicate that there are fairly significant correlations between the two sets of variables. Three variables are much correlated, and these are income and house type, income and toilet and income and kitchen. The correlation between income and house type is $r = +0.349$, between income and toilet is $r = +0.395$ and between income and kitchen is $r = +0.375$. There are also significant correlations among other variables and household characteristics, but these correlations are quite low. This implies that there are serious variations within the data and less multicollinearity is probable. The variations in data are due to the variations in households residential and background information. What is important is the fact that there are quite noticeable and significant correlations between residential quality and households' characteristics. On the aggregate data, these correlations are consistently significant but not very highly. Aliu and Adebayo (2010) however noted a slightly semblance of the findings here but due to the limited spatial coverage of their study it may not be a definitive pronouncement on the bases for residential quality variation in Lagos. In a study of the determinants of residential quality in Ibadan Northern region, Ajala and Adelodun (2007) found a similar trend in housing quality variables correlation with household characteristics. However, the correlation results provide evidence in support of the first hypothesis that housing attributes have significant correlations with household's socioeconomic characteristics.

9.1.3 Spatial Pattern of Residential Quality and Housing Preferences Exhibited in Lagos

Objective four of the study actually deals with the need to *ascertain the spatial pattern of preferences for residential quality variables* in Lagos. The revealed preference analysis presented more interesting results. Starting with the correlations between the residential variables themselves, we noticed that there are with only few exceptions low correlations. The low correlations among the residential quality variables became more pronounced when the PCA analysis was carried out. From the PCA results, eight variables were extracted from a total of twenty variables. The first component accounted for 30.5% of the total variance, while the second accounted for 16.5% and the third accounted for just 8.6%. Other five variables, each on Kaiser Criterion had less than 1.0 Eigenvalue and 5.0% on the total variance observed in the data. This result confirms the veracity of the second hypothesis set in the study. Indeed there are only few residential quality variables that explain housing preference formation in the study area. This implies that the first component Dwelling Facility Quality is the most important component for explaining variation in residential density status of the households. Although this confirms previous studies (Kain and Quigley 1970; Cirman 2006; Choi and Kang 2010; Opoku and Abdul-Muhmin 2010; Aliu and Adebayo 2010), the findings from this study advance the evidence through the submarket variation estimations. Kain and Quigley (1970) extracted five components in their residential quality study using 35 variables, while Opoku and Abdul-Muhmin (2010) extracted 9 components to explain residential quality importance of Saudi low-income households. Evidence from relatively recent works on housing quality showed that the PCA can be employed to explore the influence of residential quality on tenure preferences (Cirman 2006; Choi and Kang 2010). In order to explain the spatial variation or polarization along the submarkets the total sample was disaggregated into three subsamples and their PCA estimated. The same trend except for the HRD was noticed in the arrangement and magnitude of loadings extracted. The spatial maps produced also bear credence to the spatial polarization of the residential quality and preferences exhibited in the study areas. The stated preference analysis carried out in this study produces useful results. Starting from the perception of important residential quality that dictates housing choices of urban residents, it is noticeable that without the constraints of affordability and vacancies, residents are highly disposed to high-quality dwellings.

Respondents prefer dwellings in reputable locations, with secured, good layout and good environmental quality. They also prefer dwelling units with large rooms, 3–4 rooms, water and lights, flush toilets and baths, as well as units with tiled kitchens. The choices were made based on the spatial differentiations that exist in the study area as depicted by the respective means of the RDAs. Specifically, the MRD performed better on the neighborhood variables having overall weight mean of 49.56, while the LRD performed better on the neighborhood variables only with overall mean of 48.51. Also on structural attributes MRD lead with overall mean of 51.57, followed by LRD 49.93 and HRD 47.34. However, ANOVA results indicated that two neighborhood variables—school and hospital and one structural variable caution—are insignificant to household housing preference formation going by their F values $F = 1.085$ ($p > 0.05$), $F = 0.452$ ($p > 0.05$) and $F = 0.238$ ($p > 0.05$) which are far lower than the statistical table values. The results from the ANOVA verify the fourth hypothesis, and indeed there are significant variations in the preferred residential attributes within the study area. The SMART analysis indicates a greater preference for the flat units ($U_j = 38.3$) in comparison with the multiunit ($U_j = 23.4$) and duplex housing units ($U_j = 37.5$). The neighborhood quality variables are more important in housing preference decision making than the structural and cost quality variables. The multinomial model estimates indicate that Choice 3 is the most preferred dwelling (34.6%) followed by choice 4 (33.6%). These two choice sets are actually flat dwelling units with different structural, neighborhood and quality cost qualities. The flat dwelling from these results appears to be the most popular home preference of households, all other things being equal, as it shows dominant proportion in HRD 60.8%, MRD 77.45% and LRD 70.3%.

9.1.4 Households' Characteristics that Determine Housing Preferences in Lagos

Objective five of this treatise requires that we estimate determinants of housing preferences in Lagos in light of households' characteristics and quality of their dwelling units. The results from the MNL results fitted on four models: marital status, age and income as well as location—metropolitan characteristics provide sufficient evidence to realize this objective. Preferences for housing quality vary according to marital status, age and income. The married prefer large room, flat housing units and two toilets and baths facilities. Conversely, they do not seem to be capable of getting homes with flush toilets, pipe-borne water and neighborhoods that are closer to their places of work. These variations were also observed in studies of Chinese people of Guangzhou housing market (Li 2000) and Beijing transitional housing market (Wang and Li 2004). The active adults (41–60 years age) are capable of getting dwelling units that are far from their places of work, children school and good layout. The aged (61 years and above) prefer close neighborhoods to places of work. This is quite understandable, if one takes into consideration their age differentials and the stress required in commuting from home to work place. Due to the shrinking areas of Lagos, the spatial location of facilities including industries and schools is rather random and irregular. For all the models, it is found that household and housing attributes actually influence and shape households' choice of dwellings. The findings from this study partially find support in previous studies (Sue 2008; Opoku and Abdul-Muhmin 2010; Wang and Li 2004). These findings also confirm the veracity of the third hypothesis in the study which states that socioeconomic variables are significant predictors of housing preferences. From the same analysis income is the most important variables for explanation of choice behavior in Lagos. Previous studies in similar cities have arrived at this conclusion (Wang and Li 2004; Li and Li 2006). This inference leads to the acceptance of the hypothesis that affordability is the major determinant of housing preference decision in Lagos.

9.1.5 Comparative Analysis of RP and SP Outcomes: Convergence and Divergence

A particular conclusion resulting from the findings generated by the RP and SP data analyses in the study is the level of similarities and contradictions they produced in terms of their respective results. Many studies that used both methods ended up with similar conclusion (see Earnhart 2001; Tayyaran and Khan 2007). While the results from the RP point to the fact that households prefer more the multiunit dwelling structures, in locations close to activity places, the SP results indicate preference for flat structure at far places. Can both be right? Indeed yes, the RP and SP results could be both right because they predicted well the behaviors of home seekers within the prevalent circumstances under which they are acting. Multiunit houses are prevalent in the city core areas where residents' places of work, schools and other activities are located and these patterns of residential distribution informed their revealed choices. Conversely, all being equal, the same residents would normally prefer flat units in the outer city core areas where there are likelihoods of getting more flat units at cheaper rates. Of course, the RP could be more appropriate in knowing "what it is," while the SP could be more appropriate in estimating "what ought to be." Regardless of the other aspects of the households, home seekers tend to react to choices under hypothetical conditions without much concern for the possibility of realizing the consequences of their actions. On the other hand, the home seekers get only what they can get given their prevalent conditions in real-life situations that permeate the RP models.

9.2 Implications of Research Findings

9.2.1 Study's Implications for Policy

The findings from this study have theoretical, practical and policy implications. For policy, this study has provided useful findings from which the stakeholders in housing planning policy can have insights into the dynamics of residential quality and preferences within a complex urban milieu. The findings have wider policy implications as they form the basis, for the government and other relevant stakeholders to consider the important components of buyers' interests in different forms of housing being provided in Lagos and Nigeria as a whole. Perhaps this is a wakeup call for government to incorporate housing preference into the national housing policy framework in Nigeria as the case in other advanced countries. The current National Housing Policy (NHP 2002) does not make any direct provision for housing preferences as a policy issue.

The findings have further implications for urban housing policy. The effects of inadequate quality dwellings in an evolving megacity like Lagos are multidimensional. First, lack of housing that meet people's desires and aspirations constitutes a hindrance to urban socioeconomic and health well-being (Aliu and Adebayo 2010). Second, it degrades the physical environment and psychological dissatisfaction to residents who, though, have sufficient money to rent a decent dwelling but makes do with substandard accommodation for lack of sufficient good quality homes (see Jiboye 2009). Lagos as an evolving megacity has long required a radical policy shift in its quest to provide adequate housing for its inhabitants.

Two housing policy approaches have been proposed and implemented—the low cost housing scheme and the creation of new towns with public–private estates. These two approaches need a re-evaluation in the context of housing quality preferences of prospective consumers. Low cost housing, for instance, has worsened in terms of residential quality, and the new towns housing model has worsened in terms of affordability and locational efficiency (Towry-Coker 2012). Much as every successive government in Lagos provides public housing and in the contemporary time encourages private participation in estate provision, Lagosians seem to be less interested in the schemes perhaps for their spatial mismatch and obviously for their unrealistic cost of acquisition. As at the present, Lagosians are still interested in the CBD at least closer areas, where substandard housing is prevalent and require renewal and gentrification. Since residential dwellings reflect location pattern and choices, it is only normal that public policies involving housing provision take into consideration locational dimension of residential estates be it private or public. Perhaps the question might be; how can we engender affordability in the housing market that is characterized by high neighborhood and structural quality (Ajala et al. 2010; Ajala and Adelodun 2007).

9.2.2 Study's Implications for Professional Practice

For the professional practice, it is expected that the findings from this study would be of tremendous significance in that they could form a major input in the planning and construction of houses for the urban population. The residential quality analysis particularly reveal (in both RP and SP set ups) the orientations of the housing sector in Lagos. The revealed residential quality analyses indicate a need for improvement in the ways houses are provided in the city, and the stated residential quality analyses indicate the potential needs of the people. The builders, the civil engineers and to a lesser extent the town planners, who play a vital role in housing provisions should take good note of the needs of the potential home consumers. As discovered in the study, it appears that the neighborhood and structural quality of dwellings have a profound influence in shaping housing preferences in the study area. Hence, the house builders and planners might be advised to introduce more aesthetically and locationally pleasing residential and neighborhood designs to reduce the incidence of spatial mismatch; a sociogeographic concept first expounded by Kain (1968), to describe the nature of poverty and employment of American Blacks resulting from residential segregation (McLafferty and Preston 1996). Spatial mismatch observed in this study might have been generated by the incongruous location of residences vis-à-vis places of work and employment opportunities. Addressing this challenge requires an understanding of the role of space as an organizing framework in human activities. In Lagos megacity where the transport system is poorly developed, the idea of expanding decent housing opportunities around the CBD through gentrification would boost housing preferences of the city dwellers. This also requires a redefinition of regional development policy in Lagos. The stakeholders in housing provision (public and private) can also find out that the orientation of Lagos structural housing design has shifted from multiunit to flat units. This preferential behavior and readjustment are instructive as the contemporary desire of Lagos dwellers seems to tend toward a lifestyle that emphasizes privacy and aesthetics. The balance of educational attainment provides a sufficient basis for this new orientation. Hence, housing designs should as a matter of fact reflect this orientation of preferences.

9.2.3 Study's Implications for Theory

The findings from this study have theoretical implications. As regards theory the findings have further strengthened the Multi-Attribute Residential Preference (MARP) theory which is an extension of the existing collections of residential preference models. A cursory look at the theoretical basis of this study (see page 42), and analyses provided in Chaps. 6–8, apparently indicates the fact that choices are made within the confines of spatially polarized housing markets. The results from this study indicate that the housing entity possesses too many quality variables that cannot be conveniently found in one dwelling unit. Hence, as reflected in the insignificance of some of these variables, in reality the home seekers take note of a few of them and collapse the variables into feasible ones in forming their residential choice decisions. Despite the fact that several scholars have attempted to inquire into the ways home buyers and renters come about their decisions, the measurement of preferences has been largely controversial. One very simple area of controversy is the choice of variables and methodologies employed to explain housing choice behavior (Flaming and Griffith 1984; Timmermans et al. 1994; Rhodes 2007). There are apparently diverse variables being used in research to measure preferences but in reality consumers hardly use all the perceived quality variables and given affordability home consumers are likely to maximize their choices to the extent to which the housing condition permits. Two commonly used methods in housing preference studies, that is, revealed and stated approaches have made it possible to empirically explore the difference between what ought to be and what it is. As observed in the course of this study and in sharp disagreement with previous commentators on housing preference measurement, especially Earnhart (2001, 2002) and Tayyaran and Khan (2007), it is of no theoretical relevance to expect the same results from both RP and SP data because the two data sets are obtained from two different circumstances. While the RP decisions are made to reflect the real life situations, the SP decisions are made to reflect hypothetical conditions and to mimic the real life market conditions. Incidentally, the SP data are approached by the respondents with little concern for the reality of the outcomes and therefore does not mimic reality relevantly. Nonetheless, the SP analyses produce results that can be employed to promote housing need estimations and planning.

References

Abiodun OJ (1976) Housing problems in Nigerian Cities. Town Plann Rev 47(4):330–348

Ajala OA, Adelodun OA (2007) Determinants of housing quality in Ibadan North Local Government Area of North Western Nigeria. Baselius Res 8(2):72–84

Ajala OA, Aigbe GO, Aliu IR (2010) Affordable housing and urban development in Nigeria: contemporary issues, challenges and opportunities. Ilorin J Bus Soc Sci 14(1):1–13

Aliu IR, Adebayo A (2010) Evaluating the influence of residential quality on urban residents' wellbeing: the case of Lagos Nigeria. Int J Acad Res 2(6):400–410

Aluko EO (2000) Urban market segmentation and house values in metropolitan Lagos. Niger Geogr J 3&4:148–157

Choi S-H, Kang M (2010) An analysis on elderly housing preference using structural equation model: focusing on Silver Town. Int J Urban Sci 14(3):254–263

Cirman A (2006) Housing tenure preferences in the post-privatization period: the case of Slovenia. Hous Stud 21(1):113–134

Earnhart D (2001) Combining revealed and stated preference methods to value environmental amenities at residential locations. Land Econ 77(1):12–29

Earnhart D (2002) Combining revealed and stated data to examine housing decisions using discrete choice analysis. J Urban Econ 51:143–169

Flaming HK, Griffith WI (1984) Causal modeling as a guide to housing preference research: a theoretical note. Hous Stud 11(2):108–111

Jiboye AD (2009) Evaluating tenants' satisfaction within public housing in Lagos, Nigeria. Town Plann Archit 33(4):239–247
Kain J (1968) Housing segregation, Negro employment and metropolitan decentralization. Quart J Econ 82:175–197
Kain JF, Quigley JM (1970) Measuring the value of house quality. J Am Stat Assoc 65(330):532–548
Li S-M (2000) The housing market and tenure decisions in Chinese cities: a multivariate analysis of the case of Guangzhou. Hous Stud 15(1):213–236
Li S-M, Li L (2006) Life course and housing tenure change in urban China: a study of Guangzhou. Hous Stud 21(5):653–670s
McLafferty S, Preston V (1996) Spatial mismatch and employment in a decade of restructuring. Prof Geogr 49(4):420–430
NHP (2002) National Housing Policy: Government Whitepaper on the Report of the Presidential Committee on Urban Development and Housing, Abuja
Onibokun A (ed) (1985) Housing in Nigeria. Nigerian Institute of Social and Economic Research NISER, Ibadan
Opoku RA, Abdul-Muhmin AG (2010) Housing preferences and attribute importance among low-income consumers in Saudi Arabia. Habitat Int 34:219–227
Rhodes LM (2007) Strategic choice in Irish housing system: taming the complexity. Hous Theory Soc 24(1):14–31
Rosenbaum J (1996) The influence of race on Hispanic housing choices in New York City 1978–1987. Urban Aff Rev 32(2):217–243
Sue H (2008) Housing choices and issues for young people in the UK. Joseph Rowntree Foundation, London. www.jrt.org.uk. Accessed 23 March 2010
Tayyaran MR, Khan MA (2007) Telecommuting and residential location decisions: combined stated and revealed preferences model. Can J Civ Eng 34:1324–1333
Timmermans H, Molin E, van Nootwijk L (1994) Housing choice processes: stated versus Revealed modeling approaches. Netherl J Hous Built Environ 9(3):215–227
Towry-Coker L (2012) Housing policy and the dynamics of housing delivery in Nigeria: a case study of Lagos State. Makeway publishing, Ibadan
Wang D, Li S-M (2004) Housing preferences in a transitional housing system: the case of Beijing China. Environ Plan A 36:69–87

Chapter 10
Recommendations and Conclusions on Residential Quality and Housing Preferences

Abstract Based on the information from the previous parts of this book, a lot of empirical evidences concerning the housing quality and preferences across different parts of Lagos Metropolitan Areas have been produced and interpreted. The enormous findings from the study require some policy suggestions and recommendations for housing researchers, real estate practitioners and government who are key stakeholders in the housing sector and policy formulation. These recommendations will equip the stakeholders especially in Lagos housing governance and housing property developers as well as urban planners to improve the Lagos housing market. In addition, this chapter also highlights the contributions to knowledge and conclusions to the book.

Keywords Policy suggestions · Housing governance · Housing property developers · Urban planners · Housing researchers · Further housing research

This chapter of the treatise dwells on the recommendations based on the findings and implications so far done in Chaps. 6, 7 and 8. The study has produced a lot of information and evidences concerning the housing quality and preferences across different parts of Lagos Metropolitan Areas. The enormous findings from the study require some policy suggestions and recommendations for the housing scholars, practitioners and government who are key stakeholders in the housing sector. These recommendations represent the suggestions for the stakeholders in Lagos housing governance and housing property developers as well as urban planners to improve the Lagos urban private housing market. This chapter also highlights the contributions to knowledge and conclusions to the book.

10.1 Recommendations

Based upon the empirical results from the study and their implications for theory, professional practice and policy, the following recommendations are suggested:

© The Author(s), under exclusive license to Springer Nature Switzerland AG 2024

I. R. Aliu, *Urban Private Housing in Nigeria*, The Urban Book Series,
https://doi.org/10.1007/978-3-031-47432-3_10

- *Ensuring spatial equity in social amenities and infrastructure provision*:

Since empirical analyses in this study have revealed that private housing quality and preferences reflect more of neighborhood quality than structural quality indicators it is recommended that urban stakeholders especially the planners should endeavor to seek for spatial equities in facility distribution in Lagos metropolis. Essentially, there is a need to re-examine policy on industrial locations in the state so that the CBDs are decongested of industries. Investors should be encouraged to locate at the suburbs of the city so that employment and trade opportunities which drive urban population toward dwellings around the city core are redistributed. The need for regular and proper monitoring of housing standards within Lagos metropolis cannot be overemphasized. House owners should be encouraged to improve their properties in the areas where we have noticed some elements of revulsion for residential quality preferences.

- *Provision of housing that suits contemporary lifestyles of residents*:

Again as it was discovered through the stated housing preference analyses that the majority of Lagos residents would prefer housing units such as flats that guarantee individualistic lifestyles, it is suggested that urban stakeholders especially the builders and planners should encourage property owners to construct houses that allow some level of individuality of households. Instead of multiunit housing, localized as "face-me-I-face-you," which forms majority of dwellings in Lagos metropolis, the builders and home construction firms should increase their efforts at constructing mini flat units that are more favored by the residents in the contemporary time.

- *Incorporation of housing quality and preferences into the national housing policy*:

Although the houses surveyed in this study are privately built and rented homes, it is perhaps necessary to incorporate the housing preference issue into the national housing policy. The incorporation of housing preference component into the national housing policy is indeed crucial in improving the residential quality and housing preferences of the urban residents. The achievement of this recommendation would be made easier if the town planning stakeholders are prepared to implement the housing codes and construction standards in the city to the letter (Gallent et al. 1998). For example key residential quality and home preference indicators could be included in the national population census exercises in Nigeria. And based upon this verifiable source housing policy can stipulate minimum housing quality for all residential homes including public and private housing in the Nigerian cities.

- *Encouraging personal ownership of homes through sustainable mortgage system*:

Analysis of housing quality and preferences as done in this study has revealed that housing tenure in the private housing market tilts toward renters at the expense of homeownership. This raises a fundamental question about the reasons for lack of property ownership especially in the metropolitan areas of Lagos. In light of recent studies on the impact of fees on housing (see Evans-Cowley and Lawhon 2003) and influence of mortgage funds on housing ownership (Mylonakis 2007), my thought splits into two lines on the explanation for this. First, perhaps because the residents are majorly immigrants (this is evident in their ethnic and familiarity attributes), the city dwellers make deliberate decisions not to build homes in the central metropolis as against the state suburbs and they may prefer to own personal dwellings in their respective country homes. Second, it is my candid thought that may be the total cost of effecting residential apartment in this part of the state is too huge to discourage home ownership by households who themselves are not financially buoyant to compete in the already saturated residential land market in the metropolis. Therefore, the residents should be encouraged through some policy shift in housing finance like extending mortgage funds to the less privileged in the study area which may encourage them to build more dwellings in the suburb so as to reduce competitions for poor housing within the city. Mortgage funds would also assist in improving the quality of the homes in the city regions through gentrification. The lack of sustainable mortgage facilities has led to many housing obstacles and crises in recent times (Basolo and Hastings 2003; Immergluck 2011).

- *Recognition of the polarization of urban private housing markets*:

The results from this study have clearly demonstrated the existence of polarization in both housing quality and preferences in Lagos. Hence, it is important for both policy makers and housing scholars to realize the spatial imperatives of the housing market and a co-option of spatial aspect of the urban housing market and consumer spatial behavior into preference theories is of highest importance. It is quite difficult and absolutely unrealistic to remove spatial influence from human decision making and behaviors. The geographic theme of spatial differentiation is crucial in understanding housing preferences in highly complex cities like Lagos metropolis. Analysis of residential quality and preferences done in this study clearly showed that households' reaction to spatial variations in residential markets is obvious. However, the reaction is not like those of the multicultural societies where spatial polarization gives way to racial segregation (Clark 1991; Hogan and Berry 2011). The variations that existed within LRD, MRD and HRD areas are due to differences in available dwellings and prevailing socioeconomic status of the areas. In each of these residential density areas there are also some variation among group of households due to spatial proximity of neighborhoods to the CBD, work, hospital, markets, school and relations. Both the RP and SP analyses uncover the consistent predilection of home renters for spatial differentiation in dwelling qualities.

- *Intensification of studies on housing preference modeling*:

This research has deliberately taken into consideration very important housing preference approaches especially the revealed and the stated models in order to examine their analytical potency in understanding the behavior of housing renters, but like in many other areas of research endeavors it is crucial that more in-depth studies of these two be intensified as this will provide a better promising planning signification. Like

Kersloot and Kauko (2005) have suggested, there are three areas that housing preference analyses should face: consumption-driven, policy-driven and science-driven goals. While these have been achieved in the developed economies (Netherlands and Finland for instance), the situation in Africa has been grossly inadequate. This will be made only possible if the research capabilities of housing scholars are appreciably improved and enhanced by the stakeholders through a provision of grants for housing research. There is a need to establish housing research institutes in Nigeria to carryout advanced multidisciplinary research on general housing issues including residential quality and preferences.

10.2 Contributions to Knowledge

This book, "Urban private housing in Nigeria," contributes to knowledge in three areas of urban housing studies. First, the book provides up-to-date information about variations in the housing quality across urban private housing areas of Lagos metropolis. Second, it also reveals the influence of these residential quality variations on housing preferences beyond what obtained in past studies. Third, it contributes to the existing literature and analytical techniques on urban housing markets. The study has contributed deeply to the explanation of the urban housing sector in Nigeria, in that the spatial aspects of residential quality and housing preferences has revealed, in comparative sense, the preferential peculiarities of the city dwellers across different segmented neighborhoods and residential markets in Lagos. At the end, the study provides a new, critical perspective on urban residential quality and housing preference dynamics within urban private housing markets in Nigeria as a whole and Lagos in particular.

10.3 Conclusions and Areas of Further Research

Although research efforts in housing preferences have proliferated in the last decades, the issues have continued to wear different togas and colors over time. The area where this book has concentrated upon, that is the dynamics of residential quality and preferences in private housing markets, have largely been underexplored in this part of the world. Hence, the decision to examine the private housing markets and the dimensions of space and attribute importance in housing preference formation in Lagos is highly timely. The book reviewed several existing studies on preferences and conducted in-depth analyses into the conditions of housing quality and preferences in Lagos to provide answers to the raised questions in the study. Using both revealed and stated preference approaches at once, this book has provided solid and penetrating analyses to explain the housing preference formation of Lagos residents. Empirical results substantially confirmed evidences from existing studies and threw up fresh revelations about the behavior of city dwellers on the issue of housing preferences and residential quality. However, in spite of a strong effort at making use of Multi-Attribute Utility Technique (SMART) in this study the results from the SMART analysis are too preliminary and more works need to be carried out to establish a substantial claim to its use in housing preference studies. Hence, the use of SMART and non-quantitative analytical frameworks may serve as further areas of improving and explaining the housing preference formation of home seekers. Again a comparative study of public and private housing quality and preferences could be embarked upon to evaluate the areas of inadequacies between two urban housing markets (public and private housing markets). Further, studies need to be done on how spatial differentiation influences home choices in emerging megacities of the world.

References

Basolo V, Hastings D (2003) Obstacles to regional Housing Solution: A comparison of four metropolitan areas. J Urban Aff 25(4):449–472

Clark WAV (1991) Residential preferences and neighborhood racial segregation: a test of the Schelling model. Demography 28(1):1–19

Evans-Cowley JS, Lawhon LL (2003) The effects of impact fees on housing and land: a literature review. J Plan Lit 17(3):352–359

Gallent N, Baker M, Wong C (1998) Securing housing choices: new opportunities for the UK planning system. Hous Stud 13(3):425–438

Hogan B, Berry B (2011) Racial and ethnic biases in rental housing: an audit study of online apartment listing. City Commun 10(4):351–372

Immergluck D (2011) Critical commentary on sub-prime crisis, policy response and housing market restructuring. Urban Stud 48(16):3371–3383

Kersloot J, Kauko T (2005) Measurement of housing preferences—a comparison of research activity in the Netherlands and Finland. Nordic J Surveying Real Estate Res 1:144–160

Mylonakis J (2007) A research study of customer preferences in the home loans market: the mortgage experience of Greek Bank customers. Int J Financ Econ 10:153–166

Appendix A
Study Sampling Units by Wards, LGAS and Neighborhoods

Residential density area*	Ward/locality	LGA = 12	Total neighborhoods $N = 56$	Total questionnaires $N = 1485$
Low residential density LRD (I)	Ikoyi I, Ikoyi II, V/Island I, V/Island II	ETIOSA	4	108
	GRA, Onigbongbo	IKEJA	2	54
	Apapa I, Apapa II, Apapa III and Apapa IV	APAPA	4	108
	Subtotal	3	10	270
Medium residential density MRD (II)	Gbagada I, Gbagada II, Akoka, Palmgrove, Onipanu	SOMOLU	5	135
	Festac I, Festac II, Festac III, Satellite Town, Amuwo estate	AMUWO-ODOFIN	5	135
	Shitta/Ogunade drive, Adeniran Ogunsanya, Iponri housing estate, Aguda	SURULERE	4	108
	Alogomeji, Yaba/Igbobi, Abuleoja/Oyadiran, Iwaya	LAGOS MAINLAND	4	108

(continued)

© The Editor(s) (if applicable) and The Author(s), under exclusive license to Springer Nature Switzerland AG 2024

I. R. Aliu, *Urban Private Housing in Nigeria*, The Urban Book Series,
https://doi.org/10.1007/978-3-031-47432-3

(continued)

Residential density area*	Ward/locality	LGA = 12	Total neighborhoods $N = 56$	Total questionnaires $N = 1485$
	Subtotal	4	18	486
High residential density HRD (III)	Olowogbowo, Idumota, Epetedo, Oke Faji, Ojuto/Isale Eko, Agarawu/ Obadina	LAGOS ISLAND	6	162
	Idioro/ Odiolowo, Mushin/ Atewolara, Babalosa/ Ojuwoye, Idiaraba, Itire, Papa Ajao	MUSHIN	6	162
	Oshodi/Bolade, Orile/Oshodi, Isahagatedo, Mafoluku, Ejigbo, Ilasamaja	OSHODI/ISOLO	6	135
	Tolu/Ajegunle, Ojo Rd, Awodiora, Olodi, Amukoko	AJEROMI/ IFELODUN	5	135
	Oniwaya/ Papaoku, Okekoto, Orile-Agege/ Okooba, Agbotikuyo/ Dopemu, Tabontabon/ Oko-Oba	AGEGE	5	135
	Subtotal	5	28	729

Appendix B
Residential Density Areas and Wards

Local government area	Serial number	Locality/ward	Residential density area		
			Low	Medium	High
Agege	001	Isale Oja/Idimangoro			X
	002	Oniwaya/Papaoku			x
	003	Agbotikuyo/Dopemu		x	
	004	Oyewole/Papa Ashafa			x
	005	Okekoto			x
	006	Keke			x
	007	Darocha			x
	008	Tabontabon/Oko-Oba		x	
	009	Orile-Agege/Oko-Oba			x
Ajeromi/Ifelodun	010	Awodi-Ora			X
	011	Olodi			x
	012	Tolu			x
	013	Ojo Rd			x
	014	AlabaOro/Amukoko			x
Alimosho	015	Shasha/Akowonjo			X
	016	Egbeda			x
	017	Idimu/Isheri			x
	018	Ikotun/Ijegun			x
	019	Egbe/Agodo			x
	020	Igando/Egan			x
	021	Ipaja North		x	
	022	Ipaja South		x	
	023	Ayobo			x

(continued)

© The Editor(s) (if applicable) and The Author(s), under exclusive license to Springer Nature Switzerland AG 2024
I. R. Aliu, *Urban Private Housing in Nigeria*, The Urban Book Series,
https://doi.org/10.1007/978-3-031-47432-3

(continued)

Local government area	Serial number	Locality/ward	Residential density area		
			Low	Medium	High
	024	Oke-Odo		x	
	025	Abule Egaba/Alagbado			x
Amuwo-Odofin	026	Amuwo-Odofin estate		x	
	027	Festac 1		x	
	028	Festac 2		x	
	029	Festac 3	x		
	030	Kirikiri		x	
	031	Agboju			x
	032	Ijegun			x
	033	Satellite		x	
Apapa	034	Apapa 1	x		
	035	Apapa 2	x		
	036	Apapa 3	x		
	037	Apapa 4	x		
	038	Ijora-Oloye			x
	039	Iganmu		x	
	040	Afolabi Alasia		x	
	041	Malu Road			x
	042	Sari-Iganmu		x	
Eti-Osa	043	Victoria Island 1	x		
	044	Victoria island 2	x		
	045	Ilasan Estate/Mayegun Village		x	
	046	Ikota/Ikate Village		x	
	047	Igbo-Efon/Ikota		x	
	048	Ajah	x		
	049	Addo		x	
	050	Ikoy 1	x		
	051	Ikoyi 2	x		
	052	Obalende			X
Ibeju-Lekki	053	Ibeju 1		x	
	054	Ibeju 2		x	
	055	Orimedu 1(Eleko)			x
	056	Orimedu 2			x
	057	Magbo Alade			x
	058	Lekki	X		

(continued)

(continued)

Local government area	Serial number	Locality/ward	Residential density area		
			Low	Medium	High
Ifako	059	Ogba-Oke Ira			X
	060	Old Ifako/Karaole			x
	061	New Ifako/Oyemekun		x	
	062	Fagba/Akute			x
	063	Iju-Ihsaga			x
	064	Obawole		x	
	065	Panada/Abule Egba			x
	066	Ijaye/Ojokoro		x	
	067	Agbado/Ijaye			x
	068	Alakuko Kollington			x
Ikeja	069	Anifowose		x	
	070	Agidingbi/Omole		x	
	071	Alausa/Oregun		x	
	072	Onilekere/Onipetesi		x	
	073	Ipodo/Seriki			x
	074	Adeniji Jones/Ogba		x	
	075	Okeira/Agudatitun		x	
	076	Onigbongbo (Maryland)	x		
	077	GRA	x		
	078	Wasimi Opebi/Allen		x	
Kosofe	079	Oworosoki		x	
	080	Ifako/Gbagada		x	
	081	Anthony/Mende		x	
	082	Ketu Alapere			x
	083	Isheri/Olowo ira		x	
	084	Ojota/Ogudu		x	
	085	Ketu/Ikosi			x
	086	Aboyi 1			x
	087	Aboyi 2			x
	088	Ajegunle			x
Lagos Island	089	Olowogbowo/Elegbeta			X
	090	Idumota			x
	091	Isale Eko			x
	092	Agarawu/Obadina			x
	093	Popo Aguda			x

(continued)

(continued)

Local government area	Serial number	Locality/ward	Residential density area		
			Low	Medium	High
	094	Oke Faji			x
	095	Onikan/Okesuna		x	
	096	Epetedo			x
	097	Ilubirin/Lafiaji			x
Lagos Mainland	098	Otto/ido			X
	099	Olaleye			x
	100	Mako/ebutemeta			x
	101	Oyingbo/ebutemeta			x
	102	Oyadiran/abule oja		x	
	103	Alagomeji		x	
	104	Iwaya		x	
	105	Yaba/igbobi/sabo		x	
Mushin	106	Idi-oro/odiolowo			X
	107	Ojuwoye/babalosa			x
	108	Ilupeju		x	
	109	Olateju			x
	110	Fadeyi		x	
	111	Atewolara			x
	112	Papa-ajao			x
	113	Ilasamaja			x
	114	Itire			x
	115	Idiaraba			x
Ojo	116	Ojo			X
	117	Okokomaiko			x
	118	Ajangbadi			x
	119	Ijanikin			x
	120	Iba		x	
	121	Otto-Ilogbo			x
	122	Irewe			x
	123	Taffi			x
	124	Etegbin			x
	125	Idoluwo			x
	126	Sabo-Alaba			x
Oshodi-Isolo	127	Oshodi/Bolade			X
	128	Orile-Oshodi			x
	129	Isolo		x	

(continued)

(continued)

Local government area	Serial number	Locality/ward	Residential density area		
			Low	Medium	High
	130	Ajao Estate	x		
	131	Ilasamaja			x
	132	Mafoluku			x
	133	Sogunle		x	
	134	Alasia		x	
	135	Okota		x	
	136	Ishagatedo			x
	137	Okeafa/Ejigbo			x
Somolu	138	Onipanu		x	
	139	Palmgrove		x	
	140	Bajulaye			x
	141	Pedro			x
	142	Bariga			x
	143	Ilaje Akoka		x	
	144	Igbobi/Fadeyi			x
	145	Gbagada 1		x	
	146	Gbagada 2		x	
	147	Abuleokuta/Ilaje Bariga			x
Surulere	148	Yaba/Ojuelegba			X
	149	Shitta/Ogunlana Drive		x	
	150	Adeniran Ogunsanya		x	
	151	Iponri Estate		x	
	152	Orile			x
	153	Coker			x
	154	Aguda		x	
	155	Ijeshatedo			x
	156	Itire			x
	157	Ikate			x

Source Independent National Electoral Commission (INEC) 2010

Appendix C
Multi-attribute Residential Preference (MARP) Survey Questionnaire

Urban Private Housing in Nigeria-Spatial Patterns of Residential Quality and Housing Preferences in Metropolitan Areas of Lagos, Nigeria

I am a doctoral researcher working on residential quality and housing preferences in Lagos. The goal of the study is to analyze the spatial pattern of housing quality and housing preferences in Lagos Metropolitan Areas. Given the nature of this study, it is therefore normal to enlist the support of Lagos residents in the provision of data that can be used to arrive at conclusions that might facilitate the achievement of the objectives of the study. Hence, I solicit for your consent and assistance in providing candid and sincere answers to the raised questions in this questionnaire. The data provided are solely for the analyses required in the Ph.D. thesis and would not be deployed to any purpose capable of affecting adversely your personality and privacy. Your responses are anonymous and covered in confidentiality. Your personal data would not be exposed to the third party. You may decide to withdraw at any time in the enquiry without any prior notice and for any personal reasons. I am ready to share the outcomes of this study with you if you are interested.

I shall be very grateful to you and acknowledge your civic responsibility in the research thesis should you assist me in responding to this questionnaire appropriately. The questionnaire only takes about 15 minutes to complete. The questionnaire is organized in three sections A–C. Section A dwells on the residential quality and revealed housing preference indicators ranging from structural, neighborhood and locational quality indicators like housing type, number of rooms to property rents, Section B interrogates the residential quality and stated housing preference dynamics and patterns involving conjoint experimental choices and Section C dwells on the personal sociodemographic and economic aspects of households (respondents) in Lagos private housing apartments.

© The Editor(s) (if applicable) and The Author(s), under exclusive license to Springer Nature Switzerland AG 2024

I. R. Aliu, *Urban Private Housing in Nigeria*, The Urban Book Series,
https://doi.org/10.1007/978-3-031-47432-3

For further enquiries, please feel free to contact the under-listed person. Thanks and God Bless.

I.R. Aliu (Ph.D. Research Candidate)
Department of Geography
Obafemi Awolowo University
Ile-Ife, Nigeria
Tel: +234(0)8027525933
Email: ibrahim.aliu@lasu.edu.ng;
ibrolordimi@yahoo.co.uk

A. Residential Quality and Revealed Housing Preferences

This section considers the real residential attributes or quality indices that made you to choose your present dwelling. In fact, the questions probe into the neighborhood and structural conditions of your residence as they were when you made your first decision to acquire it.

Preferences for Structural Quality: *Please indicate the structural quality indices identifiable with your present dwelling*

SN	Dwelling structural quality indicators	Tick option
(1)	What housing type did you prefer when looking for this residence?	
	• Duplex	
	• Flat unit	
	• Rooming multifamily unit	
(2)	How many rooms did you consider to live in at the time of renting this residential unit?	
	• 1–2 rooms	
	• 3 rooms and more	
(3)	What was the space design of the rooms that attracted you to this dwelling?	
	• 3×4 m^2	
	• 3×3 m^2	
(4)	What was the source of water that existed at the point of renting this dwelling?	
	• Potable piped borne/piped borehole water	
	• Open well water/others (water vendor)	
(5)	How many toilets and baths that you considered before taking this residence?	
	• 2 toilets and 2 baths and more	
	• 1 toilet and 1 bath	
(6)	What was the nature of the kitchen that was considered before taking this dwelling unit?	
	• Tiled separate	
	• Untiled separate	

(continued)

(continued)

SN	Dwelling structural quality indicators	Tick option
(7)	What was your housing tenure preference?	
	• Owner-occupier	
	• Private renter	
	Residential Control Constraints Please indicate your constraints with this dwelling choice	
(8)	The total annual rent/price at the point of obtaining this dwelling was?	
	• NGN200,000 and less	
	• NGN201,00–400,000	
	• NGN401,000–800,000	
(9)	How would you describe the internal structural quality of this dwelling when you moved into the area?	
	• Good	
	• Poor	

Preferences for Location and Neighborhood Quality: *Please indicate the location and neighborhood quality indices identifiable with your present dwelling*

SN	Neighborhood quality indicator	Tick option
(10)	Which of these parts of the neighborhood attracted your preference while looking for home?	
	• City core	
	• Outer city core	
	• City suburbs	
(11)	How close was workplace to your neighborhood of preference?	
	• 0–4 km	
	• 5 km and more	
(12)	How close was market to your neighborhood of preference?	
	• 0–4 km	
	• 5 km and more	
(13)	How close was hospital to your neighborhood of preference?	
	• 0–4 km	
	• 5 km and more	
(14)	How close were children schools to your neighborhood of preference?	
	• 0–4 km	
	• 5 km and more	
(15)	How close was place of worship to your neighborhood of preference?	
	• 0–4 km	
	• 5 km and more	

(continued)

(continued)

SN	Neighborhood quality indicator	Tick option
(16)	How close did you intend to be to your friends or relations when choosing this neighborhood?	
	• 0–4 km	
	• 5 km and more	
(17)	How accessible was this neighborhood in terms of public transport when you chose to live there?	
	• Reasonably accessible	
	• Limited accessibility	
(18)	When you first chose this neighborhood and residence, what safety and security criteria did you consider?	
	• Presence of police station	
	• Presence of OPC/private security	
(19)	What was the nature of land use pattern in your neighborhood at time of moving into this area?	
	• Mixed layout	
	• Orderly planned	
(20)	How would you describe the external environmental quality of this neighborhood when you moved into the area?	
	• Good	
	• Poor	

B. Residential Quality and Stated Housing Preferences

You are expected to choose from the six housing choice options below, given your level of income and affordability of dwellings. The assumption is that everyone will prefer one or none of these houses, based on their combination of location, neighborhood and structural attributes. *Supposing you were to rent a dwelling unit, which of these houses from 1 to 6 would you prefer, given prevalent affordability and your economic capability.*

Choice I

House 1:	(Rooming multiunit A)
Location	City core
Accessibility	Limited
Proximity to public utility	Market within 2–4 km
Security	Private security
Number of rooms	1–2 RMs
Room design	Small rooms
Water	Well

(continued)

(continued)

House 1:	(Rooming multiunit A)
Price/rent	NGN100-200K
Your choice	

Choice II

House 2:	(Rooming multiunit B)
Location	Suburb
Accessibility	Reasonable
Proximity to public utility	Market within 1 km
Security	Police station
Number of rooms	1–2 RMs
Room Design	Small rooms
Water	Borehole
Price/rent	NGN 100-200 K
Your choice	

Choice III

House 3:	(Flat unit A)
Location	Outer city core
Accessibility	Limited
Proximity to public utility	Market within 5 km
Security	Police station
Number of rooms	2–4 RMs
Room design	Small rooms
Water	Borehole
Price	NGN 201-400 K
Your choice	

Choice IV

House 4:	(Flat unit B)
Location	City core
Accessibility	High
Proximity to public utility	Market within 1 km
Security	Private security

(continued)

(continued)

House 4:	(Flat unit B)
Number of rooms	2–4 RMs
Room design	Large rooms
Water	Bore hole
Price	NGN201-400 K
Your choice	

Choice V

House 5:	(Duplex A)
Location	Outer city core
Accessibility	High
Proximity to public utility	Market within 5 km
Security	Police station
Number of rooms	5–8 RMs
Room design	Small rooms
Water	Borehole
Price	NGN401-800 K
Your choice	

Choice VI

House 6:	(Duplex B)
Location	City suburb
Accessibility	Limited
Proximity to public utility	Market within 2–4 km
Security	Police
Number of rooms	5–8 RMs
Room design	Large rooms
Water	Pipe borne
Price	NGN401-800 K
Your choice	

For future needs, please rate the dwelling attributes according to your preference (Extremely important=6; Important=4; Less important=2; Unimportant=0). *How important are these residential quality indices to you?*

Neighborhood attributes (A)	Extremely important	Important	Less important	Unimportant
(2) LOC1 = Distance to the CBD				
(3) LOC2 = Distance to workplace				
(4) LOC3 = Closeness to friends/relations				
(5) LOC4 = Accessibility to public transport				
(6) PRES1 = Planning and orderliness				
(7) PRES2 = Security and safety				
(8) CONV1 = Closeness to market				
(9) CONV2 = Closeness to children's schools				
(10) CONV3 = Closeness to general hospital				
(11) CONV4 = Closeness to place of worship				
(12) CONV5 = Presence of recreation park				
Structural attributes (B)	Extremely important	Important	Less important	Unimportant
(13) HUSE1 = Number of rooms				
(14) HUSE2 = Number of tiled toilets and baths				
(15) HUSE3 = Number of tiled kitchens				
(16) HUSE4 = Treated potable water				
(17) HUSE5 = Light				
(18) DESG1 = Housing type				
(19) DESG2 = New house				
(20) DESG3 = Internal room design				
(21) DESG4 = Aesthetics				
(22) DESG5 = Patio				
(23) DESG6 = Lot size				
(24) MCON1 = Tenure				

(continued)

(continued)

Structural attributes (B)	Extremely important	Important	Less important	Unimportant
(25) MCON2 = Cost of maintenance (caution fees)				
(26) MCON3 = Price of dwelling unit				

C. **Household Characteristics**

This section deals with the personal background information of the respondents whose housing preference and residential quality indices are being studied. *Please tick the appropriate answers from the alternatives provided*

Residential address:____________________

Demographic/Lifecycle characteristics

(27) Household head gender:

- Male
- Female

(28) Marital status of household head:

- Single
- Married
- Widowed/Divorced

(29) Age of household head:

- 20–40 yrs
- 41–60 yrs
- 61 yrs and above

(30) How many children do you have________________

(31) What is the total household size:

- 1–2
- 3–6
- 7 and above

(32) What is the household head religion:

- Islam
- Christianity
- Others

(33) What is your nationality

- Nigerian
- Other African
- European/American
- Others

(34) The ethnic origin of household head:

- Yoruba
- Other tribes in Nigeria
- Other race outside of Nigeria

(35) Number of children above18 yrs:

- 1–3
- 4–7
- None

Socioeconomic Characteristics

(36) Maximum education of household head:

- Graduate/M.Sc./Ph.D.
- Technical/Secondary
- Primary/No formal education

(37) Occupation of household head:

- Civil servant
- Private sector worker
- Artisans/traders
- Unemployed

(38) Number of years worked:

- 10 yrs or less
- 11–20 yrs
- 21–35 yrs
- 36 years and above

(39) Which of these groups fits your monthly income level:

- NGN 0–74, 999
- NGN75,000–149,999
- NGN150,000–224,999
- NGN225,000 and above

(40) Number of years spent in Lagos:

- 5 yrs or less
- 6–20 yrs
- 21 yrs and above

Thank you for filling out this questionnaire